Children's Play:
A Study of Needs and
Opportunities

MICHAEL JOSEPH BOOKS ON LIVE ISSUES
*Series Editors:* H. L. Beales, O. R. McGregor

*Where to play?*

# Children's Play:
# A Study of Needs and Opportunities

*A Study for the Council for Children's Welfare*

ANTHEA HOLME
AND
PETER MASSIE

LONDON
MICHAEL JOSEPH

*First published in Great Britain by*
MICHAEL JOSEPH LTD
*52 Bedford Square*
*London, W.C.2*
MARCH 1970
SECOND IMPRESSION JUNE 1972

7181 0571 0

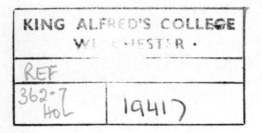
*Printed in Great Britain by*
*Redwood Press Limited*
*Trowbridge, Wiltshire*
*Bound by James Burn at Esher, Surrey*

This Report is sponsored by the Council for Children's Welfare and financed by the Calouste Gulbenkian Foundation. It is edited by Anthea Holme who was responsible for the Survey of Existing Facilities and wrote Chapters 2, 3, 10–13. Peter Massie designed and carried out the contrasting Neighbourhood Study which he describes in Chapters 8 and 9. He also wrote Chapter 1. Chapters 4–7 were written by Anthea Holme in collaboration with Peter Massie. The Children and Playgrounds Survey contained in Chapter 10 was designed by Peter Wood and analysed by Brian McLoughlin and David Foot, whose contributions we gratefully acknowledge on page 18.

# Contents

# Illustrations

# List of Tables

## Survey of Existing Facilities:

# List of Figures

## Contrasting Neighbourhood Study:

## Survey of Existing Facilities:

# Acknowledgements

We have a great many people to thank, for we have been exceptionally fortunate in the help and co-operation we have received from beginning to end of this project.

The study was financed by the Calouste Gulbenkian Foundation and is the second project for the Council for Children's Welfare which the Foundation's Trustees have supported. Once again we express our sincere thanks for their generous grant and for the freedom they have allowed us in producing this report.

Throughout we have had the continued support and advice of a specially appointed committee whose members share between them almost all aspects of knowledge about children at play. The Chairman, Mrs Joan Maizels, was unstinting of her time and valuable advice and we owe her a special debt for the help she has given in organising the material for publication. We have benefited from the practical experience of Mr Joe Benjamin, Play Scheme Organiser, London Borough of Camden; Miss Murielle E. Otter, one-time Adviser for Youth and Community Service, Liverpool Education Committee; and Miss Joan Pearse, one-time Principal Supervisor of the Save the Children Fund Playgroups; and the planning expertise of Mr Leslie B. Ginsburg, Head of Leverhulme Department of Planning and Urban Design, the Architectural Association School of Architecture. Miss Mary Mitchell, Consultant Landscape Architect to the County Borough of Blackburn, Architect's Department, was able to advise on the question of the siting, design and layout of playgrounds. Miss Joan Cass, one-time lecturer in Child Development, University of London, Institute of Education; Miss Gertrude Keir, Senior Lecturer, Department of Psychology, University College, London; Mrs M. L. Kellmer-Pringle, Director of the National Bureau for Co-operation in Child Care; and Miss Vere Hole, a Principal Scientific Officer of the Building Research Station, all with specialist knowledge of children and the subject of play, brought academic rigour to the discussions. Mr W. D. Abernethy, Secretary of the Children's Playground and Play Leadership Committee, The National Playing Fields Association, shared his accumulated experience; Mrs Betty Vernon helped to steer us through the intricacies of local government. Mr F. Le Gros Clark's wisdom and understanding of the problem were carried through from earlier days in the Council for Children's Welfare. To him and to Mr Joe Benjamin we owe the conception of the study. All the members of our Research Advisory

Committee, and the organisations which many of them represent, do not necessarily agree with all the views expressed in this book; these are the sole responsibility of the authors.

Three separate pieces of research were carried out, for all of which we were dependent upon the help and co-operation of a number of different individuals, organisations and local authority departments.

The contrasting neighbourhood study in the New Town of Stevenage and the London Borough of Southwark involved three different approaches: a survey of mothers, a systematic observation of children around the neighbourhood and administering play inventories to 1,800 school children. Without the help and co-operation from numerous individuals and bodies all this could not have been carried out. We have space for mention of only a few of those concerned—Stevenage Development Corporation, Borough of Southwark Planning Office, the Inner London Education Authority and the heads and staff of most of the schools in the two neighbourhoods. In particular, we are most grateful to Colin Ackhurst, of the Department of Social Work Training, Stevenage College of Further Education, for allowing his students to do the bulk of the interviewing of mothers in Stevenage and John Bynner of the Social Survey for the helpful discussions and suggestions in the design and analysis stages of the play inventory. We are also indebted to Cybernetics Research Consultants Ltd. for their generous help in the machine analysis.

The children and playgrounds survey was carried out in ten boroughs. To the following four people we owe a particular debt, for without them this ten-borough survey would neither have been begun nor completed. Miss M. E. Otter introduced the Council for Children's Welfare and the project to Liverpool, and it was from Liverpool that the inspiration for this survey came. Mr Peter Wood, Divisional Planning Officer, City Planning Department, devised the final version of the survey and to him, therefore, chief credit is due. At Manchester University Department of Town and Country Planning, Mr Brian McLoughlin, then Senior Research Fellow, University of Manchester, was responsible for the preliminary analysis of the material which Mr David Foot carried further to include a multiple regression analysis. We are especially grateful to Mr McLoughlin and Mr Foot for allowing us to quote from their reports on the findings (chapter 10). The whole operation was an exercise in collaboration, the success of which cannot be too much stressed. Local authority planning departments are exceptionally busy at the present time and a considerable extra load of work was created by the survey both in supervising the field work and in completing the material for the analysis. The volunteer field work help which made the survey possible came from colleges of education, schools, and voluntary bodies. We gratefully acknowledge the help of the chief planning officers and their staff of the Boroughs of Brent, Bristol, Camden, Leicester, Liverpool, Newcastle, Southampton, Southwark, Swansea and Worcester; the Principal, staff and students of the Maria Grey College, Brent; the Redland College, Bristol, the City of Leicester Training College, the Northumberland College, Newcastle; the College of the Immaculate Conception, Southampton; the Training College, Swansea; the City of Worcester Training College; the Head, staff and pupils of the Wyggeston Girls School, the Gateway Boys School, the Alderman Newton School for Girls, the Newark Girls School, the Collegiate Girls School in Leicester; the Friern School and the Rachel McMillan College of Southwark; the Hampstead I.V.S. Group.

We much appreciate the sponsorship of this particular survey by the Town Planning Institute. The Research Committee, under the chairmanship of Mr Wilfred Burns, undoubtedly influenced the response we received from the planning departments. We attempted to include Stockholm in this survey and found Mrs S. Wretlind-Larsson, Superintendent of Play Parks, Stockholm, most friendly and willing to co-operate against the odds of language difficulties and distance. Mr R. A. Pluck, Lecturer in Social Statistics, Department of Sociology, Bedford College, London, kindly advised us on the statistical analysis, and Mr Gordon Cherry of Newcastle Planning Department, Mr Donald Smith of Leicester Planning Department joined Mr Peter Wood, Mr David Foot and the authors to form a steering committee.

Of the ten boroughs listed above, nine also participated in the third survey of our study—the survey of existing facilities, thus involving themselves in yet more work. Ten other boroughs also took part, and with gratitude we acknowledge the help of the following: the chief planning officers and their staff of the Boroughs of Bradford, Coventry, Darlington, Derby, Gloucester, Kirkby, Lincoln, Norwich, Stevenage, Swindon; the Principal, staff and students of Bingley College of Education, Bradford; Coventry College of Education; Darlington College of Education; Bishop Lonsdale College of Education, Derby; Gloucester Training College; Kirkby Fields College of Education, Bishop Grosseteste College, Lincoln; Norwich Training College; Stevenage College of Further Education; and Mr R. H. May and Mr James Scott of Swindon.

We are immensely indebted to the members of our own team. Mrs Irma Bertram not only gave us stalwart secretarial and moral support but patient and constructive help with the analyses; Mrs Helen Gordon gave valuable assistance both in the preliminary and analysis stages of the work. We have also to thank Mrs Betty Marshall for her skilful typing and forbearance in the face of untidy manuscripts.

It is impossible to list the names of all the individuals, from officials at the Ministry of Housing and Local Government to play leaders and parents, with whom we talked informally and from whose advice and opinions we gained so much. It will not, we are sure, be thought invidious if we mention only two: Lady Allen of Hurtwood and the late Dr Simon Yudkin who, both in his capacity as chairman of the Council for Children's Welfare and personal friend, contributed so much to the promotion and furtherance of the project.

Our thanks are due to the following for permission to reproduce extracts from works in which they hold the copyright: Lady Allen of Hurtwood, *New Playgrounds*; Dr Robin H. Best, *Land for New Towns*; Cambridge University Press, *High Living* by Anne Stevenson, Elaine Martin and Judith O'Neill; Jonathan Cape Ltd., *The Death and Life of Great American Cities* by Jane Jacobs; The Commonwealth and International Library of Science, Technology, Engineering and Liberal Studies, *Planning for Men and Motor* by Paul Ritter; R. B. Gooch, *Selection and Layout of Land for Playing Fields and Playgrounds*; William Heinemann Ltd., *The Other Half* by Hunter Davies; Her Majesty's Stationery Office, *The Parker Morris Report, Written Evidence to the Royal Commission on Local Government in England* (Ministry of Housing and Local Government) and *Children's Play on Housing Estates* by Vere Hole; Hutchinson & Co. Ltd., *The Soviet Family* by D. and V. Mace; International Playground Association, Articles by Mrs Wretlind Larssen, Miss M. Mitchell, and H. Rupprecht in the *I.P.A. Newsletter*; London Borough of Southwark, *Recreation in Southwark: An Introductory Report of Continuing Studies* by F. O. Hayes; The Macmillan Company, New York, *Man the Sacred* by Roger Caillois and *The Neighbourhood and Child Conduct in Cities and Societies* by Henry D. McKay; Joan Maizels, *Two to Five in High Flats*; Methuen & Co. Ltd., *The World We have Lost* by Peter Laslett; Ministry of Housing and Local Government, an unpublished draft of *Families Living at High Density*; The National Playing Fields Association, *Playleadership* by W. D. Abernethy and *Statutes and Constitutions* by R. Owen; New Society, *Social Theory and the Planners* by Maurice Broady; Penguin Books Ltd., *The Family and Marriage* by Ronald Fletcher; Random House, Inc., *Crime and Society* by Gresham M. Sykes; The Ronald Press Co., New York, *Recreation Areas* by G. D.

Butler; Routledge & Kegan Paul Ltd., *Homo Ludens, a Study of the Play Element in Culture* by Johan Huizinga and *Play, Dreams and Imitation in Childhood* by Jean Piaget; The Royal Society for the Prevention of Accidents, *Road Accident Statistical Review*; Stina Sandels, *Survey of Activities 1958–1964 of the Research Institute on Developmental Psychology at Stockholm University, School of Education*; J. S. Slotkin, Article in *Social Anthropology* (New York); Sociological Review, University of Keele, *Notes on the Concepts of Play and Leisure* by A. Giddens; Stevenage Development Corporation, *Stevenage Traffic Accident Survey* 1957–1966 by E. C. Claxton; Tavistock Publications Ltd., *Stress and Release in an Urban Estate* by R. J. Spencer; Turku University Press, Finland, *Theoretical Aspects of Play and Socialisation* by R. Helanko; John Wiley & Sons Inc., New York, *Theory of Games and Economic Behaviour* by J. Van Neumann and Oskar Morganstern.

Our thanks are also due to the following for permission to reproduce photographs in which they hold the copyright: Henry Grant, A.I.I.P.; The Greater London Council; The Royal Danish Embassy; Valentine Rylands; The Borough of Blackburn and Mrs Mary Mitchell, F.I.L.A.; The American Machine Foundry Company, New York and John Olley for the map on page 207.

Finally we thank the children and mothers who have answered our questions. To them and the millions of others throughout the country this book is dedicated.

# Introduction

This Council's concern with the welfare of children is directly related to changes in society as they affect children. The present century has brought tremendous acceleration in these changes and an inevitable lagging behind in the adjustments necessary to cope with them.

Nowhere is this gap more apparent than in the opportunities for children to use their physical environment. Children will play when and *The* where they can: in the street, in the fields, on their way to and from *problem* school, in a crowd, on a piece of waste land, solitary on a railway station or waiting at a bus stop, running down a hillside, walking beside a canal, chasing round buildings, talking in quiet groups perched on walls, 'playing houses' in unlikely corners, swinging on lamp-posts or trees. But now the street is unsafe, the hillside probably inaccessible, much territory is forbidden, noise unpopular. It is the urban environment in particular which is becoming increasingly restrictive for these opportunities, and freedom to play is one of the major casualties.

The change from a rural to a predominantly urban environment during the late eighteenth and the nineteenth centuries was a major influence on the lives of children. Villages became towns and towns became cities overnight. The cities are still the great producing centres that they were, but, largely owing to the scientific and technological revolution of this century, their character is changing. Once again, the lives of children, along with the adult members of the community, are being affected.

Accompanying the industrialisation and urbanisation of nineteenth-century Britain was an enormous growth in the population. But these last years have seen an even more startling growth. This is, after all, the main reason why present and projected urban development must be conceived on such a vast scale. Population forecasts are notoriously unreliable but it would obviously be foolish for the planners to do other than work to the highest estimates. By the year 2000 it is forecast that the population of the United Kingdom will have increased by 19,000,000.[1] Thinking in terms of some of the boroughs investigated in one of the surveys of this study[2] this could mean twenty-six more cities the size of Liverpool, forty-four the size of Bristol, nearly three hundred the size of Worcester. In the London region it is expected that four million more people will have to be accommodated; in thirteen

1 Ministry of Land and Natural Resources.
2 Chapters 11, 12, 13.

more Southwarks? Or 'overspilled' into seventy-three more Stevenages?

But, in whatever way they are distributed, more and more children will be living in towns and cities. The country child, it is true, today finds many frustrations and obstacles to full freedom of activity: the jealous guarding of fields from trespass, woods hemmed in by barbed wire, or villages cut in half by uncrossable roads. Nevertheless, though the play needs of town and country children are the same, their play opportunities, and the problem of making these as abundant as possible, are different. It was not feasible to consider both within the same research programme and it was therefore decided to concentrate on the urban scene as comprising the greatest number of children and the greatest number of problems for children at play.

Most of these problems are present in today's environments. The aim is not only to prevent new problems arising, but to see that existing ones are not projected into the future. Such is the problem of space. In our vast, sprawling conurbations, in our constricted, cramped towns there are areas where the spare patches of ground seem smaller even than the patches of visible sky. Such also is the problem of traffic. Moving or stationary, motor traffic is a constant threat to the safety and lives of children. The roads, ever bigger and busier, form artificial barriers and restrict freedom of movement. Planners are aware of the need to preserve or create open space and government policy directs that they do so. Similarly there is a realisation of the need to come to terms with the motor car. But what is important is that in the competing claims for available space children's play needs get their rightful place in the list of priorities.

As well as restricted freedom outside the home there is restricted freedom within the home; overcrowded living conditions in old, poor housing are still characteristic of the towns and cities of today. And the buildings replacing them, the tower blocks and the hastily constructed housing estates, what kind of freedom are they providing? There is questioning too about the kind of play facilities which abound. Still in the majority are the familiar, dull, unimaginatively equipped, asphalted, flat squares or rectangles.

These are all material conditions. But there are related problems in other spheres: mothers at work for example, unstable home backgrounds, intolerance of children and their noise, the breaking-up of communities.

These and kindred problems are, for the most part, becoming increasingly recognised as having a bearing on the need to provide children with somewhere to play. But there is still reluctance to translate

this recognition into practical terms. And even if the willingness is *Reasons*
there, is enough known about the best way to do it? *for the*

The Council for Children's Welfare believed that enough was not *research*
known. Referring to play provision during a speech at the Town
Planning Institute in March 1966, Dr Nathaniel Lichfield made the
plea that all existing planning standards should be overhauled to
ensure that they meet the needs of our children rather than our parents.[1]

On the other hand, a local councillor of a borough renowned for its
enlightened policy on play provision, speaking at a meeting of an
organisation responsible for the administration of several London *Aims*
playgrounds, said that she 'wouldn't spend twopence on research. *of the*
Let's just get on with building the playgrounds.' *study*

But, quite apart from the hundreds of local authorities who don't
and won't get on with it, can one be sure that 'just building the playgrounds' is enough? Where should they be built to ensure that they are
available to the maximum number of children.? How should they be
built, equipped and staffed? How can it be known that the kind of
playgrounds that children really want and will go on using are being
provided? How much variety should children have in their play provision? Should age groups be mixed or kept separate?

Ask any of these questions and a dozen others, and a surprising number of different answers will be given; some are based on practical
experience, others on guesswork. In either case they are usually not
enough to convince the holders of the purse strings and the purveyors
of that most precious commodity, space.

Patching-up operations are one thing. New thinking on a scale
commensurate with that of new urban development is another; but for
both, as Dr Lichfield has suggested, adequate, reliable and up-to-date
standards are vital.

So the aim of this investigation was to provide documented evidence
for the planners and the providers; for the local authorities, the architects and the town planners. In this study we have looked at how
children in their play are responding to different environments. We
have attempted to assess children's play needs and relate them both to
the environment and to the type and scale of provision which may best
suit them. We have examined facilities already existing in certain selected
areas and have investigated the use made of some of these facilities.
We have studied the question of the administrative and financial
responsibility for children's play provision and have considered the

1   *The Guardian*, March 17, 1966.

general implications of urban planning and development for children's activities.

Our next problem was to decide what age range we should attempt to cover. Much research is currently being undertaken into the development of the very young child and a great deal of attention is rightly focused on the tremendous problem of their care and education in a society seemingly unable to grasp the dangers and difficulties which have accumulated because the problem has not been faced. It was impossible in our study to ignore the under-fives because play is, or should be, an intrinsic part of their lives, but we felt we could more usefully concentrate on the older children, the nine to fifteens who are only very rarely considered as a group needing provision for the hours they spend outside home and school. Accordingly, one part of the study investigated the out-of-home, out-of-school behaviour of this age group exclusively, whilst the rest took into account the entire age range up to fifteen.

For older children there is the difficulty of using the word *play*, which the children themselves do not like and which may convey too limited a meaning to many adults. Alternatives were considered—leisure activities, recreation, for instance—but these are equally unsatisfactory for young children and in themselves are inaccurate in describing the fundamental question we were proposing to consider. So we adhered to *play*.

*Scope of the study*

We started from the basic assumption that children need to play but we felt it necessary to explore the basis for such an assumption, bearing in mind that we were isolating for consideration certain kinds of play opportunities—those to be found outside home and school. This exploration into the theories of play begins the book (Chapter 1). There follows a brief history of play provision in this country (Chapter 2), and in Chapter 3 we survey the situation in several countries abroad.

Three separate pieces of research were carried out: a neighbourhood study in the boroughs of Southwark and Stevenage consisting of a survey of mothers' views on local play amenities and a comparison of school children's activities; a study of playgrounds and their use in ten boroughs; and a survey of existing facilities in nineteen boroughs. These are reported in the third section of the book with their own summaries (Chapter 8–13). To avoid confusion each investigation is introduced and described individually. Although each piece of research covered a different aspect of children's play there was inevitably an overlap in the conclusions. To avoid repetition, therefore, the conclusions are presented together in Chapter 4. These conclusions arise strictly from the research, but their implications are far-reaching and must also be affected by a number of other factors that we have not been able to investigate but upon which it may be considered legitimate to hold opinions or which have already been subjected to other research. These implications, therefore, are discussed in two further chapters (Chapters 5 and 6).

Finally we offer a policy for play (Chapter 7). Many of the suggestions we make can only be tentative because they depend upon projected changes in local government structure. Others are tentative because our research has not thrown up the answers and there is insufficient evidence from other sources. Any suggestions of the kind we make have to take into account the slow tempo of reform in the world of social affairs. We allow for this in differentiating between short-term and long-term possibilities. We would not, however, wish that this should excuse the urgency of the situation. For there is an urgency. The years of childhood are not long. Successive generations are leaving these years behind them and entering adolescence and adulthood whilst the powers argue over a piece of land and continue to make do with the inadequacies and mediocrities inherited from the past. Each of these generations is a generation deprived; deprived of a vital dimension in its development and in the pleasures of being a child.

# Background to the Study

# I

## Theories of Play

The importance of play in children's physical, intellectual and
emotional development is now undisputed; such activities as the
exploration of a child's environment, being with other children,
physical exercise, imaginative games—activities which we adults
normally call play—are all essential to this development. There has
not always been this certainty and even today the equating of play with
idleness is not uncommon, though there is usually an inherent qualification in the kind of play described. Social anthropological studies
suggest that this is universal:

'. . . every society categorises play on the basis of its mores. Play
which is right is *recreation*; play which is wrong is *vice*.'[1]

There were always the exceptional thinkers—Rousseau[2] was one—
who saw beyond the moral codes of the day and realised the value of
play in children's development, but it was within the structure of
formal education that the play role was first worked out in practical
terms. Nearly a hundred and fifty years ago the great educationalist,
Froebel, stressed the immense importance of play as an educational
tool and devised a system of education which centred on learning
through experience, or learning from the environment.[3] Through
Froebel's work, and that of other educational pioneers, play as a method
of learning has become an essential element in the education of young
children in Britain and elsewhere.[4]

Towards the end of the nineteenth century interest in play grew and
a number of speculative theories were evolved on different aspects of

1 Slotkin (1950), p. 282.
2 Boyd (1911).
3 Froebel (1826).
4 Reaney (1927).

the nature of play but not specifically related to its educative role. These early theories have been categorised under two headings: physiological and biological. Predominant in the physiological category are two theories of play known as the *surplus energy* theory[1] and the *recreation* theory.[2] Surplus energy simply means that there is a supply of energy in man, over and above that which is necessary to sustain life; from this surplus the play impulse derives. But it is not possible to separate the energy needed for play, whether it be physical or mental, from that needed for other activities. This is particularly so with children. However, there are the beginnings here of modern interpretation.

The recreation theory suggests that man plays only when his mental and physical powers are fatigued. This, in contradiction to the surplus energy theory, ignores the fact that a considerable amount of energy, both physical and mental, may be needed for play activity.

Under the biological heading come two main theories which embody respectively the concepts of *preparation for life*[3] and *recapitulation*.[4] The recapitulation theory supposes that in play children reproduce all the past cultures of their race. Building dens, therefore, is viewed as a survival of the period when it was necessary to construct such places to live in, and hunting games derive from the time when it was necessary to hunt in order to survive. Play as a preparation for life implies that all play behaviour is helping to fashion particular skills that will be necessary for survival in mature or adult life.

Of all these early theories this is the one that has been the most influential. Before publishing the *Play of Man* Groos wrote *The Play of Animals* in which he really set the 'preparation for life' theory in motion and crystallised many of the ideas he uses later in the *Play of Man*. In the *Play of Man* he says:

'I consider the governing force of instinct as having been fully established in the study of animal play.'[5]

and again:

'among higher animals certain instincts are present which especially in youth, but also in maturity, produce activity that is without

1   Schiller (1875), Spencer (1872).
2   Lazarus (1883).
3   Groos (1898 and 1901).
4   Hall (1905).
5   Groos (1901), *op. cit.*, p. 1.

*Notting Hill adventure playground*

*Modern playgrounds: two schools of thought*

serious intent, and so give rise to the various phenomena which we include in the word "play".'[1]

Later he writes:

'The biological criterion of play is that it shall deal not with the serious exercise of the special instinct, but with practice preparatory to it. Such practice always corresponds to definite need, and is accompanied by pleasurable feelings.'[2]

and:

'Play is the agency employed to develop crude powers and prepare them for life's uses.'[3]

If interpreted generously enough the two essential points made by Groos, that play is a pre-exercise or preparation for life's situations and that play is a thing apart are supported by more recent writers.[4] Undoubtedly, significant similarities in play behaviour between children and the young of other species do exist and the recognition of this has resulted to some extent in the incorporation of the earlier biological concept of play into later psychological theories. Nevertheless, considerable caution is necessary in interpreting results of animal studies in terms of human behaviour.

There is one fundamental difference between the play of animals and the human child which Groos did not apparently see and that is the social aspect of children's play. When the kitten is playing—pouncing upon another kitten or even chasing its own tail—it is actually exercising talents that it will need to catch food, its ability to flatten its body against the ground, the element of surprise and the quickness of the action are the identical and similar movements that will be used in maturity to catch a mouse or rat. Though the same may be said of children acquiring and practising the sensory motor skills it certainly cannot be said of a child playing with dolls or making mud cakes to be baked. So, too precise a comparison may be misleading. Animals tend to have a rigid pattern of behaviour that is instinctual, the human child does not; it must acquire social as well as physical and symbolic skills to lead a normal life. A distinction should be made here between higher and lower mammals in the animal world. Present-day ethological

---

1 Groos (1901), *op. cit.*, p. 2.
2 *Ibid.*, p. 5.
3 *Loc. cit.*
4 E.g. Huizinga (1949), Caillois (1961).

studies[1] with higher mammals reveal the necessity of social play. What is important for animal and human is that play makes adaptation possible.

The other point that Groos has made is that play is a thing in itself. It is this aspect of play that Professor Huizinga takes up in *Homo Ludens*:

> 'play is more than a mere physiological phenomenon or a psychological reflex. In play there is something "at play" which transcends the immediate needs of life and imparts meaning to the action.'[2]

What Huizinga saw in play was a quality that had no obvious unit of measure, 'Play casts a spell over us; it is "enchanting".'[3] It is this very qualification that detaches the play world from the everyday world where the realities of an on-going society have to be faced. Despite what appears to be a separateness the 'real world' and the 'play world' are inextricably mixed. Huizinga was more interested in showing how the play element has influenced our culture, indeed he sees the play influence everywhere and even argues that the give and take of parliamentary democracy is possible because of the play element in our culture. Roger Caillois, while acknowledging the influence of Huizinga, took a more rigorous sociological approach to the subject by defining play as having six essential qualities: free; separate; uncertain; unproductive; governed by rules; and having make believe.[4] He also saw games as having a fourfold classification: those with competition, chance, simulation, and vertigo.[5] Caillois, like Huizinga, insists that play is something more than it appears. He has written:

> 'No one can deny that play is pure form, activity that is an end in itself.'[6]

If Caillois is correct, then play is fundamental as relaxation and leisure for the adult. But for children it is equally fundamental in terms of

---

1  Harlow *et al.* clearly demonstrated in their experiments with young monkeys that if they are deprived of social play (i.e. playing with other young monkeys) they have difficulties later in developing normal social and sexual relationships. (Harlow, 1962)
2  Huizinga, *op. cit.*, p. 1.
3  *Ibid.*, p. 10.
4  Caillois (1961), p. 9.
5  *Ibid.*, p. 36.
6  Caillois (1959), p. 157.

their physical development and socialisation. And it is with children here that we are concerned.

It is in the psychological field that play theory in relation to children has been most fully and consistently developed. Freud[1] saw play as a cathartic experience providing an important emotional outlet. He also interpreted it as a means of acting out rôles, thus contributing to the function of *ego-expansion*. But it is from Piaget[2] that the most outstanding contribution to the understanding of the role of play in childhood comes. He rejects the idea of play being a pre-exercise and points out that the difficulties of understanding play have arisen:

> 'because play has been considered as an isolated function rather than an aspect of, or characteristic of, a particular piece of behaviour.[3]

Although Piaget, like Groos, Huizinga and Caillois, believed that play was something in itself,[4] he was more interested in the function of play in the development of children. He divided children's play into three developmental categories: practice games, that is play through acquired physical skills; symbolic games, play where there is implied representation of an absent object as well as make-believe representation; and games with rules, these are essentially social games with rules imposed by the group. Even at a very early age a child can exhibit play behaviour:

> 'Play begins, then, with the first dissociation between assimilation and accommodation. After learning to grasp, swing, throw, etc., which involve both an effort of repetition, reproduction and generalization, which are the elements of assimilation, the child sooner or later (often in the learning period) grasps for the pleasure of grasping; swings for the sake of swinging, etc.'[5]

Piaget uses two of his key concepts here, 'assimilation' and 'accommodation'. When a playing child assimilates pieces of experience through play, he adopts the experience into his own limited world; but by accommodation he meets the demands of reality and experience; in play, assimilation is predominant, so play is seen as assimilation of reality to the ego; for the child lives in an egocentric world.

1   Freud (1922).
2   Piaget (1951).
3   *Ibid.*, p. 147.
4   *Ibid.*, p. 168.
5   *Ibid.*, p. 162.

'When a child plays, he certainly does not believe, in the sense of socialised belief, in the context of his symbolism, but precisely because symbolism is egocentric thought we have no reason to suppose that he does not believe in his own way anything he chooses. From his point of view "the deliberate illusion" which Lange and Groos see in play is merely the child's refusal to allow the world of adults or of ordinary reality to interfere with play, so as to enjoy a private reality of his own. But this reality is believed in spontaneously, without effort, merely because it is the universe of the ego, and the function of play is to protect this universe against forced accommodation to ordinary reality.[1]

Piaget's interpretation of children's use of symbolism is dependent upon his own observations and tests of the way a child thinks in the various developmental stages which precede logical thought. As a child's intellectual powers increase so the symbolic play would decrease, the real world weakens the strength of the play world and at about the age of seven games with rules predominate. The rules are not the formal rules of conventional games but rules created by the children to enable them to indulge in more realistic make-believe in contrast to the 'reflective belief', as Piaget called it, that exists in symbolic play.

So we can see how Piaget's observations of play behaviour are consistent with the concept of the socialisation process. Play allows the child gradually to come to terms with the external world and at the same time have a controllable and secure world of its own. In time, experience and understanding gained through play are sufficient to allow the child to take on the more abstract complexities of the objective world around. It is this seeming inseparability of play and socialisation that makes play such an important subject for all those concerned with the education and welfare of children. For the interaction is such that regard must be paid to the influence of the socialisation process on the play world as well as to the role of play in socialisation. Helanko, a Finnish sociologist, saw the relationship between play behaviour and the socialisation process as one of continuous interaction.

'The new systems[2] that interfere with play force the individual to

1  Piaget (1951), p. 168.
2  Helanko defined play in terms of forms of interaction which he called 'systems'. Play could be a primary system, that is when the subject acts upon the object; and a social system, that is when the subject interacts with the object which is also a subject. The primary system is one-way; the social system is two-way. So a system becomes play if the individual subject can freely choose the object of the system without interference.

function according to the situation. Pure undisturbed play, on the other hand, does not compel the individual to exert himself in any way . . . Since the system that interferes with play usually promotes socialization there seems to be an apparent incompatibility between play and socialization. . . . Only the alternation of play and non-play can promote socialization.'[1]

Helanko saw play behaviour in psychoanalytical terms as tension relieving, which implies that if play is inhibited the individual would become neurotic. It seems reasonable to believe that in individual play a child has the opportunity to select the world it wishes and reject the real world with its tensions of success or failure. As the ever-present world of reality keeps up the pressure, the haven of the play world may be seen as therapeutic. In fact, the therapeutic value of play has been well established.[2] Equally in social play, games will allow individual interpretation of social roles within the context of the rules; the rules may be created to suit the needs of the players and so each player may develop a sense of his own social identity. But the real world cannot be rejected; the society into which children have been born requires them to develop certain types of behaviour to survive, and because of the complete dependence of the child it is easy to impose acceptable social behaviour. Behaviour that is desired is rewarded and thereby reinforced, so the norms and values of the different cultures that children grow up in are inculcated. Without this interaction process a child would not acquire specifically human behaviour characteristics.[3] We know from a cross-cultural study of child-rearing patterns in six different societies[4] that formal and informal play arrangements for children vary from culture to culture. In industrial societies, where childhood is prolonged on the assumption that children are not full members of society, play receives nowadays considerable recognition for its importance in their healthy development and socialisation. In some non-industrial societies the need of child labour necessarily cuts across much of the time that would be devoted to play by children in other societies; play is snatched along with the various duties to be performed. Different types of behaviour are encouraged or discouraged from one culture to another by different child rearing patterns, but despite this all children have the common behaviour characteristics of

1   Helanko (1958), p. 21.
2   See e.g. Lowenfeld (1935).
3   Gesell (1946).
4   Whiting (1963).

play. 'Children in quite separate cultures develop similar rudimentary play forms apparently spontaneously and without instruction.'[1] In their play children will imitate the roles of persons close to them, what is significant for the child will be important, he may practise roles that carry privileges or rewards, parents are obviously influential. Simple games of mothers and fathers and schools are acted out without the complexities of everyday life. The simple structure of the game helps the child towards an understanding of some of the complex social arrangements around it. Because the child imposes his own rules upon the game he expects and anticipates certain responses to certain action. The rules of the game are much the same as those described in the sophisticated 'Theory of games and economic behaviour':

> 'The rules of the game, however, are absolute commands. If they are infringed, then the whole transaction by definition ceases to be the game described by those rules.'[2]

We have all heard a child cry: 'That's not fair, you're not playing', implying the rules have been broken. So the child will go on abstracting parts of real-life roles into a simple composite role governed by simple rules that he understands; the peculiar balance between 'assimilation' and 'accommodation'. Later in the child's development more formal games with formal rules are played, thus moving nearer to the complexities of the real-life group relationship. Gradually the importance of play behaviour seems to recede although it is retained throughout adulthood. 'Economic obligation' takes over and play activity is transformed into work activity which in turn is imitated by the child as play activity. But in the sphere of games, distinctions are less clear. Footballers who play for money must take the game seriously and lose the play pleasure though spectators may retain theirs. Professionalism in many leisure pursuits has converted simple play to serious intent and the conversion has rubbed off onto situations which have no connection with the 'real' world. Even at school it is now considered more important to win than to play. Thus, what happens after the game becomes an important part of the game; it is no longer free and separate. It is possible that the corruption of play behaviour could reach further down the scale if the nature of, and the necessity for, play is not understood.

The seemingly contradictory mixture of theories which has so far

1   Giddens (1964), p. 77.
2   Neumann (1964), p. 49.

been considered may best be clarified by distinguishing four main aspects of play.

First, the nature of play. It is possible to extract criteria which are common to most theories. Giddens has identified three common strands of a major kind: 'play is an activity which is by and large non-instrumental in character'; 'on a social level, play is a relatively self-contained activity'; and 'play is essentially a non-productive activity'.[1]

Secondly, the function of play. One may look at the suggested functions of play as they occur in the various theories and decide which, either by standing the test of time or because they have been confirmed by empirical study, would seem to have a universal significance. Here we suggest that there are four main functions: play relieves tensions and provides emotional outlet; play has a vital role in the socialisation of children; it is part of the learning process; and play gives satisfactions of achievement and self-realisation which may otherwise be frustrated.

Thirdly, the stages of play. It is helpful to consider the kinds of play which are seen to occur—group, solitary, exploratory, manipulative, imaginative—in relation to the various stages in children's development, particularly the three main stages postulated by Piaget.[2]

Fourthly, the definition of play. It cannot be precisely defined. Helanko saw the essential difficulty of isolating play for the purpose of defining it. 'Play is actually like a person in hiding, who now and then gives a sign of his presence, only to disappear again in the next instance.[3] The individual, particularly the child, cannot always say whether or not he is playing, and certainly this is frequently undiscernible externally. This difficulty is unimportant in terms of the child's behaviour, in fact it is central to the concept of play as outlined above.

In the context of providing opportunities for play, however, the inability to define is important. If play is an 'aspect of a particular piece of behaviour', and if it is often undistinguishable from the piece of behaviour itself, then it becomes necessary to think of play in the context in which it occurs and more than ever necessary to protect the freedom of children so that their physical, emotional and intellectual growth may proceed unhindered. A consideration of the nature and the functions of play as summarised above confirms these necessities.

Other conclusions must also follow. Piaget's three main stages of

1  Giddens, *op. cit.*, p. 74.
2  See page 35.
3  Helanko (1958).

development suggest a clear differentiation in the types of provision suited to each stage, though this does not necessarily mean that there should be segregation of facilities. But however the facilities are organised the various kinds of play must be given full scope for their realisation.

If play is essentially a 'non-productive' and 'non-instrumental' activity—that is, 'not linked psychologically to purposes which are external to the activity',[1] care must obviously be taken that the play situation is not exploited. And here there arises a difficulty in reconciling the implications of this with those of the second two of our main play functions—socialisation and learning. As the child grows up the solution, as we have suggested earlier, is largely self-generating. The demands of the real world become irresistible and the child learns to balance these with those of the 'unreal' world—his play world. (Piaget's accommodation concept.) He can be helped in this at the earlier stages as well as at this later stage of development by sympathetic adult supervision, but it is imperative that there should be full awareness of the extreme delicacy of the balance. Without such an awareness the value of play to the child is placed in jeopardy.

Finally, since external tension is destructive to play it is necessary when creating an environment which is to be used by children to ensure that parts of it may be used without having to acknowledge all that is going on around. Some parts of the environment must be free from household and outside urban dangers where a child can truly play.

1  Giddens, *loc. cit.*

# 2

## Outline History of Play Facility Provision in this Country[1]

The industrial revolution is the great watershed in Britain's modern
social history. The magic phrase 'pre-industrial days' is often used to
evoke a falsely idyllic picture. Different those days certainly were and
for the children as much as for anyone. Painstaking research[2] is slowly
revealing patterns of living which have only been guessed at before—
often wrongly. But still surprisingly little is known, for instance, about
'what happened when children went out to play; whether it was in
family groups, or whether it was neighbourhood gangs, even village
gangs embodying rich and poor, the privileged along with the rest.
We do not know very much about what they played, or even about
what they were encouraged to play or to do.'[3] Laslett has shown that
children shared in the work of the family and the community at a
very early age; and that there were swarms of children everywhere—
they dominated the rural scene. In those days, however much or little
they were expected to play, there was space in plenty.

The space began to shrink with the implementation of the notorious
Enclosure Acts and the changing of society from a rural to an urban one.
Towns and cities in the nineteenth century grew at a prodigious rate.
The overriding need was to house the people pouring into them and the
ever-multiplying working force. Considerations of care and comfort,
hygiene, recreational amenity and of simple human dignity were
subordinated to this need. Children had worked in the villages as
members of the family working unit. Now they were exploited in the
vast industrial melting pot. Undernourished, overworked, uneducated,

1  For a more detailed historical account see Owen (1967).
2  Notably that of Laslett (1965).
3  *Ibid.*, p. 104.

disease on the doorstep, squalor and overcrowding within, smoke veiling the sun—such was the lot of numbers of town children during those years. Doubtless, being children, they somehow contrived to play but time and opportunity must have been very scarce; small wonder that the social conscience began to prick and questions such as 'Is there any place to which the children of humbler classes may resort for any game or exercise?'[1] were asked.

The first reference to children and play on the statute books appears in the Recreation Grounds Act of 1859:

> 'Whereas the Want of open public Grounds for the Resort and Recreation of Adults, and of Playgrounds for Children and Youth is much felt in the Metropolis and other popular Places within this Realm, and by reason of the great and continuous Increase of Population and Extension of Towns such Evil is seriously increasing, and it is desirable to provide a Remedy for the same.'

This realisation of the importance of open space in an urban environment was reflected during the ensuing years in a series of Acts of Parliament: some, like the Public Improvements Act of 1860 and the Open Space Act of 1906, concerned exclusively with the subject; others, like the great Public Health Act of 1875 and the several subsequent Public Health Amendment Acts, recognising its significance in relation to the general health and welfare of the nation. There is little recorded history about the early playgrounds. In Birmingham for instance the first site belonging to the Parks Committee to be laid out as a playground was Burbury Street Recreation Ground in 1877, but what was meant by a playground then is unclear.[2] There is no mention of equipment and it may have just been surfaced to allow ball games and so on.

The Education Act of 1870 and other reforms that followed gradually transformed the lives of young children; school rather than the factory or the mine was to become the rival centre to home. Notwithstanding the increasing number of open spaces and the changing orientation in children's lives the street, 'their street', certainly was the principal playground for most urban children. They, probably, were less bothered than the reformers, for the street would have had the advantages then as now of proximity to home, familiarity, constant supervision and providing an automatic meeting ground for friends.

1  Smith (1964), p. 178.
2  Taken from unpublished material.

Hitherto, allocation of space had been the main aim in the agitation for play facilities but now a new element was added—the belief that children of the working classes would benefit from healthy play and recreation—and at the turn of the century the first 'play centres' began to appear. The difference in nomenclature is significant. These centres, unlike the playgrounds, were places which set out deliberately to attract and which had a decided educational bias.

The early play centres were all creations of voluntary bodies. Perhaps the first of its kind established was the Children's Happy Evenings Association opened in 1888. Their first six centres were an experiment but by 1914 they had ninety-six centres situated in London schools besides centres in at least ten other towns. The centres were only open one night a week for boys and another night for girls between the hours of 5 p.m. to 7 p.m. The activities organised at the centres included drill, skipping, dancing, singing, games, tailoring, cobbling, rug making, sewing, basket work, painting and boxing.[1] Later, in 1897, a more thorough and progressive voluntary organisation, the Pasmore Edwards Settlement, inspired by Mrs Humphrey Ward, set up a Play Centre open five nights a week and Saturday morning. In 1907 seven more play centres were opened and by 1915 the number had risen to twenty-two. Each centre was led by a woman superintendent; she was assisted by paid and voluntary helpers. The superintendent was paid £45 to £55 per year and worked an eighteen-hour week, the helpers were paid 2/6 to 4/- a night. A woman was also employed to look after the younger children. Most of the centres were sited in elementary schools and were free of charge. The children, both boys and girls, were allowed to attend two to three evenings a week; where social circumstances were difficult they could attend more regularly, the under sevens being allowed to attend every day.[2]

In a report published in 1917 play centres were seen to have two major objectives: 'to improve the bodily and mental development of the children and to prevent juvenile crime or mischief by offering an attractive alternative to the streets.' The latter objective was thought to be the most important because of the 'relaxed parental control' due to the war and the restricted street lighting at the time. The centres in fact tended to cater for the most deprived sections of the community.

In London and many of the other large urban centres Guilds of Play organised games in the city parks. Parks Committees generally co-operated with the movement. In Manchester recreation grounds

1  Campbell (1917), II.
2  *Ibid.*

were first organised by private voluntary groups in 1911, later they were adopted by the Parks Committee and by 1913 there were eleven recreation grounds. Woman instructors were employed and five centres had sand gardens, an idea that had come from Berlin where public sand heaps were a feature of the parks.[1] Thus, in a limited if somewhat negative sense play was already seen as something of value in itself. But at the same time one of the greatest influences of our time—the science of psychology—was developing. Its full impact on children's play was not to be felt for some time, but already in the first years of the century the early theories were being evolved in this and other countries.[2] They were applied in the first instance more to very small children and indeed still today, the significance of play in a child's development is thought of primarily for the under fives. In the primary schools, however, it became increasingly recognised as a vital element in education. In the inter-war years the numbers of municipal playgrounds increased but they still came from the same mould—heavy fixed equipment, asphalt covered, occasionally a sand pit, sometimes attended to ensure the observance of the regulations, located in parks and recreation grounds. During these years only two pieces of legislation, embodied in the Physical Training and Recreation Act of 1937 and the Street Playgrounds Act of 1938, showed any official recognition of the recreational needs of the young. The latter empowered local authorities to close certain streets to traffic. It was introduced more as the result of alarm at the growing number of street accidents to children than from a positive desire to remedy the shortage of play space. The former included the important step of giving the Board of Education powers to make grants not only towards the provision and equipment of gymnasiums, swimming baths and so on but of 'other buildings and premises for physical training and recreation' and 'towards the expenses of a local authority or local voluntary organisation in respect of the training and supply of teachers and leaders' and 'to the friends of any national voluntary organisation having such objects as aforesaid'.

Since its inauguration in 1925 the National Playing Fields Association has become an increasingly influential pressure group. Its early efforts were directed largely to the securing of playing fields but fairly soon it extended its horizons and the Physical Training and Recreation Act of 1937 was chiefly the result of its agitation.

There has been considerable speculation about the possible harmful effects of their experiences on the thousands of small evacuees who

1  *Loc. cit.*
2  See Chapter 1.

44

streamed out of the cities into country towns and villages at the outbreak of war in 1939 and stayed for varying periods, reinforced by new contingents during the ensuing years. For those aged under five who never left the cities or who returned, day care was provided on an unprecedented scale to enable their mothers to contribute to the war effort. Education for the older children suffered severe dislocation whether they remained in their temporary homes or returned, but the war affected play activity in curious ways.

'Serious shortage of material and equipment, both during and after the war, led to much improvisation and "do it yourself" enterprise which had a direct influence in the schools and in the construction of informal apparatus. It was not difficult to trace a connection with "commando" training, in the use of nets and ropes for clambering, swinging and climbing, to encourage pluck and initiative.'[1]

Undoubtedly also the splendid opportunities for adventurous play afforded by the innumerable bomb sites were a fruitful source of ideas for the pioneers who saw value in this kind of play.

The 1944 Education Act was important not only for the changes in formal education which it introduced but also for the sections which conferred powers upon the Local Education Authorities to provide facilities for out-of-school hours. This Act, the 1946 National Health Service Act and the 1948 Nurseries and Child Minders Act all gave powers of different kinds to local authorites concerning children under five. In spite of these powers, however, and in spite of growing pressures resulting from obvious need, statutory provision for these children steadily declined in the post-war years. Attempts as usual were made to fill the gap by voluntary effort; the work of the Save the Children Fund in this field and the formation of the Pre-School Playgroups Association are monuments to these attempts. But, as has been clearly revealed by recent study, something more comprehensive is needed.

Voluntary effort was active during the latter part of the war and the years immediately following on behalf of older children too. The Under Fourteens Council and Lady Allen of Hurtwood between them were virtually responsible for crystallising the Danish ideas[2] on play into a workable form for this country. The first public playground of

1 Owen, *op. cit.*, p. 18.
2 See pp. 47, 48 and Appendix I.

this kind was set up by a voluntary group in Camberwell in 1948 and lasted for three years.[1]

The vicissitudes of those early years of the junk or adventure playground movement have been well documented by Joe Benjamin, an early practitioner in the field.[2]

Several adventure playgrounds were founded and run by voluntary associations during the fifties; only some have endured. The movement, however, is by now firmly established and, significantly, is being taken over in a growing number of instances by statutory authority. In recent years the question of supervised facilities has assumed importance in all discussions of children's play provision and there is now considerable variety within the provision. These differences will be explored in later chapters.[3]

1 Benjamin (1966), p. 16.
2 *Ibid.*
3 See Chapters 6, 7 and 12, and Appendix I.

# 3

# The International Scene

In recent years the subject of children's play has quite frequently earned the distinction of an international conference. UNESCO sponsor a regular conference concerned with the under fives under the auspices of the *Organisation Mondial pour l'Education Pré-Scholaire* (OMEP). The United Nations held a European Seminar on Playground Activities, Objectives and Leadership in Stockholm in the summer of 1958 and out of this there grew a permanent organisation—The International Playground Association.[1]

Appropriately the Director of the Seminar was Swedish, Mrs S. Wretlind-Larsson, and the first President of the International Playground Association was Professor C. Th. Sorensen, from Denmark. These two countries were the first to recognise that good play provision was not simply a matter of fixed equipment in a piece of available space.

## Denmark

Denmark is justly renowned on two counts: for the original 'junk' playground, conceived by Professor Sorensen in 1931 and realised at Emdrup in 1943, and for the Copenhagen Building Regulations. The latter which came into force as long ago as 1939 ensure that housing blocks intended for more than eight families shall be provided with children's play space. The space must be segregated from courtyards used for trade purposes, garages, etc. The regulations have been extended to other parts of Denmark under the Town and Country Building Act of 1961. They include the important provision that the building authorities may oppose development of open space nearby if it is required and would be suitable for children, thus inhibiting the

[1] For particulars see Appendix V.

appropriation of the space for garages and car parks.[1] This is an exactly reverse order of priorities to that which obtains in this country. There is a continual rethinking of the aims of play provision in Denmark which manifests itself in new experiments such as the building site playground[2] and new legislation (Children and Juvenile Welfare Act, 1965) which ensures various forms of 'socio-educational' facilities and enables central and local government grants towards their establishment and main-tenance.[3] At the time of writing there are four hundred and fifty-four leisure time centres for the young in Denmark. Of these over half are to be found in Copenhagen, all with one or more trained leaders. These leaders have a full-time training course of two years and professional standards of pay.

## Sweden

One of the first things to strike a visitor to Stockholm is the quantity of recreational and ornamental open space throughout the city and the ever recurring glimpses of water. The visitor who is interested in children's play provision cannot fail to observe the frequency with which the pretty little symbol of the 'Parkleken' (play park) occurs within the recreational spaces, on housing estates and at street corners. Apart from innumerable unsupervised play areas—often just a sandpit and two or three pieces of equipment well sited on housing estates or in the parks—there are at the time of writing sixty-two full-time supervised playparks and sixty-five during the summer only. This means that for part of the year there are enough of these playgrounds to cater for the child population of Stockholm at a rate of just over eleven hundred children per playground and during the winter months at a rate of just under two thousand five hundred children per playground.

The play leaders (usually two or three in number with additional part-time help where necessary) have all had five months' full-time training in a vocational school. Three most important elements are invariably provided—indoor accommodation, a 'play pen' for the under fives and sand; water almost always. In the larger play parks there is a hard-surfaced ball-games area, moving equipment is fenced off for safety; building blocks and similar play materials are in plentiful supply; Wendy houses are a feature of many of the playgrounds and in winter, turning the climate to good advantage, the playgrounds

1  Sigsgaard (1965), p. 16.
2  See p. 97.
3  Sigsgaard, *op. cit.*, p. 18.

provide facilities for skating, sledging and so on. Although adventure play sections are provided in several of the play parks it is undoubtedly a much more ordered, circumscribed sort of play than that which is to be found in adventure playgrounds in this country. An extensive organisation is behind these Stockholm play parks headed by Mrs Wretlind-Larsson, and generous official financial backing. To the casual observer they reflect a way of life very different from our own.

Gothenburg is well known for the landscaping of its play provision and its imaginative equipment.

## France

France's chief contribution to the field of children's play would seem to be its *centres de loisirs* on the outskirts of the cities and its famous *colonies de vacances* which are administered by the *Haut Commissaire de la Jeunesse et des Sports*. Strings of children can invariably be seen by the sea or in the country during the summer months and there are few students who at some time or other have not done their stint as moniteurs or monitrices in a holiday camp. These camps undoubtedly serve a tremendously useful purpose, particularly for those families in which the mothers go out to work. The general emphasis in France is on club activity and sport, on 'preventive teams' to combat delinquency.[1] There is a shortage of park land within the cities and an unimaginative use of space within easy access of home—and 'home' in France, as elsewhere, is likely to be on the eighteenth floor of a tower block. A law has recently been passed to ensure the provision of play space within new building.

## Germany

The space aspect of play provision has perhaps been more highly developed in post-war Germany than in any other European country. The devastated cities had to be rebuilt entirely and advantage has been taken of new town planning philosophies and techniques. The importance of children's play has not been overlooked in this new thinking. For many years it had held an honourable place in specialist literature which culminated in 1960 in the publication of the *Golden Plan*—a guide for the erection of recreation, play and sports centres. Included in this plan are play space standards for size and distance.[2] These very

1 Marty (1966), pp. 12–16.
2 See Appendix V.

detailed standards are regarded as guides only. A less precise formula is to be found in the various provincial building regulations. In Ulm, for example 'on the erection of buildings with more than three dwellings, areas are to be provided on the site on which children can play and such areas are to be provided where need arises. This is not so when a community area is provided in the immediate neighbourhood, or when the type of dwelling or the activation of the buildings does not require it.'[1]

## Yugoslavia

In Yugoslavia also, specific space standards have been set which, however, cannot apparently be fully met in the high-density cities of Belgrade and Zagreb with their bursting child populations. By law each housing project must possess play space. The authorities are responsible for the equipment of playgrounds, but policy dictates that housing tenants' associations should look after the equipment and employ the leaders which when adopted probably results in an increase in rent.[2]

## Poland

Interestingly, the same dependence on tenants' initiative is evident in Poland and in the U.S.S.R. A flourishing community play centre in Warsaw was created out of a 'backyard slum', in this case by the individual efforts of the housing superintendent who stimulated action amongst the children.[3]

## U.S.S.R.

An account of a similar success story, based on this instance on action by the tenants themselves, in a town in the U.S.S.R. is given in a pamphlet about Soviet children.[4] But in the U.S.S.R. there is also a highly organised system for the care of children which includes extensive recreational and play facilities. Two English observers found that 'if you enter a Soviet village where all the buildings except one are drab and depressing, that one fine structure will probably turn out to be

1　Rupprecht (1966), p. 13.
2　Milincovic (1961), pp. 22, 23, 25.
3　'Poland' (1967), No. 2.
4　Didusenko (1964), pp. 41, 42.

the Palace of the Young Pioneers. The children's schools, their parks, their recreation centres are the best that can possibly be provided.'[1] The care of under fives outside the home has been highly developed and opportunities for play in the facilities provided are given serious priority.

## Italy

In many other western European countries not yet mentioned, as in the United Kingdom, a slowly growing awareness of the need to provide adequate facilities for children's play is to be found. In Italy, for example, active experiments are being made with supervised play provision, though as yet on an exceedingly limited scale. These experiments have had official financial help[2]—always a landmark in any voluntarily sponsored endeavour. At the time of writing, an ambitious research project into children's play is being carried out, sponsored by the *Comitato Italiano per il Gioco Infantile* (Committee for Children's Games) which has already produced an impressive bibliography. This Committee, financed jointly by Olivetti's and the Provincial Administration of Turin, is also responsible for the experimental play provision mentioned above. The Comitato frankly take their ideas for these experiments from our own adventure playgrounds and from the 'Robinson' playgrounds of Zürich.

## Switzerland

The 'Robinson' playgrounds first came into being in 1955 through the drive and inspiration of Professor Ledermann. They can best be described as 'comprehensive' playgrounds and in spite of their element of adventure the emphasis is perhaps more on other aspects of play and recreation: craft rooms, libraries, theatres, team games and sport, sand and water play for the under fives, the keeping of pets. Great importance is attached to the integration of the family and old people into the leisure life of the young. There is no central federal responsibility, or ministerial organisation for children's play in Switzerland, or for sports and leisure activities and no obligatory powers. Everything is left to each canton and, within each canton, to city councils or parish communes. The 'Robinson' playgrounds are to be found in Zürich, Basle and Berne and are run by a heavily subsidised voluntary

1 Mace (1963), p. 247.
2 Paviolo (1965), pp. 6–8.

organisation—*Pro Juventute*. There are no supervised playgrounds in other parts of Switzerland but again, as in France, club activities, sports centres and so on are catered for on quite a substantial scale through the *Service de l'École et des Œuvres de Jeunesse* and the *Services de Loisirs*.

## Belgium

Travellers through Belgium may have noticed an unusual type of play facility. These are the little, conventionally equipped playgrounds attached to cafés and restaurants. One occasionally finds large department stores in some countries which follow this practice though here the expense is greater because there is usually some form of supervision. The costs in both cases must surely pay high dividends in food and drink consumption and goods purchased. It is surprising that more commercial enterprises don't follow suit. Beach clubs—consisting mostly of organised games and sport—are also a speciality of Belgium.

## Holland

Next door to Belgium lies The Netherlands, a small country with the severest density problem in Europe. A recently founded organisation, *Ruimte voor de Jeugd* (Space for Youth) is rapidly becoming a pressure group of significance and has the sympathetic ear of many in official positions. Supervised play with the emphasis on integration into the community is the aim and already some progress has been made towards its achievement. Meanwhile the nine-year-old scheme 'Youthland' succeeds in drawing thousands of children to its holiday play centres, and the numerous conventionally equipped playgrounds dotted about the towns and cities, although not especially imaginative in design, are well cared for and abundantly supplied with sand. Recent legislation for new building demands a small play space for every hundred dwellings and special centres are being built for socially deprived children.

## Japan

On the other side of the world can be found another city with desperate problems of space and density: Tokyo. And here again there is a growing consciousness of the need to provide facilities for children's play. The playgrounds have been described as being 'without exception all well-designed with the greatest of care and thought for those who had to play in them. Play leaders are few and far between and for a population of ten million far more playgrounds are needed. Generally they are entirely open, with little or no supervision, intensely developed, immensely stimulating, and full of children.

'The Mitake Children's Home designed by Architect Tange and Landscape Architect Shigeya Hayashi was most impressive. Children had access to the entire building which caters for all age groups, with studios, music room, numerous models of engines, telephone, television and transport, all encased with a push button which makes everything work. The adjoining play area was the most exciting of all in its simplicity, yet imaginative layout.'[1]

## Australia

It is a common misapprehension that space for children in Australia is no problem. Nearly half the population can be found in the two big cities of Melbourne and Sydney which have similar problems of high density, slum clearance and so on to our own. Attention hitherto has been focused as in France, for instance, on getting the children out of the cities. Holiday camps are a feature of Australian life. Active pressure is now being exerted on statutory authorities to do something about the play needs of children of all ages within the cities.

## New Zealand

In New Zealand, on the other hand, with a population of under three million, space in itself is less of a problem. Seventy per cent of the population is housed in individual dwellings with their own grounds.[2] Nevertheless, a strong Play Centre Movement exists, formed originally with the under fives in mind, but recently enlarged in scope to include the needs of older children.

## U.S.A.

Although Minneapolis was the home of one of the first junk playgrounds,[3] adventure play as it is understood in this country has not been developed in the States to anything like the same extent as here.

1  Mitchell (1965), p. 7.
2  Morris (1965), p. 21.
3  Benjamin (1966), p. 22.

Experiments are taking place,[1] however, one of which has been carefully studied with interesting results.[2] Supervised activities for children's leisure hours however have featured in several states since the turn of the century.[3]

The latest figures for adult-organised play show a striking increase in an already remarkably high number. In 1950 there were 14,747 playgrounds conducted under leadership; in 1960 the total had reached 20,107.[4]

As elsewhere, playground design is slowly undergoing a transformation; play sculpture, retention of trees, utilisation of existing variations in levels or creation of new ones, use of light attractive materials and an attempt to translate what children actually *do* into terms of practical pieces of equipment are all evident in a recent book on children's playgrounds in America.[5]

There is a recommended but not obligatory standard for play provision.[6]

The above brief description of some of the international developments in play provision makes no claim to comprehensiveness; many countries have been omitted and only a superficial look has been given to those which have been mentioned. Nevertheless, it is possible, by means of this account, to detect certain trends and it is also possible to identify policies and practices which may have value for the providers of play facilities in this country.

1   See Allen of Hurtwood (1968), pp. 100, 111, 116, 117.
2   *Ibid.*, pp. 72–7.
3   Patrick (1916), p. 6.
4   Owen (1966), p. 12.
5   Aaron (1965).
6   See Appendix V.

# The Conclusions of the Study and their Implications

# 4

## *Summary of the Main Conclusions*

Three separate pieces of research were undertaken for this study. Each was concerned with a different aspect of provision for children's play in towns and cities. The common aim was to establish a foundation of knowledge of children's play and the kind of opportunities best suited to play needs upon which local authorities, planners, architects and landscape architects could build. By examining children's behaviour outside the home and school in two contrasting neighbourhoods[1] it was hoped to discover whether or not a relationship existed between children's play patterns and the urban environment. In the wider survey of nineteen boroughs[2] it was the facilities themselves that were investigated both from the point of view of their availability to children and of their characteristics. Here, too, other possible places in which children can play—parks and recreation grounds, for instance—were investigated in relation to play facility provision and the wider environment. The question of responsibility for children's play provision was also examined in this survey. Thus, in the contrasting neighbourhood study we looked at children and in the nineteen-borough survey we looked at facilities. The third survey, which took place in ten boroughs, was concerned with both children and the facilities.[3] In studying how children use such facilities as are provided it was hoped to formulate a basis for certain standards of location and siting.

The detailed findings of these three pieces of research are given separately in the relevant chapters. Because of their common aim, however, the main conclusions arising from the findings can more properly be considered together. Their full implications are discussed in the two ensuing chapters.

1   Two areas within Southwark and Stevenage were selected. See Chapters 8 and 9.
2   See Chapter 12.
3   See Chapter 10.

# Children's Play in Relation to the Environment

One of the most important conclusions arising from the research is that children in their play appear to respond to the environment. This was revealed in a number of different activities in the two contrasting neighbourhoods in Southwark and Stevenage which were studied. In the new, planned, medium-density, pedestrian-segregated environment of Elm Green in Stevenage the play tended to be individual, passive and home oriented. This would be likely to lead to stronger parental influences than those of the children's contemporaries, and also to a slower *social*[1] maturing. In the Heygate area of Southwark, on the other hand, which is old and unplanned with bad, overcrowded housing and traffic-congested streets, children appeared to play away from home and in groups; their play was more active and included more games of a traditional character. The away-from-home, group-orientation of the play patterns suggests that here other children will have a stronger influence than parents and that through the frequent conflict situations that must inevitably occur when children play in crowded, dangerous streets children will learn to take decisions for themselves and in the process may develop mature social attitudes at an earlier age.

*Differing play patterns*

Cultural, social and physical elements in the environment are inextricably linked. The evidence here points to physical factors which are more easily defined and more easily remedied. We cannot, however, ignore the possible underlying influence of social class; in the two areas studied the main difference in occupational level was between unskilled and skilled workers.[2]

We cannot ignore also the fact that viewing television may be a major competition to children's real playtime.[3] Children cannot find in television viewing the necessary social interaction of the play situation or opportunities for manipulation of the environment that play can bring. We still know little of the effects of television and all we can ask is for more enquiries into this field.

*Sight and sound play*

Children need to be able to move about and play within the general environment. It is also important, particularly for the very young, that they should be able to play within sight and sound of home. Traffic-

---

1 Not to be confused with emotional or physiological maturing.
2 In Southwark there was an above-average proportion of unskilled and semi-skilled workers.
3 See Chapter 9 and Appendix II.

congested streets are obviously unsuitable.[1] From the point of view of *Pedestrian* urban planning pedestrian segregation allows the maximum freedom *segrega-* and safety of movement and play. There was clear evidence for both *tion* these conclusions from the study.

## Space for Children

There is a great unevenness in the distribution of space for children· This was evident both from the contrasting neighbourhood study—the Southwark area was seriously lacking in this respect—and from the existing facilities survey in the nineteen boroughs. In towns and cities there are, very broadly, two kinds of outdoor space in which children can play, other than in and around the general environment: the specially designated play spaces; and public recreational space—parks, recreation grounds, commons and so on. Deficiencies were to be found in both of these.

There were no apparent *regional* differences in open space provision but this fact should not conceal the very pronounced regional differences *Public* in urban environment which do exist.[2] The facilities survey was not *recrea-* intended as a measure of environment but simply as an indication of *tional* certain of its aspects. Those differences which existed were to be found *space* between boroughs, and between areas within boroughs, irrespective of their regional disposition. As would be expected, the nature, size and population density of the cities and their various parts appear to be major determining factors in open space distribution. The more highly industrialised and the more highly populated the city or part of the city, the less likely is there to be found adequate amounts of public recreational space. Thus it can be said that children who have least access to the countryside and who live in congested, high-density areas are likely to have to go furthest to find stretches of public recreational space. For children it is, of course, important whether or not it is space which can be played on with reasonable freedom as, for example, on Newcastle's Town Moor or Camden's Hampstead Heath. For the most part parks and recreation grounds are orderly and comparatively formal; children must 'keep off the grass' and are forbidden to climb trees or ride bicycles, though there may be stretches in larger parks which carry fewer restrictions.

The areas which are poorly provided with commons, parks and

1  High flats present problems for this kind of play of a different but no less serious kind but, since there was no direct evidence about high flats arising from our study, these problems are discussed in Chapter 5.
2  See e.g. Arvill (1967).

*Sports facilities*

recreation grounds are likely also to be lacking in sports facilities,[1] which are important for the older half of our age group, particularly as this provision in schools falls far short of needs.

There was evidence in some of the worst areas of an attempt to compensate for a lack of general recreational space by a more generous provision of play space. In general, however, it may be concluded from the nineteen-borough survey that in the older urban areas, particularly in the larger industrial cities, there is too little space allotted for children's play and this is true also for many of the more newly developed areas. Thousands of children can be said to be deprived in this sense.

*Play space*

It must be said that in the great majority of the boroughs investigated in the nineteen-borough survey (which included Southwark and Stevenage, studied in greater depth in the contrasting neighbourhood study), there was a consciousness of the importance of recreational space and in particular of children's play space. This consciousness both in the nineteen boroughs and elsewhere has undoubtedly increased in the years since the field work was carried out. However, housing estates are still being built without play space; available and suitable land is still not being converted to play use.

*Additional space*

In view of the widespread and growing shortage of space it is surprising that more use is not made of already existing space. Every urban area has a number of sites scheduled for development but which are not likely to be built on for a number of years. Our study showed a singular lack of initiative in taking advantage of this temporary waste land for play use. Another much under-used source of additional space is that of school premises, both inside and outside.[2] *Seen purely in terms of space* a quite dramatic increase in the amount available for children's play could be achieved by using school playgrounds which lie fallow for so much of the time.

*Different environments create different demands*

There will always be different urban environments. This variety is obviously desirable and can be exploited through the different demands it creates. Some conditions of urban living, however, are so *un*desirable as to demand special attention. From our study we conclude that there are areas which should be given priority treatment for play provision although these may not necessarily coincide with other designated areas of special need. In Southwark the mothers' plea was for more facilities; in Stevenage, it was for better facilities. This points the difference but

1  Provision for team games, athletics, etc., and indoor provision.
2  Only four of the nineteen boroughs surveyed had a school play centre service. See Chapters 10 and 11.

should not necessarily shape the solution. In areas such as those studied in Southwark the need is not only for more facilities but for better facilities as well.

## Location and Siting of Play Facilities

The distribution and location of designated play space should be dependent upon the needs of children. In fact, it would appear from our study that at present the major determining factors are the availability of space and the question of costs. There are also a number of arbitrary considerations as to the nature and type of facility based on administrative convenience rather than suitability for children. There is no systematic relation of the provision of play facilities to the needs of children.

Certain conclusions arising from our study may help towards the achievement of such a systematic relation. It is first of all necessary to ensure that space for children's play is allocated at the initial stage of any development or redevelopment plan. In existing urban areas there must also be a willingness to 'create' play space, where necessary, by converting to play use open space in use for other purposes, such as schools, waste sites, parts of public recreational space, forbidden areas on housing estates. The results of our study suggest that universal standards[1] for the location of play facilities would be inappropriate and misleading. The results further suggest that individual standards should be worked out by systematic reference to a set of requirements. These requirements should be based on the following: distance between home *Require-* and the facility; size and density of child population; accessibility of *ments for* the play facility as affected by the disposition and type of buildings in *standards* the neighbourhood and the network of 'natural' barriers such as road- *in* ways and railways; the presence or otherwise of public recreational *location* space in the neighbourhood; size of the facility; a necessary diversity in the play provision.

We by no means underestimate the problem for planners, architects and landscape architects of adjusting costs and avilability of space to these requirements, but they should always be considered in the light of the requirements and not the other way round.

More research is needed before a comprehensive frame of reference can be established but the following pointers arising from the study indicate the lines upon which planners can work in the immediate future and the areas in which more research may fruitfully be carried out.

1 For examples of existing standards see Appendix V.

## Distance

The proportion of children attending playgrounds (other than those situated in parks) who live within comparatively short distance of the playgrounds is so high[1] as to suggest that the provision of play facilities is essentially a neighbourhood service. These distances also confirm the previously held view of the National Playing Fields Association and others that playgrounds should be situated at not more than half a mile's distance from each other to enable a journey of not more than ¼ mile between home and playground.[2] The other requirements for location outlined above make it clear, however, that this is a minimum reckoning since these other requirements may demand a greater number of playgrounds within the half-mile radius.

A parallel conclusion to that of the neighbourhood needs is that the number of playgrounds situated in public recreational space should be increased. It was evident from our study that a significant number of children are prepared to go considerable distances to reach such playgrounds and use them in substantial numbers. The fact that these playgrounds are attended by a high proportion of very young children accompanied by an adult confirms the idea that parks should always be designed for multi-purpose, all-generation use. Clearly, also, the accommodation at these playgrounds should cater for children coming from long distances; there should, for instance, always be shelter from rain, adequate provision of w.c.s *and* wash-basins and drinking water. The marked popularity of these park playgrounds apparent in our survey may have been in part due to the fact that the survey was carried out either on school holiday week-days or at the week-end. This fact to some extent conceals the term-time weekday needs of children to have somewhere to go for short periods near home. It confirms, at the same time, the findings of the contrasting neighbourhood study that week-end activities tend to be family activities.[3]

## Child population

In relating child population to playground location it is necessary to take into account not only the total child population and its density

---

1  For equipped playgrounds nearly 70 per cent travelled ¼ mile or less and 85 per cent ½ mile or less. For unequipped play spaces and play streets as many as 75 per cent travelled 220 yards or less and nearly the total number of children, 97 per cent, were accounted for within the half-mile radius.
2  Three-quarters of the playgrounds surveyed in the ten-borough survey had up to three other playgrounds within half a mile's distance.
3  See Appendix II.

within the given area for development or redevelopment but also the estimated catchment population[1] for each proposed facility. A basis for predicting attendance at equipped playgrounds has been worked out from the material of the ten-borough survey.[2] These attendance figures could usefully form a part of the playground location requirements but should not, of course, be used for this purpose on their own.

Not surprisingly, it emerged from the study that where a play space is in immediate proximity to the children's homes, the proportion of children using the play space[3] is maximised.

Sparsely populated neighbourhoods will inevitably result in lower *total* attendance figures, but the type of environment is likely to influence the *proportion* who attend. In a deliberately planned, low-density residential area, for example, children may have a satisfactory choice of alternatives—gardens, pedestrian ways and so on. On the other hand, where a neighbourhood's density is low because it contains industry or railways, the proportion of children living there who attend play facilities will be as high as in densely-populated neighbourhoods.

## Accessibility

Evidence from the study underlined the importance of accessibility in locating playgrounds. This not only concerned the more obvious factor of safe walking distance but revealed that isolation could be a strong deterrent to attendance. This showed particularly in the mothers' attitudes. Other studies have produced interesting results concerning siting on housing estates.[4]

## Size of facility

There was evidence from all three parts of our study to show that large, multi-purpose playgrounds are likely to be the most popular and to provide the most worthwhile service. The regression analysis of the ten-borough survey showed playground size to be a significant factor in attracting children to playgrounds; there tends to be a falling off in attendance as playground size decreases. It was also evident from the survey that the larger the playground the longer children spent playing

1  Catchment areas for different types of playground have been calculated. See Chapter 10.
2  See Chapter 10 and Appendix III.
3  This has been expressed as an activity rate. See p. 190
4  See pp. 94, 96

there. No precise acreage can be regarded as a universal optimum size for the reason indicated above, namely the interdependence of factors involved in establishing standards. Nevertheless, it should be noted that the numbers of children attending playgrounds appears to increase up to a size of about 3,000 sq. yds. and that the length of time that they stay there continues to increase as the size increases beyond that figure.[1] There may be occasion, however, for smaller facilities; special areas for toddlers, for example, or unequipped kick-around spaces— both essential parts of a play service which can be usefully provided on their own.

## Diversity

The planners must provide the space but it is not their function to determine what kind of service should be provided within the space. Nevertheless, since the nature and diversity of the service should be essential considerations in the space allocation, there must be consultation in the initial stages with those qualified to assess the particular needs.

# A Service for Play

*The diverse requirements*

A service for play should take account of the following: sex and age of children; the importance of play itself and its relation to a child's development; and the concept of play provision as a *social* service. Implicit in these different considerations is the need for diversity. It can be concluded from all three parts of our study that this necessary diversity in play provision was seriously lacking.

## Provision for different age groups

There was a marked deficiency of provision for the under fives. This included all forms of day care as well as the more simple provision of facilities equipped with such play material as sand and water. Nor did provision cover the full range of interests for older children. Our study found that the majority of children using the playgrounds were between the ages of five and nine. It was also apparent from both the ten-borough and the nineteen-borough surveys that the vast majority of playgrounds are conventionally equipped, i.e. with fixed items of equipment such as swings and roundabouts. There were also indications

1 See pp. 274–275.

*Making the most of their play space*

*A New York play street*

that these items were popular with this middle age range, but became increasingly less so as the children's ages increased. These findings confirm those of other studies.[1] There were unfortunately insufficient data in our study from which to conclude whether they would have been different had there been a fuller choice of alternatives, or whether they reflected conscious preferences. Allowing for this reservation, however, the evidence suggests that certain traditional elements in play provision—swings and slides in particular—should be preserved, but not in isolation.

## Differing habits of boys and girls

Boys, from five onwards, used playgrounds altogether more than girls, particularly the unequipped spaces and particularly in the older age range. It is not possible to be sure from the data whether girls are less frequent users of playgrounds than boys because they are traditionally more home-oriented or because they do not find sufficiently attractive features in existing play facilities. The overwhelming popularity of the 'kick-around' areas amongst the boys is not hard to explain, either in terms of a reflection of adult values expressed in the almost universal enthusiasm for football, or of a need, greater amongst boys than girls, for an outlet for physical energy. Team games, football in particular, emerged from the study as an outstandingly popular activity.

## Play provision as a social service

The urban environment inhibits children's play. Play is important. It is necessary, therefore, to provide special places in which restrictions are minimised and opportunities for play are maximised. This applies to all town children. At the same time, there are groups of children for whom special play arrangements are desirable such as the children of working mothers; the group which can best, if unsatisfactorily, be described as culturally deprived; and children whose physical home environment is restricted.

On both these counts adventure playgrounds and similar facilities *Supervised* provide the best answer. One essential requirement of such facilities *play* is that they should be supervised. Our study revealed an extreme *facilities* shortage of supervised play facilities containing unconventional equipment and confirmed the need for their large-scale extension. The contrasting neighbourhood study showed mothers' fears for their children's safety from traffic dangers, molestation and bullying to be very real. Pedestrian segregation, as has been suggested, is one part

1  See p. 100

of the answer; supervised play facilities is another. There was evidence from the ten-borough survey that children stayed longer at supervised facilities than at conventionally equipped, unsupervised playgrounds.[1] The data were unfortunately insufficient to establish the exact reasons for this, though the presence of a team ball games area and the extent of the equipment, much of it of an unconventional kind, would seem to have had an influence. There were too few of these playgrounds to use as a distinctive group in predicting attendance. Both of these aspects should be studied further.

*Indoor provision*

A most important conclusion arising from the study is that children have scarcely any opportunity for play outside the home in winter and in bad weather. There was minimal indoor provision in the facilities investigated in both the ten- and the nineteen-borough surveys. The majority of playgrounds are available to children during daylight hours[2] but this is a negative virtue in view of this country's climate.

*Play-ground hygiene*

Hygiene has, on the whole, a low priority in playground provision. W.c.s are in short supply, often filthy, and, where they exist, only the minority are accompanied by washbasins.

The great majority of playgrounds are reasonably well tended and clean but that there should be any exceptions at all, which there were, is to be deplored.

*Design, layout and equipment*

The type of play facility will, to some extent, dictate its design and layout. An unequipped space intended for unorganised team games will need to be flat, hard-surfaced and well fenced. A true adventure playground will not be very sightly and is probably best hidden from view. In between these two extremes are a range of play facilities (sometimes incorporating one or both of the extremes just mentioned) for which the design (including that of the equipment) and layout are intrinsic to the quality of the service provided. They also have a secondary aesthetic significance. All would be the better for variations in levels and surfaces. It can be said, from the evidence of our study, that the majority of play facilities in this country are dull, uniform, unimaginatively designed and lacking in stimuli for play.

## Responsibility for Play Provision

The final point that emerges from our study is the need to define the

1  See Chapter 10.
2  The exceptions tend to be concentrated in certain areas so that some children cannot even play in the playgrounds provided for them in fine weather after school hours or on Sundays.

areas of responsibility for the provision, administration and financing of children's play facilities.

Our study showed that local authorities are not, as a whole, meeting play provision needs. The survey of facilities confirms the impression that the necessary drive to get good play facilities installed depends largely on individuals, whether councillors or departmental officers, with the help and inspiration of outside pressure groups. It is these individuals, irrespective of the nature of their ostensible duties—drains, cemeteries, highways, housing—who will use their initiative to persuade their fellow councillors or officers of the importance of children's play provision. With all that is owed to these individuals the situation is too haphazard to be satisfactory, for there are hundreds of local authorities which do not boast such individuals and many more which swamp any incipient enthusiasm for children's play with other priorities.

From all this one may conclude that there is an urgent need for a policy for play.

# 5

## The Conclusions in Perspective:
## Play and the Environment

A policy for play must take into account more than the preceding conclusions. These were based solely on our research. By considering the implications of these conclusions and by setting them in the perspective of current practice and thought in the fields of planning, local administration, education, social welfare and children's play, a broader base for a policy for play may be achieved. This is what we do in the following two chapters.

The restrictions imposed by increasing urbanisation make it necessary to consider children's play in relation to the environment. The distinction between the two environments of our contrasting neighbourhood study lies partly in the fact that one, that of the Stevenage neighbourhood, is new and the other, that of the Southwark area, is old with established traditions. There are also the tremendous differences in the housing conditions, the population density, the street layout, the open space provision and so on. The indications are that had a new or redevelopment high-density area, consisting mainly of tower blocks, been taken as the contrasting *new* neighbourhood its play patterns would have approximated more to those of the old Southwark area than to those of the Stevenage area.

*Children's response to the environment*

The implications to be drawn from the markedly different play patterns which were revealed by the study lie first and foremost in the vital role of play in a child's development.[1] Tensions destroy play and overcrowded, congested environments are likely to produce tensions. Such environments are continually forcing children into situations, both inside and outside the home, which inhibit play. An environment which provides more opportunity for play must be a better environment.

1  See Chapter 1.

68

There are also other important implications. Parental influence can be seen as a stabilising factor in present-day society. Such influence is bound to be stronger where children are more at home. In Stevenage the children's play was more home centred than in Southwark, and also it was more individualistic. In the converse situation children naturally form groups and thus the influence of their peers cuts across that of their parents.

We know that different patterns of child rearing can produce adults with different types of propensity. Play forms an important part in the child-rearing process, that of turning children into responsible adults, and it seems reasonable to believe that individual response to situations in adult life and an ability to make assessments without reference to the group are attributes which may thus be fostered or hindered by the kind of play in childhood that the environment permits. In Stevenage children are not hampered in their play by traffic or adults going about their work. In Southwark these factors create tension and frequently the patterns of play may revolve around them. These can only be tentative deductions, but the field is open for more exploration.

More, however, is in question than play and the physical environment. As H. D. McKay has said:

'. . . the child takes over what the neighbourhood has to offer—its traditional leisure-time activities, its standards of sportsmanship, its characteristic ways of expressing anger, pleasure or hostility, its philosophy of life, its moral codes and its language. These come not only from the institutions in which the child participates directly, but also from his vicarious participation in all the activities which the neighbourhood encourages or tolerates.'[1]

The results of our study bear out, from a limited point of view, the insight revealed in this passage. 'Traditional leisure-time activities' are clearly reflected in the Southwark children's play behaviour and the new environment of Stevenage appears to have discouraged, to a considerable extent, group activities and traditional games.[2] In the long run, however, it is the *total* environment that matters, that is to

1 McKay (1961), p. 820.
2 We know that the Opies (Opie and Opie, 1959) have illustrated how consistently children carry on tradition in their games and language, so it could be that in our area of Stevenage New Town there has been insufficient time for these traditions to seep through. It could also be, however, that the break has had a more drastic effect than previous experience has suggested.

say the subtle interrelation between culture and the physical environment, and it is of the total environment that McKay is talking.

Planners, architects and landscape architects are realising more and more the significance of the total as against the merely physical environment and many make continuous reappraisals of their aims and *The* motives. But they are faced with a dilemma, which is to know how far *planners'* they should, or indeed how much they do, interfere with the self-*dilemma* determining process of the communities for whom they plan and design. On the one hand there are the major influences at work on society such as population growth, scientific and technological advances, rising standards of living, shorter working hours, increasing leisure demands, changing familial and educational patterns, together with those subtle ones referred to by McKay. On the other hand there is the undoubted influence of the physical environment, exemplified by our findings on children's play behaviour. Maurice Broady has most ably summed up this dilemma:

'This genuine social concern—even social idealism—is one of the nice things about architect planners. But they are often inclined to suppose that the design of the physical environment—which is their particular metier—will automatically secure the social ends which their idealism leads them to desire. This has often resulted in their adopting a set of assumptions that can be called "architectural determinism". This theory, more implicit than explicit, supposes that architectural design has a direct and determinate effect on the way people behave and largely ignores the social factors that also affect environment and which a properly formulated theory of "total environment" must incorporate.'[1]

Strongly dissociating himself from the concept of architectural determinism is Professor N. J. Habraken, who is already experimenting in Arnhem, Holland, with an urban environment designed, so he claims, to allow the community—as individuals and as a whole—to create its own conditions of living.[2]

For most architects and planners, however, the dilemma remains and they are increasingly seeking the help of other disciplines. But there is a need to harmonise these disciplines. Architects and landscape architects, planners and geographers, engineers and traffic experts, sociologists and demographers all speak their own language and there is often a serious failure to communicate with each other. Psychologists

1  Broady (1967), p. 232.
2  *Interbuild Arena* (1967), pp. 12–19.

and ethologists have still formally to enter this field. If more research, informal as well as formal, into attitudes and behaviour were carried out and reactions anticipated perhaps more disasters could be avoided.

It is not necessary to be an expert to recognise the disasters, even though there must be some room for disagreement on which these are. On our visits to New Towns and new housing developments we have frequently sensed a failure to achieve a successful, lively atmosphere for living. We are conscious that, in criticising present-day planning, there is need to be wary of the fact that the newness in itself can be depressing—not only aesthetically, but socially. It really is not fair to assess an area whilst the bulldozers are still at work and half the shops have white daubs on the window panes instead of goods for sale behind them. Thousands of our post-war buildings, however, have been up long enough for a judgment to be made and it has become sadly apparent that the vitality essential to good urban living will have difficulty in thriving amongst them.

There are, of course, numbers of exceptions to this depressing rule— one, a South-West London estate, was visited by the authors in the company of the architect, whose sensitivity to the social needs of his clients was as apparent in his design as in his conversation. Nevertheless, one wondered, as he himself was the first to suggest, whether the comparative success of the scheme was not primarily due to the fact that dwellers on the estate were all local people known to each other for generations. This may be one of the key answers to the classic problem of creating a viable social environment within a brand new physical environment. Social contacts build up over a number of years and the problem of adapting to a new physical environment can be enormously eased if old links with neighbours and kin are maintained.

Another way of preserving some form of social continuity whilst at the same time providing the necessary new housing is by 'rehabilitating' old neighbourhoods. This means that, instead of wholesale demolition and total redevelopment, as much as possible of the old is retained and renovated, with only partial replacement.

The planning problems for this kind of urban renewal are formidable, particularly on the scale which the combined factors of population increase and essential slum clearance are demanding. It obviously cannot be the only method and in some European countries, owing to the wholesale destruction of their cities, total renewal has been the only solution.

But in this country there is often a choice. Several boroughs have successfully demonstrated the practicability of partial renewal. The immediate advantages to the community are obvious. The new building which replaces the old can be absorbed into the neighbourhood without disrupting the existing social, economic and cultural patterns. By this means the neighbourhood's diversity is maintained and even added to. It is argued that established customs and habits are enriched by the injection of new customs and habits; the newcomers in turn are able to absorb much of the existing neighbourhood tradition without conscious effort. Remembering that 'the child takes over what the neighbourhood has to offer', all this can be said to apply with particular force to children. There are those, however, who would argue that we should cast off outdated traditions and habits and that a totally new physical environment gives us the necessary opportunities to do so.

Visionary architects, other than Habraken and his colleagues, are already conceiving buildings—high, low, all shapes, constructed of light, expandable materials. These buildings would be grouped and connected with each other by as yet untried methods; they would not be built to last.

Such fundamental re-thinking of the city environment is exciting. Planning for a future of unknown quantities rather than for a future extension of existing conditions is a way of ensuring flexibility. It is particularly valuable if the architects are conscious of the importance of social needs, and are prepared to learn as they go, as many are.

Nevertheless, the concept of 'throw-away' architecture raises serious doubts. Nobody would question the speed of change in this second half of the century as it relates to things. But people are slower to change. It is true that an affluent, consumer society encourages the 'throw-away' tendencies of its members but it is open to question whether further encouragement, in the shape of an expendable physical environment, is desirable. In this we see the need for a much greater knowledge and understanding of attitudes than can be found now. We are back to our plea for investigations by the social psychologists. Here, too, is a case of what Broady calls 'architectural determinism' for, undoubtedly, such conceptions would accelerate the speed of change and would play a considerable part in bringing about new social patterns.

Post-war research into family life, notably Young and Willmott's Bethnal Green study,[1] has revealed that the removal of sections of a homogeneous community to distant areas leads towards the unnecessary break-up of kinship patterns and a process of estrangement between the generations.

New environments of the kind referred to above could be viewed

1  Young and Willmott (1957).

with apprehension as contributing to this process of break-up and estrangement or they could be regarded as the logical outcome of 'the great imaginative leaps where you feel free to think it out from scratch' which, according to Mr Wedgwood Benn, 'are an exciting and essential part of our technological progress'.[1]

Meanwhile, the pressure for space increases.[2] For the architects and planners this means a preoccupation with densities—the number of persons per acre or the number of dwellings per acre. The tower blocks have been one attempted solution to the problem; building high was seen as a means of releasing more ground space. Today it is claimed to be possible to achieve compact, high-density areas by judicious planning and new methods of house design—without the use of tower blocks. In practice this usually means a mixture of terraced housing and blocks of flats of two to three storeys with a reasonable amount of communal open space—in good-sized chunks and not in unusable small amounts—and even some private gardens or 'outdoor rooms'. The value of a garden—an extension of home—has been shown to be of great significance for children in the most recent of the Newson studies in Nottingham.[3]

*How many people to the acre?*

Today, also, in terms of the wider urban environment, there are those who claim that the encroachment of buildings on rural open space is not the bogey it was once thought to be;[4] neither is the actual quantity of acres consumed as great as is feared, nor need the effects of 'spread' be so disastrous for the countryside or unattractive for the people living there. According to the exponents of this view the garden city concept has been almost universally corrupted in practice. A return to first principles adapted to suit varying conditions could produce a living, modern environment. This is not the place to argue the pros and cons of such a marriage of town and country, which has acquired the unlovely name of agropolis. It does, however, merit particular consideration as far as children are concerned. For entailed in this kind of planning is a greater amount of space immediately around each dwelling than is generally considered feasible in present-day urban conditions and this, as has been shown, is what children need.

The whole problem of living in high flats has been much discussed in recent years and is increasingly now being investigated. Serious studies come up with different answers but on balance, especially where

1  *The Observer* (1967).
2  Some examples of open space standards are given in Appendix V.
3  Newson, J. and E. (1968), pp. 130–2.
4  March (1968).

young families are involved, the evidence supports the view that this planners' expedient has proved disadvantageous for the people who live there.[1] However conscientiously the housing managers may try to sort out the tenants according to their needs or likes and dislikes, thousands of young families will inevitably find themselves among the upper storey tenants. Two studies[2] have not found as marked a difference between the attitudes of high-storey mothers and low-storey mothers about children's play as might be expected. Both groups have expressed dissatisfaction with provision and find it difficult to keep an eye on the children. Nevertheless Joan Maizels concluded that:

*High flats*

'. . . living high, that is above the fifth floor, appears to be associated with a higher incidence of concern over the safety of young children and a lower incidence of the use of playgrounds.'[3]

A Stockholm study,[4] however, has shown that the higher the building, the less likely are young children to play outside their homes. This was particularly the case with children under four years old, but even for the seven-year-olds the difference in the time spent outside amounted to almost an hour.

A recent study in Australia[5] found that the majority of the children under three years of age living on an estate were consistently kept indoors; after three there appeared to be little parental restriction on play outside the flats. In this estate, there were no 0- to 5-year-olds in the high-rise block. One interesting finding from this study was that parents' attitudes about where their children played and should be able to play was coloured more by an ideal standard than by reference to previous, usually sub-standard, living conditions:

'—the parents' sights were set very firmly on an ideal of the sort of life they could lead in the suburban house they so strongly aspired to.'[6]

Living high off the ground or on the ground in a giant housing complex may have many drawbacks for older children too. So much play is spontaneous and this spontaneity is bound to be inhibited if a major effort is needed to reach a suitable and permissible place.

This implies that, ideally, for children the immediate home environment should be planned so as to ensure maximum opportunity for

1 See e.g. Fanning (1967).
2 (a) Maizels (1961); (b) Ministry of Housing and Local Government (1964).
3 Maizels, *op. cit.*, p. 22.
4 Sandels (1964).
5 Stevenson, Martin and O'Neill (1967).
6 *Ibid.*, p. 94.

74

what we may describe as 'doorstep play'—play within sight and sound of home. Various attempts to achieve this in the tower block have been made—play decks, wide balconies, closed circuit television—but with comparatively little success. So many things operate against success, particularly for the young child—danger from stairways and lifts, icy draughts (a perennial problem of housing estates), unco-operative caretakers and, for the closed circuit television idea, the sheer inappropriateness of a mother being able to see her child in trouble and not being able to do anything about it.

Residential tower blocks as we know them today are probably on their way out, though their massive foundations and heavy concrete structures will ensure continued use for years to come. If more must be built then it is imperative that they be conceived from the start with the play needs of children in mind. A few such have been designed.[1]

For the hundreds of high-density, high-rise areas where no such care has been taken, a new assessment should be made and as much special provision as possible be introduced.[2]

Playing around the home and around the neighbourhood is important in that it encourages a sense of belonging, provided there is a reciprocal tolerance from the adult members of the community and provided there is adequate safety. It is this latter quality, of course, that is missing *Street* in the streets of today though they still provide many of the ingredients *play* of good play—'light, movement, colour, noise, adventure'.[3] Certainly, there are plentiful nostalgic memories of 'our street' as a happy play-ground.[4] The simple fact is, too, that at any one time there will be fewer children within the designated play spaces (even under ideal conditions) than in and around their homes.[5] What can be done to enable play within sight and sound of home—doorstep play—and a reasonable and safe integration of older children into their environment? In new developments and large-scale redevelopments, streets can be made relatively safe. But there are thousands of urban acres, tightly packed with houses and children, where something needs to be done *now*. Every summer agitation mounts in many of these areas, with some degree of success. Private gardens are opened for public use or traffic is temporarily banned from certain streets. Nowadays, in the com-paratively few areas where they exist, official, permanent play streets are often abused by vehicle users and are said to be a direct cause of

1   E.g. Parkhill Estate, Sheffield; Winstanley Road Estate, Battersea.
2   See p. 122
3   Abernethy (1968).
4   Jennings (1962); and Berg (1965).
5   See p. 190.

accidents by the fact that they engender a false sense of security. One experiment which has been conducted in Salford[1] contradicts this belief and it is possible that its success may be due to an exceptionally widespread and consistent application. The main pressure should be directed towards the acquisition of any available space—waste site, school playground, private gardens and so on, but there are areas where this is not enough. For these areas, provided it is recognised as a temporary expedient, something on the lines of the Salford scheme, or the more recent experiment in North Kensington,[2] could be tried.

*Pedestrian segregation* For the future the most relevant single planning operation is to separate the traffic from the pedestrian pathways. Arguments against pedestrian segregation, or rather against its indiscriminate use, are sometimes put forward and, since the general environment is here being considered, it is necessary briefly to examine these.

'. . . such schemes are only practical . . . if they pre-suppose a spectacular decline in the absolute numbers of automobiles using a city. Otherwise, the necessary parking, garaging and access arteries around the pedestrian preserves reach such unwieldy and deadening proportions that they become arrangements capable only of disintegration, not of city saving.'[3]

Jane Jacobs centres a further argument on her triple theme of the need for 'city diversity, vitality and concentration of use':

'Life attracts life. Where pedestrian segregation is undertaken as some form of abstract nicety and too many forms of life and activity go unaccommodated or are suppressed to make the nicety work, the arrangement goes unappreciated.'[4]

Even though Mrs Jacobs concedes that 'it would be ideal to dispose of cars entirely on city streets where children play', she fears that the advantages would be counteracted by the lack of 'other utilitarian purposes of sidewalks, and along with them, supervision'.[5]

Jane Jacobs' concept of casual supervision is of immense importance but there is no need for pedestrian ways to be any less alive with people than pavements flanking roads. Continuous comings and goings could be just as much a part of these paths as of traffic roads if they were planned as arteries to carry people engaged in a variety of different

1 Manchester and Salford Police (1965).
2 Notting Hill Social Council Summer Play Project (1968).
3 Jacobs (1961), p. 357.
4 *Ibid.*, p. 362.
5 *Loc. cit.*

activities and not as single purpose routes or quiet culs-de-sac. This kind of casual supervision is provided too by neighbours from within doors. The value for children of the separation of roads and pathways can be taken further from home, as suggested by Paul Ritter:

> 'The play activity essential to all young animals involves running and jumping to a great extent; these are not separate activities for "playgrounds". This is activity indigenous to the whole life of the child—it is not practicable along roads, as it is along a path, playing all the way to and from school: catch games, ball games, singing and shouting—telling yourself stories as you go along. We need "linear children's playgrounds". The paths to school[1] are the most important.'[2]

The great majority of city children become accustomed to traffic whilst they are still in their prams. Cars, buses, motor bicycles, lorries— moving or stationary, solitary or massed—are permanent features of their lives. They soon find that these objects are a challenge to their wits and it is a measure of the sharpness of those wits that more children are not killed or injured in the streets of today. The figures for street accidents, nevertheless, are bad[3] and provide one good reason for increasing the number of play facilities. As a straight alternative to playing in the street—as streets are today—the case for more play facilities is unanswerable. Once in the play area children are safe from traffic dangers, from the menace of parked as well as moving vehicles. In a recent traffic survey the parked vehicle was found to be 'a prime cause of accidents'.[4] They must get to the play area, however, as they must get to school. Also, the total eradication of street play would entail other losses, as already suggested, which might be regrettable. The peak hours and the peak ages for pedestrian road accidents are well documented as are types of accidents. The Road Research Laboratory and others are engaged in continuous efforts to isolate causes so that effective counter-measures may be taken. Meanwhile, police and local authorities in most parts of the country are active. Seven of the nineteen boroughs which participated in the survey of

1   The primary school is already of great significance in modern planning. The 'neighbourhood unit'—conceived in America long before the war and adopted in this country at the time of the 1944 Education Act—has the primary school as its chief focal point. Each school must be within easy walking distance for the children of its 'neighbourhood'.
2   Ritter (1964), p. 38.
3   See Appendix V.
4   Stevenage Development Corporation (1967), 3c.

play facilities showed a decrease in 1966 compared with the previous year in their child casualty figures. It was possible to detect a slight correlation between the scope and imagination of accident prevention campaigns and improvement in casualty figures although many other factors must obviously be taken into account.

The arguments in favour of separating pedestrians from traffic are strongly reinforced by the nine-year survey of traffic accidents in Stevenage,[1] which concludes that:

'. . . the Survey clearly shows the additional safety conferred by modern road design incorporating segregation of various types of road users in the Industrial Area, the Town Centre, the residential areas and along the main routes of movement.'[2]

Under present and foreseeable circumstances some form of pedestrian segregation seems highly desirable, provided that the form it takes is subject to considerations of its use by the community in its total aspect and not as a means simply of keeping the motor-car at bay.

*Children and the community*

No amount of physical planning, however, will bring about the integration of the child into the life of the community without a fundamental change in adult attitudes. Whilst it is increasingly being accepted that the child's ties to its family are important the same cannot be said for its relationship to the community. It is often stated that children are not liked in this country. Certainly, the traditional upper-middle and upper class habit of sending children off to boarding school does little to dispel this view. English ears seem peculiarly sensitive to noise. Our climate and licensing laws do not prompt the kind of communal outdoor life common, for instance, in Latin countries. For many years the trend has been to segregate children from adults. This finds its roots partly in protective measures—historically, the child has been exploited as a member of the community—but it has persisted and hardened beyond the necessity. Everything should be done to encourage a reversal of this trend and in this connection such experiments as community play centres are important. Tolerance of children, *other people's* children, would be easier if children were to participate more in the life of the community and not merely mingle when they play. It is not necessary for the community, in this context, to be only local and neighbourhood-based. Participation is just as feasible in an associational society—where the groups are centred on common interests and activities. Robert Coles

1 Stevenage Development Corporation (1967), I, 30.
2 *Loc. cit.*

has suggested that children can withstand, and even benefit from, the stress of harsh and tragic experiences, which are shared with adults, much better than most societies today are prepared to concede.[1] It follows that happy or agreeably challenging adult experiences could be shared with children much more than they are.

It should not, of course, be forgotten that there is at times an inevitable conflict between the interests of old and young. It is important that these conflicting interests should not be submerged. Nor do we intend by all this that children should become over-burdened with responsibility. The play world of children must be sacrosanct. They must be free to retreat into it unhindered, just as adults, when they wish, must be able to pursue their various interests without interference. But mutual respect for these private worlds will be far greater if the everyday life of young and old is more fully shared than it is in this country today.

1   Coles (1968), pp. 750-4.

# 6

## The Conclusions in Perspective: Provision for Play

Given the imperfections of the existing urban environment the need to provide special places for play is self-evident. As long ago as 1917 this need was apparent.

'One argument is beyond controversy: the streets are dangerous for young children. It follows that special play spaces, *indoor* [our italics] and outdoor, are primary factors in the promotion of child nurture.'[1]

But, even supposing greater changes than can at present be envisaged, the need would still exist. For one thing, there would always be insufficient *safe* space in which children had the necessary freedom. For another, there is the concept of play provision as a social service for children with special needs.

### Play provision as a social service

Social services tend to arise as a result of discovered deficiencies which threaten, in some way, a vital section of the population. The revelation, for example, of the C3 health standard of so many of the Boer War recruits caused a public outcry which ultimately led to the creation of a national health service.[2]

There is as yet only a marginal recognition of play as a social need, chiefly because it is not always easy to identify cause and effect in this sphere. Nevertheless, it is becoming clearer that play deprivation can take toll of children and affect their development.[3] This deprivation

1 Mackenzie (1917), p. 343.
2 Bentley (1966), p. 87.
3 See Chapter 1.

occurs in a number of ways. Society may also fail fully to recognise play as a social need because it is felt that families should, or do, cope on their own.

In the fields of education and child care it is slowly coming to be recognised that the child's relation to its family is of first importance. *The* Evidence of this can be found in legislation,[1] policy recommendation,[2] *family* and, amongst the more enlightened authorities, in practical measures. All this does, to some extent, counteract the weakening effect that these two major state services—education and child care—may possibly have had on the family, though it must be said that the family on its own has proved remarkably resistant to these and other incursions. Indeed, Ronald Fletcher concludes from his interesting analysis of the family that:

'the modern family fulfils *more* functions, in a far more detailed and sophisticated manner, than did the family before or during the nineteenth-century development of industrialisation'.[3]

It is reasonable to assume that certain conditions in the home and family are more conducive than others to spontaneous and unrestricted play; the simple one of plenty of space, for example. A great many social enquiries end up by laying a large measure of the blame for the *Inadequate* problems revealed by their enquiries on poor housing conditions. This *housing* one was no exception. Small children continuously under their mother's feet and older children inhibited by cramped quarters in their freedom to move and make a noise are suffering severe deprivation of play opportunities. Then there is the question of whether or not the dwelling has a garden and, if it has, whether or not the children are discouraged from playing freely in it. But the problems caused by inadequate housing go much deeper than a simple lack of space or the luxury of a garden. And play in the home can be restricted by other than physical conditions. There may be instability and unhappiness in family *Insta-* relationships, for instance, or sheer poverty. Such problems, often *bility and* bringing with them acute misery, will affect the whole tenor of life in *poverty* the home. Under such circumstances small children may reach school age having had only the most meagre opportunities for play, and, in extreme cases, without having learnt how to play—hence the importance of play facilities outside the home. For older children, too, tensions and

1   E.g. Children and Young Persons Act, 1963.
2   E.g. Central Advisory Council for Education (Plowden) Report, 1967.
3   Fletcher (1962), p. 177.

difficulties may be reduced if they are able to seek an outlet for their energies elsewhere.

*Parental*
*attitudes*

In all this the parents' consciousness of the role of play is of vital importance for it means that tools for play are provided, that talk is encouraged, that noise and mess in the home are tolerated, or, if this is not possible, that alternative opportunities are sought outside the home.

Many of these conditions—space in the home, a garden for play, play equipment—are, largely for economic reasons, more likely to be found in middle-class than in working-class homes; others cut across social class differences. But irrespective of the social class basis for any similarities or differences it could be said that such conditions are, for children, a desirable goal. It is a goal at which an increasingly large section of the community is aiming, though this is not to say that the aim should merely be to achieve the standards so far considered to be satisfactory. Although this suggests a less urgent need for play provision outside the home, the wider freedom and opportunity will always be necessary and important for all children. It is also possible that the families of the future may become less centred on the mother and the home and more on the community. This would mean that the provision of children's play facilities for all age groups would be considered a necessity and not a luxury as it is, on the whole, still today.

Forecasts are difficult to make but it is unlikely that changes in the role of the family and in the physical environment will be very rapid. Irrespective of their speed or degree of change we believe that a flexible family unit is worth strengthening.

The question of the role of the family is intimately connected with social and religious attitudes and with changing employment patterns. If present trends continue, more and more mothers will be going out to work. There are already over $2\frac{1}{2}$ million who do.[1] Automation will undoubtedly affect the working hours of both mothers and fathers and this in turn will affect not only individual leisure patterns but those of the family as a whole. Drastic changes, however, do not appear to be very imminent and for the foreseeable future it is likely that if both parents work full-time their hours away from home will fail to coincide with those of their children.

*Working*
*mothers*

A previous study undertaken for the Council for Children's Welfare[2] found that too many children of school age were at risk through the inadequacy of arrangements for their care at the end of the school day,

1  Hunt (1968).
2  Yudkin and Holme (1963, 1968).

during the holidays, and when they were ill. This has been confirmed more recently.[1] Women's employment needs a drastic overhaul. The need is reinforced by the steadily increasing flow of married women into the labour force. For these women it is not only a question of pay and the availability of skilled jobs but of hours and conditions of work. In areas where labour is scarce employers have adjusted more to the family claims of their married women employees. But in the vast majority of cases it is the women who must do the adjusting and must balance the claims of children and employers, with consequences which are, too often, unsatisfactory to both.

An intrinsic part of any successful policy for working mothers must be the provision of supervised facilities to cater for the out-of-school, out-of-home hours of those children whose parents return after they do, are at work during the holidays, and for whom no private arrangements can be made. The existing school play centre service[2] needs improving and extending. It is not essential, however, that this service should be attached exclusively to schools. All regular supervised facilities can perform this function and already do so where they exist. Holiday camps are another important aspect of this kind of provision and there are many examples from abroad[3] that could be followed.

It is another problem for the under fives. Here, if different conditions were created, the evidence suggests that the majority of their mothers who work, particularly those with children under three, would prefer to stay at home.[4] The two most important of these conditions would be relief from financial strain and an adequate amount of organised play provision. The former would enable them to stay at home and the latter would encourage them to do so.

Pre-school children are before the public eye at the moment for far more serious reasons than an inadequacy of play space. For those whose mothers work, the system of substitute care has proved wholly deficient. This was confirmed by our survey of existing facilities. There is confusion on the part of the policy makers and of a bewildered public about what kind of provision exists and what should exist. The result of this confusion is a continuous widening of the gap between supply and demand and an alarming increase in the numbers of children being looked after under conditions which will stunt or retard their development.[5] The situation is serious, sometimes desperate for thousands of

1  Hunt, *op. cit.*
2  See p. 97-99 and Appendix I.
3  See Chapter 3.
4  Yudkin and Holme, *op. cit.*; Hunt, *op. cit.*
5  For a full exposition of the present position see Yudkin (1968).

small children and their mothers whose social, economic or cultural handicaps may already be placing them at a severe disadvantage in society.

Thus, for the under fives there are two problems. First, those children whose mothers work, either from choice or necessity, must be adequately cared for in the fullest sense. Secondly, the alternatives to work outside the home must be made more attractive to the mothers and at the same time beneficial to the children, by providing supervised play groups and, at best, proper nursery education. Such improvements, of course, would equally benefit the families where the mothers in any case would not be going to work whilst the children are small. The present isolation of many young mothers and their small children could thus be enormously eased by such provision. Where these opportunities already occur their success has been undoubted. The examples, largely voluntarily sponsored, are too numerous to mention here. The subject is discussed later in this chapter but this opportunity may be taken to pay tribute to the pioneering work of a statutory authority—the Greater London Council—in their 1 o'clock clubs.

Paradoxically, therefore, it can be said that, though play facilities take the children temporarily out of the home, they are more likely to strengthen family ties than to weaken them.

One further aspect of play provision is the question of whether or not facilities for play may act as a preventative or as a diversion from certain forms of delinquency. It is most commonly suggested that vandalism by children could be reduced by the adequate provision of *Vandalism and other forms of delinquent behaviour* play facilities. Other kinds of juvenile delinquency are also associated with the lack of such provision. The view has even been expressed by a repentant offender: 'I think if I could always have played football every afternoon of my life I would never have gone thieving.'[1] What little evidence there is available on the subject suggests that the solution is not quite as simple as giving adequate play provision. But it does seem that the physical arrangements of neighbourhoods do play a part in the complex process of creating delinquents. It appears that hooliganism occurs to a greater extent in high-rise rather than in low-rise areas and more on larger housing estates than on smaller ones.[2] In our neighbourhood study it was possible to observe other subtle processes at work. Because of cramped housing conditions mothers preferred their children to play outside. The children forced to their own devices formed groups for popular play activities. There were no amenities; in

1 Davies (1966), p. 168.
2 Cohen (1968); Mycroft (1964).

the streets some activities such as lighting fires, breaking up abandoned cars, playing in the road clashed with adult interests. Should any of their pastimes take a delinquent turn it is more likely that the group would be involved. In conditions like these the group can have a reinforcing effect:

'The potential reaction of the individual's primary group plays a major role in determining whether or not the individual will engage in deviant behaviour; and if the individual lacks primary groups which support such adherence to the norms or identifies himself with others who place a positive value on violating the laws of society, the likelihood of crime increases.'[1]

Many 'natural' activities of children have to be inhibited because they are out of place in an urban environment. However, with the advent of the adventure playground this is no longer so; what would be intepreted as near-delinquent behaviour can now be acceptable within the confines of the playground. Tense scenes between adult authority and children over such things as lighting fires, swinging on trees or building dens in abandoned cars need not occur.

Much research into the aetiology of juvenile delinquency, particularly that of the Gluecks, suggests that family relationships are all important. Play and play facilities can have an important role in reducing tensions within families. Families in overcrowded conditions can obviously gain if there are amenities in the neighbourhood.

For all these children and their families the value of supervised facilities is undoubted. In fact, if play provision is to function adequately as a social service it must be supervised.

## A Comprehensive Service for Play

There is as much reason and need for a comprehensive service to cover children's activities outside home and school as there is for the existing services of education and child care. Education caters for the compulsory attendance of all children: the child care service caters only for a minority in difficulties. A play service would be catering for all children of whom only a minority[2] would take advantage of the service at any one time. A parallel may perhaps be seen here with the Youth Service and clearly, for a variety of reasons, the initiation of any new

1 Sykes (1956), p. 74.
2 See p. 190

service for children would have to be considered in relation to all existing services and the facilities they provide.

It is evident that, for the most part, the play needs of children have been seen as static; playgrounds are still being designed in the pre-war mould; children are thought of too little as persons developing in response to the changing society in which they live. This means not only deprivation for the children but waste and under-use of much existing play space.

What should a comprehensive, flexible service for play provide?[1] The need for diversity has been emphasised in Chapter 4. Predominant within the diverse range should be supervised facilities.

## Supervised play provision

*Variety in provision*

The variations between different kinds of supervised provision are considerable[2]—in the range of activities, in the months and hours of opening and in the aims of the providers. At the time of writing there are over four hundred play schemes of one sort or another in the country; some run by local authorities, some by voluntary committees; most operating on a holiday/seasonal basis. The latter tend to be of the organised games variety but their scope is being widened more and more each year.

The number of permanent schemes has grown remarkably within the last few years; about forty are now in existence. Ten years ago there were fewer than five.

*Provision for the under fives*

For the under fives our study confirmed that play outside the home is, on the whole, not tolerated by mothers unless there is some form of supervision. This does not, of course, mean that there should not be play places to which mothers will go *with* their children—attractive, sheltered places with comfortable seats. Parks are an obvious location for such places. From our study and from observation it would seem to be pointless to provide unsupervised toddlers' play areas on housing estates in the expectation that mothers will allow their small children to play there unattended. If they are designed and sited, however, with the intention of gathering the mothers as well as the children, they are likely to be well used.

---

1  Children's libraries, in many areas, provide excellent and imaginative ancillary services. There are also a growing number of children's clubs providing for a wider range of creative activities. These have been left out of our discussion only because they do not strictly correspond to our definition of play facilities; their importance is far-reaching.

2  For a description of the different kinds of supervised play provision see Appendix I.

Notwithstanding, the most important kind of provision for the under fives is supervised provision. The Plowden Committee gave considerable thought to the question of nursery provision.[1] Whilst there may be room for disagreement on certain points, their recommendations on nursery groups and centres and the suggestions, both short and long term, for meeting staff and other requirements offer a practical solution to the problem—with the important proviso that there should be opportunity for the local community to be involved in the creation and running of such centres. Meanwhile, community-sponsored activities in this field need all the help and encouragement they can get.

Considerations of supervised provision for older children must be differently based. If the evidence were to show unequivocally, as we believed it would, that children flocked in far larger numbers to playgrounds with play leaders than to those without this would be sufficient reason to provide them. In fact, what little evidence we were able to assemble on this point indicated that it was factors such as playground size and equipment which drew children to playgrounds rather than the presence of a play leader. Unfortunately, at the time of our survey there were so few full-time, permanent play-leader playgrounds that the sample was very small. We do not consider that there was enough evidence and it may be that a different representation of playgrounds would have produced different results.[2] However, there are, we believe, sufficiently strong grounds for arguing in favour of a change towards more supervised playgrounds. One of these is supported by limited quantitative data from the ten-borough survey on the duration of stay. There were indications that children stayed longer at play-leader playgrounds than at others. Again this may be because of the nature of the activities rather than because of the play leader himself, but this merely underlines the important fact that in an urban setting these are activities which can only take place under supervision. And it is the merit of such schemes that they do, on the whole, provide for a far greater range of activity than can be found in unsupervised facilities.

*Provision for the over fives*

This range may include opportunities for arts and crafts, drama and dressing up, adventure play, community service, riding bicycles and driving 'cars' in model traffic areas, domestic activities—either real cooking or dressmaking, for instance, or make-believe domesticity, gardening, ping-pong, chess, snakes and ladders, sand and water play,

*Range of activities*

1 Central Advisory Council for Education, *op. cit.*, I, Chapter 9.
2 Regular counts kept by certain permanent play-leader playgrounds suggest that this may be so.

and so on. Many also provide items of traditional equipment, a kick-around area or a five-a-side pitch. Of extreme importance is the indoor accommodation which is almost invariably to be found where there is regular supervision.

There is still too little scope for the basic 'adventure' activities of digging, building and lighting fires even within the permanent schemes. The vast majority of urban children grow up without the opportunity to 'experiment with earth, fire, water and timber'[1] and, although the attempt to re-create 'natural' conditions within a confined space is difficult, it is the only way that most of these children will get experiences of the kind. It is arguable that such experiences have little relevance to modern urban life, but what is involved does have relevance to a child's development. It should not, of course, exclude other forms of creative and exciting activities more directly related to this techno-logical age, or counterbalancing it.

There are other play experiences denied to town-dwelling children. One such is the value and pleasure to be had from caring for pets. A few adventure playgrounds have been successful in this direction, with the play leader's dog, perhaps, or rabbits and guinea pigs. A slightly more controversial experience relates to the provision of model traffic areas. These are being installed in growing numbers. Whilst appreciating the idea of learning through play that lay behind it personal observation of one such experiment led us to question the value of a *permanent* fixture. A few children, particularly the younger ones, conscientiously heeded the rules, but a great many jumped the lights, disregarded the pedestrian crossing and rode or drove blithely on the wrong side of the road. Thus the training of the children for real road use was not to all appearances being very successfully accomplished and in fact there was even the danger that carelessness instead of carefulness was indirectly being fostered.

More stringent and consistent observation of rules and regulations could have been enforced but it is questionable whether this is desirable for either children or leaders. With portable 'rules of the road' equipment, however, strict supervision and training can be limited to special periods and on its removal the paths can be used without more than mild restraint. If these paths, however, are an integral part of the main playground the children are constantly exposed to minor road hazards in the one area where they should be free of them. Separate siting would overcome this difficulty.

Our case for supervised provision, then, is based partly on the fact

1  Allen of Hurtwood (1964), p. 5.

that, through the type and range of activities, the scope and quality of the play is improved. Also, and these are further very important reasons, children are protected from bullying and molestation (this was frequently given as a reason for wanting supervision by mothers in the contrasting-neighbourhood survey); they find there an alternative to an empty home; they are being actively helped in the process of growing up; they are likely to suffer fewer accidents than at conventional, fixed-equipment playgrounds.[1]

There will always, of course, be children whose preferences for quiet or aversion to crowds keeps them away from these playgrounds. Or, as is recognised by most practitioners in the field, there will be children who tire of the playground and move on, temporarily or permanently, elsewhere. There will also be those, and this is less willingly accepted, who keep away because they see, either consciously or unconsciously, the play leader as an authority figure. This leads one to a consideration of the whole question of supervision in relation to play.

The problem would seem to be that there is an inherent conflict in the play leader's role to which, perhaps, insufficient thought has been given.

One definition of a play leader sums up a number of contradictory elements which could be seen to be present in his role: *The role of the play leader*

'a combination of father, mother, policeman and Robin Hood to the youngsters, helping them to find something that they like to do. He must be a man who really loves children, though not in a sentimental way. He must be able to impose discipline by his own personality, rather than by rules. He should understand that his aim is to teach them to use their leisure time properly, and to behave as civilised beings. He is not just "occupying kiddies". The leader must try to instil the habit of working and playing as freely as possible. But this freedom must in no way interfere with any other group of children or older people using the parks or open spaces. He must be able to stimulate their imagination and ideals: this is the best form of citizenship training.'[2]

There are those who would strongly oppose the suggestion that a play leader should possess any of the attributes of a 'policeman'. Others

1  An unpublished Accident Survey of London play parks and conventional playgrounds found that in 1964 there had been an average of one broken limb per playground per week; in that year there were none in the play parks.
2  Abernethy (from an unpublished source).

might question whether to 'teach' is part of a play leader's function, or wonder what is a 'proper' use of leisure time, or feel dubious about the idea of 'work' in a playground.

However much one may agree with, or wish to modify,[1] this definition, the basic difficulty comes through. On the one hand there is the principle of full freedom implicit in the activity of play; on the other there is the problem of catering for this freedom within the confined space of a playground and with possibly conflicting demands of anything from 50 to 300 children. There is also the question of whether or not a genuine responsibility towards the young users of the playgrounds should not entail an attempt to help in their development. Some form of socialisation process, of course, is occurring all the time in such playgrounds, but how explicit should the play leaders' part be? This is not really a new problem. It is similar in kind to those faced by thoughtful parents and progressive teachers. But whereas parents and teachers are held directly responsible for the upbringing and instruction of children this is not automatically the case with play leaders.

In practice, at the moment, most play leaders are active as social workers and many are engaged in what could almost be described as intensive case work spreading out beyond the playgrounds into the families and the community. Although playground populations tend to be constantly changing it has been observed by the authors that certain children become habitual users of supervised playgrounds with the obvious intent of attaching themselves to the play leaders. There is evident in this a need for security and affection, and a sympathetic play leader can often most effectively meet this need. There can be no doubt that affection and adult sympathy and interest should be the prerogative of all children and the fact that most find it in their homes and many in their schools does not mean that they should not also find it at their places of play. But the children here referred to, who seem to be specially lacking in a sense of security, are a minority (though a very important one), even within the social service grouping outlined above. The children of working mothers, for instance, are largely in need of a temporary parent substitute for practical rather than emotional reasons. And the average child just needs somewhere good to play. In an account of an adventure playground experiment the following question was asked:

'Should there be an agreed order of priority as to needs? Can the

[1]  The author has since modified it himself. See Abernethy (1968).

Playground really contain the non-conforming few and the conformist many, the very destructive and attention-seeking minority with the happy and stable majority?

'This dilemma of needs gradually emerged as the central theme of the Playground's history, yet it was never resolved.'[1]

This problem surely is resolvable by means of a high staff/child ratio and later experiments have shown this to be so. Nevertheless, it is an ever-present reality in the use of playgrounds of this kind and should be recognised as such.

Who are the play leaders in this country today? They have a variety of backgrounds—ex-commando sergeants, art students, actors, middle-aged housewives, the young awaiting inspiration for what they really want to do, occasionally teachers and youth leaders.

It is generally agreed that there is a need to put play leadership on to a professional footing, but this means clarifying its aims and functions. In doing this it should be possible at the same time to go some way towards resolving the conflict in the play leader's role, by declaring these aims and functions to have an educational purpose. This means that the play leader should be truly *child*-oriented; that his concern will be to develop all the potentialities within the child rather than fitting these potentialities to the community. It does not mean an extension of school, for the word 'education' is used here in its fullest sense. Nor need it mean that the concept of community play centres is alien to such an educational purpose; the one can work quite harmoniously within the other. At present selection is based on an intuitive judgment of whether or not the applicant is the 'right kind of person', a judgment usually founded on many years' experience. The kind of intangible qualities which differentiate the good teacher from the bad are more than ever necessary for the play leader and however formalised the process of selection and training becomes the value of these qualities should not be lost sight of. The same is obviously true of the youth leader. Various aspects of the Youth Service, including training, are now under review[2] and it is likely that any recommendations arising from this review will have a bearing on training for play leadership. The relationship between the two is obviously close and important.

*Selection and training of play leaders*

1 Spencer *et al.* (1964), p. 237.
2 Two Committees have been set up by the Youth Development Council: the Fairbairn Committee to study the relationship between the Youth Service and the schools; and the Milson Committee to look into the relationship between the Youth Service and the adult community.

For some time strong pressures have been exerted to establish a national full-time training course aiming to give play leaders qualifications and status in line with those enjoyed by youth leaders and teachers. A beginning has already been made, though there are as yet no universal standards nor formal qualifications. The National Playing Fields Association runs an annual play leadership conference and course which lasts only one week. In-service part-time training courses have been in existence for some time, such as those, for instance, to be found in Liverpool and the Greater London Council. There is a practical bias in these courses but some attention is also paid to child development and to the workings of local administration. The most interesting course so far is that initiated by Camden Borough Council. It is the only one to be academically based—at the London North Western Polytechnic—and, although part-time, extends over three terms. The emphasis here, also, is on supervised practical work but the impinging social services are described in some detail and more than a passing consideration is given to the subject of child development. This is an important pointer to future development.

What direction could this future development take? Basically, there are two alternatives, which depend on whether play leadership is seen as a self-sufficient profession covering a full working life span or as work which may be interchangeable with other work concerned with children, thus forming part of a wider profession.

The fundamental lack in the present system of play leadership is a career structure. Although the starting salaries of most full-time play leaders are higher than those of teachers, for instance, the ceiling is lower.[1] But it is not only a financial question; the work is exhausting and few play leaders can maintain the constant and exacting face-to-face relationship with their charges for more than a few years. This would point to the desirability of the latter training alternative, which could be achieved by the creation of a play-leadership option in existing and projected training courses in the fields of education[2] and social work. There is no reason why this should not operate in both fields; the bias in the respective courses could be counteracted by emphasis in the option subjects. These should include theoretical and practical psychology—particularly child development, social administration, arts and crafts and physical recreation.

Clearly for the under fives the specialised nursery teachers' courses

1   See p. 112
2   A start in this direction has already been made at Sheffield College of Education.

must be the best, but it has to be recognised that the numbers of people so trained are unlikely to keep pace with the increasing demand for some time to come, nor can the financial considerations be ignored. The two-year training for nursery nurses and assistants leading to the Certificate of the National Nursery Examination Board, although providing a good basic training, must include aspects of physical care for babies and young children, with consequently less attention given to the educational aspects of children's development. It cannot, therefore, in spite of changing emphasis, be regarded as a complete training.

There are a few part-time courses, notably that held at Morley College, which is sponsored jointly by the Pre-school Playgroups Association and the Save the Children Fund. The G.L.C. run their own in-service training scheme for one o'clock club supervisors.

There is understandable opposition to the idea of supervised play facilities for the very young being run by the untrained. Ideally, there can be no question that a group of under fives should be in the charge of a properly qualified person. Parent rotas bring numbers of problems in their wake, organisational and psychological, and without experienced backing they are often short lived. Present numbers of such groups, however, testify to the urgency of the need. They testify also to the growing desire of the community to be concerned in its own affairs. In these days of acute shortage of trained staff there is a case for using mothers and other voluntary help, though, in our view,[1] there should always be ultimate professional supervision. As a temporary measure, particularly where older children are concerned, there could be a qualified, peripatetic supervisor, responsible for a small number of play groups or playgrounds.

In this connection the attendants on the old-fashioned playgrounds could be brought up to date along with the playgrounds; the latter by imaginative re-designing and equipping, the former by attendance at play leadership courses. Park keepers and caretakers could well be associated with such a scheme. At present there is an arbitrariness in the way in which play provision on housing estates is managed. Playground gates are locked at unsuitable times (sometimes indefinitely), sand pits are emptied, swings are tied up. Whether or not such things occur depends largely on what kind of caretaker has been appointed, how overloaded with duties he is and how conscientiously those responsible for his appointment maintain a watching brief. The mobile playground is another way of coping with space and staff

1   And see Central Advisory Council for Education (1967), I, Chapter 9.

shortage. In Victoria, Australia, for example, a Playmobile Service is operated by the Playgrounds and Recreation Association and consists of fully equipped Volkswagen Kombivans, manned by two leaders, which visit estates where there is no indoor provision.[1] In North Kensington a form of simple but effective mobile service is operating in some temporarily closed streets as part of a vigorously organised voluntary scheme. In another London borough, Southwark, a different kind of mobile service has been tried—volunteers touring the streets on the look-out for bored children and prepared to gather them up, if welcome, and to take them to various places of interest and amusement.

## Where should the play facilities be?

In outlining the frame of reference for the location and siting of play-grounds suggested by our study[2] no mention was made of a standard of play space *per capita* (or dwelling unit). A number of such standards do exist both in this country and abroad. They are based, for the most part, on a considered assessment of needs rather than on any precise research.

*Space standards*

The National Playing Fields Association considered it 'impracticable . . . to attempt to assess requirements on the basis of a minimum space provision per child as the number of children served by a playground is seldom constant for any length of time'.[3] Vere Hole, in her study of children's play on housing estates, questioned whether 'a play space standard based on the amount of accommodation on an estate offers a realistic measure of need'.[4] Our own conclusions confirm these doubts and it is interesting that the pioneers of statutory powers for the provision of play space—the Danes—also do not specify *per capita* amounts of space.[5]

Vere Hole suggests that the evidence from her survey is 'unequivocal as regards location of playgrounds to ensure maximum use: they should be well within the estate, highly visible, and at a point where pedestrian routes converge'.[6]

*Location and siting*

The siting of playgrounds in housing areas is not a simple problem and certainly cannot be solved if the question is shelved until the buildings are up and officials then look round for a 'suitable' piece of

1 Stevenson *et al.* (1967), p. 90.
2 See p. 61
3 Gooch (1963), p. 65.
4 Hole (1966), p. 33.
5 See Chapter 3.
6 Hole, *loc. cit.*

left-over open space; 'sloap' (space left over after planning) playgrounds are legion. The importance of conceiving play provision as part of the design at drawing-board stage seems too obvious to need emphasising, but the sad fact is that buildings are still going up with no provision. Even if it has been included in the original plan, there is the risk that it may be cut out as an economy measure at a later stage. There are also the innumerable instances (which occur outside housing estates as well) where playgrounds have been introduced at an early stage but have been sited and designed without proper regard for the children or the adult residents whose demands often conflict. Examples of this kind of siting—too close proximity to ground floor windows, too distant for safe and easy access for instance—were to be found in our survey.

There is a real dilemma here and it would be unfair not to recognise it. Not all the blame must be put on the designers. A Ministry of Housing Study found that, 'while many of the complaints about lack of children's outdoor play opportunities focused on features of the environment . . . these were often blamed for difficulties concerning children's upbringing and leisure which affect mothers everywhere in our Society'.[1]

Adults' intolerance of children's clamour is one of these difficulties and when further complications, such as those arising from a great deal of shift work in the area,[2] are also present, it is not surprising that play sites are abandoned or moved to such a distance from the houses or flats that children don't use them. Two things follow from this. First, that continuous propaganda must be used to convince adults in the community that children must have space of their own and freedom to play there and that this cannot always be on someone else's doorstep. Second, that the architects and planners should regard this as a challenge and that all the problems of use should be taken into account in the earliest stages. Planting around a play space, for example, is a great absorber of noise though it is not always practicable and can be expensive. How often is this to be found? How many boroughs employ a landscape architect? As a profession, they appear to be particularly conscious of the need for children's play provision and are notably aware of this need in terms of use as well as of aesthetic value which so often is regarded as of paramount importance. Many problems in siting simply do not arise where landscape architects are employed and work in close association with the architects from the earliest stages. From the survey of existing facilities the following field workers'

1 Ministry of Housing and Local Government (1964), p. 42.
2 As, for example, in the New Town of Peterlea.

comments illustrate one good and one bad example of estate playground siting. First the good: 'An 'An attractive, natural play space—accessible from surrounding houses without having to cross a road but sufficiently distant for freedom to move and to make a noise.' And the bad: 'Playground was locked. The reason being because of its being adjacent to an Old People's Home.'

In a Swedish study it was found that

'Whenever the children had a direct exit towards a courtyard, the playgrounds situated there were considerably more often used than when the exit faced the street; young children do not trouble to walk round the building to find a place to play in. The exceptions were those playgrounds in the yards where the play equipment had a quality above the average: there more children were found than in the remainder of the playgrounds.'[1]

Problems of siting playgrounds in parks and other recreational open spaces centre chiefly on the question of accessibility as can be seen from the ten-borough survey. But problems in siting other than accessibility arise: children's nuisance value, for instance, to adults seeking peace and quiet in a park. The practice of sinking playgrounds below the level of the surrounding grounds has been adopted on some housing estates and in a few parks[2] in this country and is common in Denmark. Much depends on the type of playground and sometimes difficulties are not what one would expect. One London play park, for example (not investigated in this study), has been sited in a corner of a large park to take advantage of good natural slopes and splendid big trees. But a local mother (in favour of adventure playgrounds in principle) complained to the authors about the loss of the corner as a family picnic site.

## Making the most of existing space

Paradoxically, it can be said that, despite the desperate pressure on open space and the various competing claims, there *is*, more often than not, enough space available for play facilities. There is also likely to be enough in the foreseeable future. The overwhelming problem is to use the space to the best possible advantage.

1   Sandels, *op. cit.*, p. 267.
2   See p. 226

On the street, Manchester

Off the street, Holland Park, London

*Playing together*

Only 7 per cent of the 467 playgrounds surveyed in the nineteen boroughs were sited in places other than public recreational space or *Waste* housing estates. This shows a sad failure to take advantage of land *sites* which has lain unused for years or has been converted into temporary car parks. The precedent has been set. In this survey there were a few 'off street' playgrounds situated on demolition or old bomb sites but why not dozens more? There are approximately 2,000 waste sites awaiting development in the greater London area alone.[1]

The Parks Department of Greater London Council are conscious that many of these could be put to good use and have already installed 'play parks' and 'one o'clock clubs' on some of them. A vocal Tenants' Association in the Heygate area of Southwark[2] succeeded in persuading their local council to convert a bomb site into a temporary playground. Building sites are glorious natural playgrounds, but, quite apart from danger, are an open invitation to damage both intentional and unintentional. Denmark is experimenting with mobile playgrounds which they set up temporarily on building sites, with their own supervisors, thus giving the children all the fun to be had from mud and drain pipes without causing too much disruption to the building work.[3] In Britain mention should be made of a recent successful experiment where, by voluntary initiative, play space was created under the motorway arcades in North Kensington. The uniqueness of this scheme lies in the use which has been made of already existing covered space— space large enough for all kinds of activities and with built-in dividers in the motorway supports.

There is another source of space which has hitherto been too little explored—schools. Here is space for the asking, indoor as well as outdoor. Children spend far more of their time through the years out of *Schools* school than in school. Many schools are unsuitable for dual use, but objections are often raised on principle and not because of particular difficulties. In enumerating these objections we shall attempt also to dispose of them.

First (the priority is ours), most school playgrounds are dismal, uninviting places and children do not want to go back into the school atmosphere anyway. This is true, but it is no argument for not *using* school playgrounds; it is an argument for *improving* them. The same could be said for public playgrounds. If they are unattractive to children they should be changed, not closed.

1  Unpublished source.
2  See Chapter 8.
3  Sigsgaard, *op. cit.*, pp. 18, 20.

A second objection concerns wear and tear. There is real difficulty here owing to the fact that the premises may be let for other purposes, such as evening institutes, as well as being used as play centres. Replacements are a problem under a regime of economy. Expenses like these, however, have to be set against such alternatives as allowing children to play in dangerous streets or return to empty houses.

Thirdly, there is the question of damage to premises and equipment, particularly if indoor rooms are used. This objection comes from teaching staff and caretakers, and pupils too sometimes when they fear for their various projects—art, nature study, etc.—which it is neither practicable nor desirable to put away every evening. One of the authors was told by a London headmistress, a person deeply concerned with the welfare as well as with the education of her pupils, that she dreaded 'their turn' for the school play centre. Nevertheless, they coped. It is mainly a matter of supervision and sensible use of accommodation. On a visit to an I.L.E.A. play centre at another London school, it was noticed that space, freedom to move and quiet were all adequate. This was achieved by using the hall which had direct access to the playground and one small adjacent classroom. There were enough play leaders to prevent mischief if it was brewing, and the tidying up and putting away was entirely the responsibility of the play centre staff and children, not of the school (the centre had been provided with a small hut in the playground for equipment storage).

It is as pointless to belittle both the extent and the seriousness of vandalism as it is to blame the school caretaker, for instance, who grumbles when the hall windows are broken for the third time. This is a problem which must be tackled fundamentally. Meanwhile, opportunities for vandalism can be minimised (unbreakable or protected glass, for example) and alternatives offered.

The fourth main objection relates to the use of playing fields at those schools which are lucky enough to have them. Common sense could prevail here. Nobody would expect a pitch to survive if it were used for six hours a day six days a week. But a lot could be used a great deal more than they are.[1]

All this concerns existing school provision. None of the above objections would be valid if schools were designed with dual use in mind. Adventurous architectural experiments are projected for the future: 'An exciting cluster of towers . . . a striking set of buildings

1   National Playing Fields Association (1960).

that would provide a lifetime of education as well as cultural and recreational activity.'[1] This is in America, but in our own country more modest schemes (covered by the term 'community school') are being tried out at primary and, more important, at secondary[2] level. These latter experiments exploit where possible the architectural potentialities of a large comprehensive school site and echo much of the philosophy which lies behind the Cambridgeshire Village College, famous from an earlier decade.

The Plowden Report, although so disappointingly reticent on out-of-school activities generally, does press firmly for dual use of primary schools.[3] But, as always, it is the eleven- to fifteen-year-olds who are left out under this dispensation. They would find activities more suited to their age in a secondary school setting. The secondary community school projects are therefore interesting.

## The playgrounds

The levelling of an area scheduled for play is still, more often than not, regarded as the first essential step in creating a playground though fortunately not by all. The landscape architect, Mary Mitchell, amongst others, not only preserves any hills or mounds and hollows that she may find on her proposed sites, but deliberately creates them where none exists. In doing this she has recognised one of the first principles of good children's play provision—plenty of opportunity to move from level to level. Running, rolling, sliding, climbing, hiding, seeking—all these play activities are happily satisfied by the provision of ups and downs. Different levels have practical uses too—separating activities, for example. The lack of artificial or natural barriers on the mixed-activity playgrounds surveyed in the nineteen boroughs presented an alarming picture from the safety point of view.

*Design and layout*

In the famous Stockholm playgrounds particular attention is paid to surfacing. There is soft landing ground under the pieces of moving equipment, natural surfaces are left where suitable, but there is always some form of hard surface for the ball games area.

Lady Allen in 'Design for Play' suggests for the small child's playground a mixture of grass and paving[4] and both in this pamphlet and

---

1   Chapman (1964).
2   Bessey (1968), pp. 364–8; Swain (1968), pp. 369–71.
3   Central Advisory Council for Education, *op. cit.*, I, p. 49.
4   Allen of Hurtwood (1962), p. 25.

her later one for older children, makes a plea for the imaginative and varied use of different materials—concrete, cinders, sand and natural surfaces.[1]

Traditional equipment, as we have defined it, is often derided nowadays as 'ironmongery', but investigation[2] has shown that certain types of conventional equipment are exceedingly popular with the five- to ten-year-olds. Camden, with its progressive and imaginative play provision, has included some form of such equipment in its community play centres and our observation has confirmed that *Equipment* even where conventional equipment is in competition with other kinds, certain items are used consistently. Swings, slides and gymnastic items are high on the list and are preferred and used more frequently by children than the fantasy type of equipment, unless these also provide scope for gymnastic activity.[3]

Enterprising architects and landscape architects design their own pieces of equipment, often with disappointing results but sometimes with flair, making good use of cheap materials or 'natural' objects, such as tree trunks, or appealing to older children, as do Mary Mitchell's high slides. These are built into the lines of banks, but, in spite of their height, are safe for children of all ages. Some commercial firms are manufacturing lighter, gayer and more imaginative pieces of fixed equipment, but the average playground still boasts only minor concessions to current trends, if at all. It is strange that nylon ropes are not used for swings instead of the lethal chains.

Improvised play materials are probably as great a source of joy to small children as formal items—apart from those of painting and modelling, sand and water. Play groups, based on adventure playgrounds, gain much from the abundance of such materials, which are usually made available to the under fives. Grassed, unequipped, fenced-in spaces, such as those to be found on Hampstead Heath, in which pre-school children can improvise their own play without risk of wandering off, fulfil a useful purpose (though they would be improved by the installation of a sand pit). The arid little hard-surfaced squares and circles to be found on some housing estates, on the other hand, are seldom frequented by children.

The provision of portable equipment underlines the need for supervision. It is just as unrealistic to expect the provision of building blocks

---

1 Allen of Hurtwood (1962, 1964).
2 Sheppard (1964); Hole (1966); this Study, see p. 273.
3 *Ibid.*

or stilts on an unsupervised playground[1] as it is to be surprised that children resort to the abuse of conventional equipment as an interesting variation in their play. Eventually straightforward swinging, for instance, gets boring. If there is no permissible alternative then children will naturally try such variations as twisting the swing and unwhirling it at high speed.

It is time that something was done to increase the provision of sand and water, so markedly absent in the playgrounds surveyed in the nineteen boroughs. The reasons for their scarcity are not entirely the result of lack of imagination or failure to understand children.

First, there is the question of hygiene. Many public health departments forbid the provision of sand pits on health grounds and numbers of parents also believe that sand pits are a dangerous breeding ground for germs. But it is possible to overcome this objection by the use of a certain type of sand.[2] In Liverpool objections on the grounds of hygiene were silenced by the simple expedient of pointing out the alternative of playing with dirt in street gutters. *Sand and water*

Another important hygiene precaution is to have the sand pit large enough—the larger the better, and designed, where possible, as a natural feature—and also, of course, to ensure that it is properly cared for; regular raking and changing of the sand when necessary.[3] Covers, where practicable, can be used. Water in paddling pools should also be changed and/or sterilised at regular intervals, the frequency depending upon the size of the pool.

A further objection to sand pits connected with hygiene is that dogs and cats foul them, as well as the children themselves. This cannot be denied and the fact that in some other countries one frequently finds little sand pits dotted about, unfenced and unsupervised, may in part be due to the comparative scarcity of pets (Switzerland provides sand for the animals too!). Examples of sand pits in play spaces which are not permanently supervised do exist in this country, too. Vere Hole found sand pits in constant use kept in impeccable condition by the estate porters.[4] Unfortunately there are few such examples and in general more consistent supervision is desirable.

The second major objection to sand pits and paddling pools concerns

---

1 Though this is, in fact, being tried in Gothenburg.
2 See National Playing Fields Association Leaflet 'Sandpits Construction and Maintenance'; or apply: The Sand and Gravel Association of Great Britain, 48 Park Street, W.1.
3 The G.L.C. chlorinate their sand pits once a week.
4 Hole (1966), p. 18.

their abuse, either by vandals or by other citizens, young and old, who use them as convenient dumps for rubbish.

Here the immediate answer to the question of litter comes back again to the supervision, fencing and the locking of playgrounds when not in use, but much more could be done at once to tackle the problem of litter. How many playgrounds, for example, have *prominent* large litter bins? How many have litter bins at all? Attempts to train children are made in schools but local authorities could take these much further. Continuous propaganda is needed to make the community really litter-conscious. Where better to begin than on the playgrounds?

The third major objection to sand pits is the danger from children throwing sand at each other or simply in exuberance throwing it into the air. Again this is an objection shared by parents and authorities. Supervision once more is the long-term answer but it is surely not unreasonable to assume that a good part of that supervision can and should be by accompanying adults. An unfenced sand pit in Rotterdam is situated in the middle of a park and is constantly filled with small children and surrounded by mothers. It is a reasonable presumption that if any older, unaccompanied children come there to make mischief rather than to play peaceably, the presence of these mothers will be a sufficient deterrent.

*W.C. and washing facilities*

Attention has already been drawn to the deplorable lack of w.c. and washing facilities in schools.[1] The survey of 467 playgrounds in nineteen boroughs further confirmed that hygiene comes very low on the list of priorities for children in this country. As far as housing estates are concerned, the underlying assumption in this lack of provision would seem to be that the children can go home when the need arises. But a child needs a lot of time and resolution to cross possibly a large stretch of ground, manipulate the lift or climb the stairs in order to reach a w.c., and anyway may not yet have acquired the necessary control. Caretakers will, understandably, say that w.c.s are locked because of vandalism, which is also used as an argument for not providing them or for shutting them down on playgrounds elsewhere. Vandalism, however, is a separate question. If w.c.s are not provided some children, particularly the younger ones, will accidentally, if in no other way, use hidden (and not so hidden) corners, access stairways or lifts. At one London estate playground some pieces of play equipment had been removed because of this.

1  National Union of Teachers (1963).

# Whose Responsibility?

There are no mandatory powers concerning the provision of play facilities in this country as there are in some other countries[1] and as there are for school open space.[2] Mandatory powers for the inclusion of play space have, in fact, been scheduled for all new housing schemes, in accordance with the Parker Morris recommendations.[3] Unlike those for car parks, however, 'the date upon which these powers might become mandatory has not yet been fixed'.[4] The responsibility for play provision 'has been placed by Parliament clearly and unequivocally on local authorities (apart naturally from voluntary organisations and clubs)'.[5] In one sense it may be said that the vast majority of local authorities in the country have met this responsibility, for there are *Permissive* few, from small parish councils with a swing and see-saw on the village *or com-* green to the great all-purpose county borough, who do not provide *pulsory* some form of play facility for children. *powers*

There exists an impressive body of legislation under which assistance can be given from public funds to children's playground and play leadership schemes.[6] It is important to stress, however, that the powers are permissive and not obligatory, and, as our study has shown, the manner in which and the degree to which these powers are exercised varies enormously from one local authority to another.

Local government is a complex, hierarchical structure—a baffling mixture, peculiar to this country, of voluntary service and bureaucratic control. It is anachronistic but has attempted, in recent years, to keep pace with the changes in the society it governs either by centralising or fragmenting its services.

These piecemeal efforts were bound to have only partial success and the need for radical reform has been evident for a long time, not least to those engaged in governing.

The recommendations of the Royal Commission on Local Government in England, set up in 1966, are therefore awaited. Because of the uncertainty of future local government structure any long-term suggestions we may make about the responsibility for children's play

1 See Chapter 3.
2 See Appendix V.
3 Ministry of Housing and Local Government Circular, 36/67.
4 *Ibid.*, p. 14.
5 Owen (1967), p. 23.
6 The National Playing Fields Association publication by R. Owen, 'Statutes and Constitutions' (1967), lists twenty-six relevant Acts of Parliament, the most important of which are referred to in Chapter 2 and are given in Appendix V.

facilities must be tentative. The chief recommendation of the Seebohm Committee to set up a new local authority department providing a 'community based and family oriented service'[1] will also have a direct bearing on play facility provision.

One further point needs to be made. Any realistic discussion on the improvement of local government services cannot ignore the financial aspect of provision. 'Exchequer grants . . . since the war have met about 53 per cent of [local] expenditure.'[2] At the time of writing, owing to the general economic situation, there is severe restriction on central government loan sanctions for such requests as play facility provision. On the basis of the Parker Morris recommendations, the Ministry of Housing and Local Government is prepared to allow, financially, for the provision of play space in new housing schemes though only to a very limited extent. But this does not include playgrounds located outside housing estates. Thus, it is from within the local budget that the major costs must be met.

Enough examples in many parts of the country show that this *need* not mean the denial to children of adequate play facilities. It is, of course, easier for the larger, richer authorities to find the money, though several smaller authorities have succeeded in persuading their ratepayers to give play facilities a high place on the list of priorities. In the overwhelming majority of cases, however, for both large and small authorities the evidence would suggest otherwise.

Thus, for a variety of reasons—size of authority, finance, physical and social environment, personal enthusiasms or a lack of them—there is today, as our study has underlined, an extreme unevenness in the amount, distribution and quality of provision for children's play. One of the virtues of our governmental system is the strength of local autonomy. Local differences and variations are nevertheless kept within a general framework of high standards by the existence of a single central authority. *Recommended* standards, however, are in danger of being disregarded.

In 1947 an enquiry into the leisure interests and activities of children out of school hours was carried out for the Central Advisory Council for Education. Their Report—'Children Out of School'[3]—seems to have made little impression on the public. In our view, the excellent recommendations of this report are still valid, for the simple reason

1   Committee on Local Authority and Allied Personal Social Services (1968).
2   Ministry of Housing and Local Government (1967), p. 46.
3   Central Advisory Council for Education (1948).

that they have been largely ignored during the intervening twenty years.

Twenty years is too long. In spite of the increasing interest and concern in the question of children's play provision and the already existing number of good quality local authority play facilities, it is evident that good intentions are not enough and that ultimately the same kind of compulsory powers will have to be introduced as have been in existence for formal education facilities for more than half a century.

Largely by historical accident, play facilities in this country are provided and maintained by a multiplicity of authorities and a multiplicity of departments within those authorities.[1] It has been shown in the nineteen-borough survey that the type and quality of the provision bear little relationship to the primary function of the department concerned. It is with horticulture, roads, cemeteries, housing and so on that these departments are primarily concerned and not with children. It has also been shown that because of this, good provision depends mainly on the initiative of individual councillors and officers. But, despite good individual efforts, this is clearly an unsatisfactory situation. It leaves too many loopholes for the bad providers and too much opportunity for uneven standards. *Allocation of responsibility at local government level*

It has been suggested earlier that variety in types of facility should be preserved and that there is a need for these different kinds of facility in different locations. This means, in effect, that there should still be equipped and unequipped play spaces, supervised and unsupervised playgrounds (albeit in different proportions from now), and these would still be situated in parks and municipal gardens, on housing estates, in schools and, for the future, on land awaiting development. The common factor between all these is that they are used by children, which suggests that the responsibility for their provision should go to a department which has children as its chief concern. This applies, today, to two local authority departments—the Education Department and the Children's Department. Neither of these as at present constituted is suitable. Children's departments are almost wholly concerned with children at risk; education departments concentrate on the in-school period of a child's life. Two Acts of Parliament have attempted to broaden horizons in both cases. The 1944 Education Act imposed duties relating to 'facilities for recreation and social and physical training' upon local education authorities and recognised that these

1 Voluntary organised provision is discussed on p. 108 and in Chapter 7.

authorities had a responsibility to contribute of the 'spiritual, mental and physical development of the community'. Three reports of the Central Advisory Council for Education—Crowther, Newsom, Plowden —have, with varying degrees of emphasis, referred to the importance of out-of-school activity and another, 'Children Out of School', was entirely devoted to the subject. The current trend in official education circles is towards a wider concept of education—integrating the child and the school with the community by greater parent participation, new designs for dual use of schools, the extension of Education's responsibility downwards to take in the three- to five-year-olds,[1] and the development in many local Youth Services towards inclusion of the under fourteens and the over twenty ones.

The 1963 Children and Young Persons Act extended the powers of local authorities 'to make available such advice, guidance and assistance as may promote the welfare of children by diminishing the need to receive children into care'. The Seebohm Committee's recommendations have reinforced this trend towards positive, preventive care oriented towards the family. This could lead to some form of family or community centred service with infinitely wider terms of reference than now exist for children's departments.

The problem for the child at play is to reconcile in practice the educational aspect with that centred on the family and the community. These two aspects are not in themselves contradictory but complementary and once this is fully accepted the question of responsibility for play provision becomes chiefly one of practicalities. It is a matter for speculation how far and how soon the necessary changes in social work attitudes and empires would occur to allow children's play provision to become a natural part of that system. Similarly, it cannot be forecast how rapidly the widening of horizons in the field of education will cease to be trends and become priorities.

Society's leisure demands are increasing at such a rate that quite serious efforts are already being made by some local authorities to meet these demands in a co-ordinated manner. This is reflected at central government level by the existence of two special Ministers—one for Arts and one for Sport and Recreation. At local level, a third alternative to the two suggested above could be the allocation of responsibility for the provision of children's play facilities to any future local government department which might be especially concerned with leisure, such as a Department of Leisure and Recreation. In so far as it recognises the

[1]  Central Advisory Council for Education (1967), I, Chapter 9.

importance of growing leisure needs the idea has much to recommend it, but there is a danger here that the broad educational aspect of children's play needs might be swamped by a too general, and perhaps too superficial, approach.

It may be as well to await developments in local government structure before finally allocating the responsibility of children's play provision to any one department. In the meantime, gaps could be closed, overlappings avoided and positive steps forward be taken by the establishment of a fully representative committee strictly concerned with all aspects of children's play provision.

If overall responsibility for children's play provision is vested in a single department, how can one ensure that the particular space claims of this department are recognised in the wider context of local council responsibilities? Compulsory powers are an essential step, but, given the powers—either compulsory or permissive—the first step is to entrust the claims in the initial stages to the department best suited to deal with them—the planning department. Planners are in the unique position of being able to measure the claims of all sections of the community against each other. But because the act of planning an urban environment impinges on all aspects of living, it is essential that there should be safeguards. Full use should be made of the skills and advice of both the practitioners in the field of play and members of local government departments whose functions are related, such as parks superintendents and housing managers. This could best be achieved by the establishment of a permanent committee with representation covering all aspects of play provision.

We realise that a concentration of play provision powers in education or social service and planning departments would reinforce the trend towards centralisation, as these departments belong to larger authorities. This would be so particularly if these functions were ultimately to be transferred to a regional authority. Here again the remedy would be a fully representative committee.

At present four Ministries are actively concerned in the provision of play facilities for children—the Ministry of Housing and Local Government, the Department of Education and Science, the Ministry of Health,[1] and the Ministry of Public Building and Works. A few schemes have been initiated by children's departments. Thus, the Home Office also, though to a much smaller extent, is involved. Only the Ministry of Public Building and Works has direct responsibility in its capacity as guardian of the Royal Parks and also as the provider of

1  Now the Department of Health and Social Security.

*Allocation of responsibility at central government level*

playgrounds in its new housing projects for the Services; the rest operate through local authorities.

Clearly the central Government agency with the most interest and power is the Ministry of Housing and Local Government. As the responsible Ministry for all local government affairs and as the central planning authority, this interest and power would inevitably be sustained through any changes at local government level. The Ministry of Health is concerned in provision for the under fives through local public health departments and, if local education departments were to take over responsibility for the three- to five-year-olds as recommended by the Plowden Committee, the Ministry of Health's concern in play provision would logically diminish and eventually disappear except in their responsibility for day nursery provision. Conversely, the powers of the Department of Education and Science as the primary grant-giving agency would increase and ultimately become paramount. It is not possible at this stage to know which Ministry would be ultimately responsible if local government responsibility were vested in a newly created social service department.

Statutory provision of play facilities is general throughout this country. The concept of adventure and kindred forms of play provision, however, originated with voluntary groups. Although a number of boroughs have now initiated full-scale schemes of this kind and others run seasonal schemes, many such playgrounds are still inspired and organised by voluntary effort. In most cases, once they have proved their worth, they receive financial help from the local authority in the form of grants for staff salaries, supply of equipment and so on.

There are broadly three ways in which voluntary participation in providing for children's play provision occurs: through nationally-based advising and co-ordinating organisations, e.g. the National

*The role of voluntary and community organisations*

Playing Fields Association, the Pre-School Playgroups Association; through other kinds of 'external' organisations, usually intimately connected with specific schemes, which they are likely (but not necessarily) to have initiated, e.g. the London Adventure Playground Association, various Councils of Social Service, the Save the Children Fund; by means of 'internal' groups which have sprung up within the local communities and whose members are actively concerned, particularly as parents of the children who will use the facilities, e.g. The Islington Adventure Playgrounds Association, The North Kensington Playspace Group. The dividing line between these last two categories is not sharp. Numbers of voluntary groups, such as those in Liverpool and Glasgow, and the Sparkbrook Association in Birmingham span the two. Current trends, as is well known, are towards a greater involvement of the community in the conduct of its affairs, whether this involvement be neighbourhood-based or arising from other groupings. These pressure and action groups can be very powerful and, if they are well organised, can achieve their ends extraordinarily quickly.

The initiative for community involvement may also come from the local authority who, through such experiments as community play centres, by means of specially mounted community projects, or through schools, may involve parents and other members of the community in the concerns and activities of children. Obviously the combination of these two approaches will achieve the most, and local authorities are already learning to foster their voluntary groups instead of opposing them.

The two vital aspects of play provision are first an adequate supply of suitable space, and secondly a varied service of high quality. To ensure the supply of space and consistently high standards an overall statutory responsibility at central and local government level is essential, but we see no reason why there should not within the foreseeable future be room for a private sector. It has been shown how successfully and at what a high qualitative level this can be maintained both in this country and abroad—particularly by the *Pro Juventute* organisation in Switzerland. Change and experiment are the essence of good social provision, particularly for children, and, although much good experimentation takes place under official auspices, the increasing restrictiveness of our society makes valuable the freedoms of voluntary groups.

It must, of course, be recognised that these freedoms are often restricted by shortage of money and that voluntary organisations are perennially short of money. So, for that matter, are statutory bodies.

## Costs

Shortage of money both at local and central governmental level is, of course, relative; it is a question of priorities. The absolute cost of providing play facilities, even at their most expensive, is not high compared with that of formal education or, more pertinently perhaps, with that of repairing the damage sustained by children[1] or the damage

1   (a) A total of £23,890,967 was spent by local authorities on children in care for the years 1967–68; the cost per week for a child in a local authority home is £14 5s. 6d. (Home Office, Cmnd 3893, 1968.)
    (b) The estimated average net weekly cost per head of maintaining boys and girls in approved schools was £23 9s. 6d. in 1967–68. (Home Office Statistics, 427, October 1968.)

done *by* young people.[1] But because the benefits of play provision are less easily definable the treasurers are more difficult to convince of the need to spend money in this way than on the services of 'proven' value.

## *What is the cost?*

Expenditure on play facilities can, very broadly, be divided into the two basic categories of initial costs and running costs. Into the former fall those of space; landscaping layout and design; equipment. Into the latter those of maintenance and replacement; and staff. It is difficult to give a precise indication of the costs of play provision because the range of facilities and the quality of the service offered carry an implicit variation in cost. It is also extremely difficult to isolate some costs for analysis, though an attempt was made for the cost/benefit analysis in the ten-borough survey[2] and examples are given in the ensuing sections.

*Space*      Land is expensive in towns and cities. In new developments the planners and architects (and landscape architects where they are employed) must make cost allocations within the rigorous framework of ministerial yardsticks and subsidies and without, at the moment, mandatory sanction for play space. Indoor space would not qualify for a subsidy. Thus, the expenses incurred by converting a ground floor flat to play use, for example, would have to be fully borne by the local authority. The advisability of single-department responsibility and the short-term need for co-operation between departments and committees becomes immediately apparent when the question of costs is being considered.

Within open space scheduled for recreational use the land costs of a play area are absorbed in the overall land costs; similarly with existing recreational open space. In existing residential areas, however, if space is to be converted to permanent play use, there will immediately be competition with other possible uses. These, if industrial or commercial, may carry high financial returns; if

---

1 Estimated cost of vandalism in 789 local authorities in 1962–63 was £561,565 (Local Government Information Office, 1964). It may be assumed that there will have been a proportionate increase in the figures over the intervening years related to the cost of living. In 1965 the total cost of vandalism to the main targets—the railways, the G.P.O. and local government authorities—was about £1½ million (Cohen, 1968).
2 See Chapter 10.

social—housing for example—they may be thought to carry higher priority, though in our view this may frequently be a misjudgment of the situation.

Economies can be made by the temporary use, or leasing of, land awaiting development. Dual use of schools eliminates land costs altogether.

The costs of landscaping and design are minimised in new develop- *Land-* ment if the facilities are conceived as part of the general plan. Allowance *scaping* for landscaping and playgrounds on housing schemes varies between *and design* local authorities and will depend, of course, on individual site charac- teristics. Today the cost ranges from £65 to £90 per dwelling.[1] Layout costs for supervised playgrounds vary enormously according to size, surfacing, fencing, planting, activity range and so on and the degree of sophistication and permanence of the scheme. They can be as high as £15,000 or as low as a few hundred pounds. If the scheme is to be a permanent one the cost of expert advice (i.e. the landscape architect), as so often, is likely to save expensive mistakes and waste. Imaginative landscaping will use up excavated material, for example, and save the cost of carting this away. Surfaces, planting, fencing and so on must be considered from the point of view of durability and resistance to wilful destruction as well as cost and attractiveness. A higher initial cost may often be justified. This applies with particular force to the question of indoor accommodation. Two playground buildings of comparatively recent date and of approximately the same size (60 ft. by 30 ft.), one sponsored by a voluntary organisation and one by a local authority, cost £9,370 and £8,200 (including services) respectively.

The more imaginative the playground the lower are the equipment *Equip-* costs likely to be: for example, by using trees which have been felled *ment* in site clearance; a tree-rope is a great deal cheaper than a conventional swing. There are exceptions, of course. A pottery kiln, for instance, is expensive, but through the child-hours it keeps creatively and pleasurably occupied it will be of comparatively much greater value than an equiva- lently expensive piece of conventional fixed equipment. As well as per- manent fixed and portable pieces of equipment there are in supervised playgrounds, what may be described as consumable items—painting, modelling and handicraft materials, food for the 'cooks', scrap and junk for the 'builders' and the 'carpenters'. This kind of equipment is often obtained free or at low cost.

1 From an unpublished source.

*Mainten-
ance and
replace-
ment*

*Staff*

As suggested above, maintenance costs will naturally vary with the original design, the quality of the materials used, the numbers of children using the playground and the incidence of vandalism.

Expense is the main reason given for limiting the number of supervised facilities. It cannot be denied that they are more expensive to run (though they may be cheaper to install) than unsupervised facilities. This was demonstrated in the cost/benefit analysis already referred to. In this analysis the estimated costs of playground provision were equated with the 'benefit' of attendance figures. The results showed that the numbers of children attending did not increase in a sufficiently high ratio to the presence of supervision. But clearly such a measurement of benefit is too crude.[1]

The number of play leaders required for a playground will vary according to the number of children attending and the hours of opening. It can be as many as the equivalent of six or seven full-time leaders (working in shifts—some on a full-time, some on a part-time basis). This is to cover opening hours of 10 a.m. to 8 or 9 p.m., seven days a week all the year round, and to cater for school-age children's attendance with daily peak figures of, for example, approximately three hundred in the summer holidays and an average of sixty during the winter week-day school periods. The under fives peak attendance figures range from eleven to forty. On the other hand, a small playground with a comparatively small attendance, open only after school hours and during the holidays for five or six days a week, may be run with one or two full-time leaders with limited part-time paid or voluntary help. A high staff–child ratio is desirable from every point of view.

Senior play leaders' salaries range from approximately £1,075 to approximately £1,200 per year; and assistants' salaries from approximately £900 to approximately £1,075 per year.

It must undoubtedly be faced that in the long run the costs of supervision are not likely to diminish. In the short run, however, it is possible to keep the increasing costs within reasonable limits at the same time as stepping up the numbers. This can be done by means of up-grading, peripatetic leaders, use of voluntary help, sharing of staff and premises, and so on.

1   See pp. 87-89.   It is also of interest to note that a comparison of costs in Lancashire has shown that the cost of opening the premises of a county school during the summer holidays as an experimental play centre was less than the cost of repairing the damage done by vandals during previous years. Children entering the school premises illegally did about £120 worth of damage, whereas the cost of running the play centre was about £75 per annum. (*Times Educational Supplement*, November 29, 1968.)

## *Who should pay?*

The question of who should pay is directly related to the question of administrative responsibility.[1] Apart from the very small central government allocation for housing schemes already mentioned, and loan sanctions which are at present suspended, money for play facilities is raised either by local authorities under various Acts of Parliament[2] (which may be used directly or in the form of a grant to voluntary groups) or by voluntary effort. It is clear that this latter source must continue to be tapped for some time to come. The introduction of mandatory powers would automatically result in increased statutory financial support.

1   See Chapter 13.
2   See Appendix V.

# 7

## A Policy for Play

There is urgent need for a centrally-directed policy which will ensure the following:

1. the acquisition of enough space, suitably located, exclusively for children's play;

2. the establishment of a play service to cover all forms of play provision for children of all ages;

3. radical reform in the allocation of responsibility for play provision which would include, ultimately, the introduction of mandatory powers;

4. a recognition that, in the immediate future, certain areas should be regarded as play priority areas to receive special attention;

5. the creation of new, and the modification of old, environments which allow children to play and move about with a reasonable degree of safety;

These five objectives require central direction but their implementation would depend upon different sections of government and the community, either severally or jointly. A sixth objective, dependent on the community rather than on any policy directives, must also be the greater integration of children into the life of the community. The following suggestions for a policy for play all stem from the six objectives. These suggestions are, for the most part, supported by quantitative data from our research (which can be clearly distinguished in Chapter 4), though they are prompted also be considered opinion and evidence from other research. For clarity they are grouped under headings which represent, very broadly, those sections which would be primarily concerned with their implementation.

# I—POINTS FOR CENTRAL GOVERNMENT, LOCAL AUTHORITIES, VOLUNTARY ORGANISATIONS AND COMMUNITIES

## A. Compulsory or Permissive Powers

### 1. *Long-term*

We envisage a time when it will be mandatory upon local authorities to provide facilities for children's play in the same way as it is today for the provision of formal educational facilities and as it is for play provision in some countries abroad. In fact, for housing estates, mandatory powers for play provision have already been scheduled.[1] These should be brought into effect without delay. They can be modified as required to conform with our suggested standards for location and those arising from current Ministry of Housing and Local Government research. Compulsory powers mean greater expenditure than is now thought necessary for children's play, either by central government or most local authorities. We believe this expenditure to be justified.

### 2. *Short-term*

In the meantime the permissive powers which already exist are sufficiently varied[2] to allow the establishment of play facilities wherever they are needed. These powers should be used much more fully than they are at present.

## B. Responsibility at Local Level

### 1. *Long-term*

(a) We should ultimately like to see the primary responsibility for children's play provision vested in a single department. The two most appropriate departments for these duties are education or a newly-created social or family service department.

The problem of organising a service for children aged 0–5 has been faced by both the Plowden and the Seebohm Committees who have (in their majority recommendations) suggested different solutions.[3] We add a further dimension to the problem by suggesting that the provision of out-of-school, out-of-home play facilities for children of *all* ages should be included in that service. But whether such a play service should be an integral part of an extended education department

1 See p. 103.
2 See p. 103 and Appendix V.
3 Central Advisory Council for Education (1967), I, Chapter 9, and Committee on Local Authority and Allied Personal Social Services (1968), pp. 192–210.

or of a new social service department must depend upon the developments arising from these two major Government Reports and the report still awaited from the Maude Commission.[1]

(b) Planning departments should be responsible for the initial provision of play *space*. There should be a built-in system of co-operation and consultation at all levels between the planning department and the department with primary responsibility (education or social service), other relevant departments such as parks and housing, and local community groups.

(c) There would need to be the closest co-operation, at some levels possibly integration, with the Youth Service.

## 2. *Short-term*

(a) In those authorities, big and small, whose control of play provision is fragmented through a number of departments the first aim should be a permanent interdepartmental committee at officer level, and at councillor level[2] a permanent sub-committee composed of members from each of the relevant full committees. These co-operating committees should always include representation from the planning department and for those small councils which are not in themselves planning authorities this should be contrived on an inter-authority basis. All new development plans should be submitted to this committee.

(b) In authorities with only one department responsible for play facilities a similar close co-operation with the planning department or authority is essential.

(c) As a transitional stage between what is now practicable and what is ultimately desirable we suggest the appointment of a special officer for children's play. His duties should cover not only the initiation and organising of playleadership schemes, to be found now in some boroughs, but as far as possible the co-ordination of all types of provision. It is probable that this play organiser would find himself attached to the department most interested in play provision, but if there is doubt, and until the ultimate departmental responsibility is decided, the Town Clerk's Department would provide good neutral cover.

## 3. *The Role of Voluntary Organisations and Community Groups*

### (a) *Long-term*

An assumption that eventually it will be mandatory on local authorities

1 Royal Commission on Local Government in England (Chairman Lord Redcliffe of Maude) set up in 1966.
2 For a description of local government structure see pp. 242, 243.

to provide adequate play facilities need not, and we feel should not, imply the end of the voluntary role. But this may fruitfully change its direction from one of 'providing' to one chiefly of consultation, though there would always, we should hope, be a place for experimentation in actual provision. The local community should be involved wherever possible *before* decisions are made and at all stages thereafter. The need to do away with the old-style imposition of facilities without consultation is as important in the matter of play as for any other aspect of urban living. Local commitment to a project can make a difference of success or failure with regard to its use.

### (b) Short-term

For some time to come, however, voluntary efforts[1] will be needed in every capacity and every advantage of these efforts should be taken. But, increasingly, assistance also must be given. Voluntarily-raised funds may be insufficient to maintain standards indefinitely and it is to be hoped that the present practice of subsidising voluntary provision in many of those boroughs where it exists will be extended.

The extent of existing provision should be discovered, as is now being done in one or two boroughs. This is particularly important where the under-fives are concerned as so many small groups are springing up and there is obvious need for a common policy.

### 4. Children as an Integral Part of the Community

The kind of pressure and response indicated in the foregoing section, however, is directed towards procuring and developing special play facilities. What is also needed is a recognition that children are people. They must be accepted as participating members of the community. This is two-edged. Not only does it entail a tolerance of child-like behaviour—with its inconveniences as well as its charm—at play or moving about in the general environment, but also a willingness to include children in grown-up activities inside and outside the home. It also suggests a positive response from the children.

There are many practical ways in which this response may be encouraged. In America and Holland, for example, children man pedestrian crossings at appropriate times. This is a regular duty and is taken seriously by adults as well as children. Investigation into the play needs of an area, as another example, can be carried out with the assistance of children—asking as well as answering the questions.

1 See pp. 108, 109.

Some forms of community service for young people would appear to be appropriate. Old voluntary youth organisations such as the scouts and various church groups, and the statutory Youth Service, are moving increasingly towards the idea of service *by* youth whilst still retaining their service *for* youth activities. New organisations concerned with community service, both national and local, statutorily and voluntarily sponsored, are appearing almost daily. Many schools are actively engaged in projects of various kinds within their neighbourhoods.[1] Serious appraisal of the factors underlying this development and of the direction in which it is going is needed, for phrases such as 'community participation' and 'community service' may come to have an empty ring if they are not fully understood. Nevertheless, for children, as for adults and young people, we are in no doubt that active involvement in community affairs, provided there is no coercion, is a desirable goal.

The intermingling of children and adults can also be achieved through the provision of all-age centres, e.g. the Harlow Sportcentre.

## C. Responsibility at Central Government Level

Under the long-term proposals for local government responsibility outlined above, central government responsibility would be shared between the Ministry of Housing and Local Government and the parent ministry of whichever local authority department is made responsible. The ultimate introduction of mandatory powers would call for the setting-up of an inspectorate.

## D. Dual Use of Schools

Whilst we recognise that many schools are unsuitable for dual use and appreciate the difficulties that must be overcome, we nevertheless urge that, if there is a lack of play space in the vicinity, school premises should be made available wherever possible. Ideally these should be used for supervised provision. New schools, secondary as well as primary, should be designed with this dual use in mind.

Another idea is to explore the possibilities, where layout permits, of using only outdoor school space. In Zürich, for instance, some school playgrounds are designed with 24-hour free access but the buildings are kept closed during out-of-school hours thus saving wear and tear and the cost of supervision. A similar experiement is currently being tried in Sheffield.

## E. Play Priority Areas

We think that certain areas should be designated for special treatment

1 Schools Council Working Paper No. 17.

in providing for children's play. Since so many areas of need[1] are being put forward—education, housing, the personal social services, immigrants, and now play—there may be a danger that the priority areas themselves will be submitted to a test of priority and that some may be considered less urgent than others. Because the effects of play deprivation are less obvious than some other kinds of deprivation there is a risk that play priority areas may get pushed to the bottom of the list. We urge that this should be avoided. It is, of course, certain that there will be considerable overlapping between these areas of need and in some cases there will be identical 'boundaries'. Nevertheless, distinctions must be drawn and individual assessments made.

1. For the purposes of play, assessment should be made on the basis of:

(a) Physical environmental conditions such as—

shortage of open space in relation to population density;
traffic-congested streets;
overcrowded housing;
lack of play facilities;
high-rise housing estates.

Our standards for the location of play facilities[2] could be used as one yardstick of need.

(b) cultural and social factors relating to children and their families. These are likely to be associated with many of the above material conditions. They would include—

a high incidence of vandalism (this may occur as often in new, high-rise housing estates as in old, slum areas);
a high proportion of working mothers;
new immigrants in substantial numbers;
poverty.

2. Once the assessment has been made, any projected improvements in play provision must clearly be related to the educational, social and planning needs of the neighbourhood, especially where subsidies are deemed necessary and especially if the neighbourhood has been designated as an area of need in any other sense.

1 At the time of writing the Local Government Grants (Social Needs) Bill is before Parliament.
2 See pp. 61–4.

## F. Training of Play Leaders and Supervisors for Under Fives Provision

### 1. *Long-term*

A professional service requires professional standards which can only be acquired through a proper training system geared to an adequate career structure. To meet this problem we suggest that a formal play leadership option should be made available on existing training courses at colleges of education and on the different schemes of current social work training.[1]

For under fives provision training should approximate as nearly as possible to that required for nursery schools. However, whilst it is ultimately desirable that all people dealing with groups of small children should be trained, it is reasonable that the degree and nature of the qualification for assistants should be less stringent than for those in charge.[2]

### 2. *Short-term*

Meanwhile existing part-time training schemes concerned with all age groups should be fostered and developed and new ones introduced, including refresher courses and special crash courses adapted to different degrees of experience.

## G. The Need for Information

There is need for a central information bureau for play.[3] Information should be available on location, landscaping, design and equipment of playgrounds; on financial and legal aspects; and on the needs of different age groups and special groups, such as the physically or mentally handicapped. The coverage should be international; research findings should be publicised and new research initiated where necessary. Short-term financing of such a project would have to come from interested professional bodies, local authorities and voluntary organisations. There is particular need for such co-ordinated information until a unified play service is established.

---

1 These suggestions are discussed in greater detail on pp. 91-3.
2 See recommendations: Central Advisory Council for Education (1967), I, pp. 1029-55.
3 This idea was originally suggested by Lady Allen of Hurtwood at a conference in 1967 and has been developed in her book *Planning for Play*, 1968.

# II—POINTS FOR RELEVANT LOCAL AUTHORITY DEPARTMENTS

## A.  Existing Residential Areas

### 1. *Traffic*

Local authorities are continuously engaged in an effort to adapt existing urban areas to suit changing conditions. The majority of these changing conditions result directly from the growth of traffic. Roads are widened thus creating new barriers for children. Pavements are narrowed, thus further limiting children's freedom of movement and increasing their 'nuisance' value in the streets. Both types of improvement may endanger children's safety.

We therefore suggest that if roads have to be widened, the question of access to existing children's play facilities should be examined. Either alternative facilities on the 'safe' side, or a safe route to the old site(s), should be provided. Also, where possible, the narrowing of pavements in well-frequented neighbourhoods should be avoided.

### 2. *Permanent or temporary improvements specifically related to children's play*

(*a*) In a great many seemingly hopeless urban areas, space for play could be 'created' out of existing space used for other purposes. All local authority departments concerned with children's play (notably planning, engineer and surveyor's, parks, health and education) together with local residents should carefully consider all such possibilities in the locality and, in a co-operative effort, convert such spaces to play use.

The most obvious of such spaces are—

sites awaiting development
school playgrounds

Also within this category comes the whole question of the play street. Few streets in urban areas are suitable for play. Nevertheless, where shortage of any kind of usable space is particularly acute, selected streets should be closed to traffic during specified hours either as an emergency holiday measure or on a semi-permanent basis. The Street Playground Act (1938) should be looked at with a view to its stengthening. At present there appear to be difficulties in enforcing it.

Through the initiative of either local residents or local authorities all these categories of space are already being used as play space and their value has been well demonstrated.[1] The way in which these emergency, semi-permanent or permanent spaces are used is, of course, of vital importance and is discussed below in Section B 1(b).

(b) Much public recreational space could be 'de-formalised' to enable a greater freedom for children. There could still be plenty of room for ornamental gardens and opportunities for adult peace and quiet. Where parks and gardens are large enough and yet contain no area for children, such an area should be created—where possible, more than one. In smaller spaces, consideration could be given to the possible relaxing of certain prohibitions. In general, with these small spaces, however, it might be more practicable to recognise the need to provide for separate spheres of interest.

(c) Existing pre-war and post-war housing estates should be surveyed for their actual and potential play provision for children.

(i) Where specific play facilities exist they should be examined in in terms of their suitability and usability—location, accessibility, diversity (including supervision, under-fives provision, and ball-games area), equipment (including sand), safety, times of opening, disturbance potential to adult residents—and, as far as possible, be modified accordingly.

(ii) Where there is no special provision, the possibility of creating play space should be examined. We realise that in many old estates the possibilities are exceedingly limited, but careful survey may reveal hidden potentialities (the removal or conversion of still extant air-raid shelters, for example, with a resulting release of space).

(iii) Incidental space should be examined for possible availability for children.

Grass areas are often forbidden ground, notices prohibiting ball games are commonplace. Occasionally there may be good reason, but frequently such restrictions are a legacy of past habits. They should be abandoned wherever possible.

## B. The Play Facilities

Diversity both in location and type of facility is of first importance.[2] All existing play provision should be surveyed and assessed with this requirement in mind. By remodelling playgrounds, big changes can be made without vast expenditure and the acquisition of new land. One

1 See pp. 94, 97.
2 See pp. 61–6.

essential, however, is the provision of covered space—a good sheltered area in unsupervised playgrounds and adequate, heated, indoor accommodation in supervised facilities.

### 1. *Supervised provision*

Priority should be given to the question of supervision.

(*a*) The size and complexity of the joint problem of the substitute care and education of the under fives calls, in our view, for a full-scale national enquiry.

Our concern here, however, is with *play* facilities which do not necessarily cater for children whose circumstances demand regular substitute care (except in so far as they may and should be used by child minders). These facilities, both local authority and voluntary, should be increased, the latter receiving additional statutory financial and administrative support (help and advice on staffing, the sharing of premises, for example as well as subsidies). The present proliferation of play groups, initiated by parents, churches, voluntary bodies, commercial concerns, needs co-ordination.

Expansion of the service should eventually ensure that there is adequate supervised play provision for under fives within easy reach of *all* families with small children, but such availability is a matter for *immediate* action where there is no opportunity for play in the home, for 'doorstep play', or for the companionship of other children (e.g. high-rise housing estates and twilight areas). Ground floor flats could be allocated as nurseries, as is common in Stockholm and as can be found in one or two boroughs in this country, or rooms originally scheduled for use by tenants' associations, and now perhaps used for storage, could be converted for play purposes. Accommodation for nurseries as part of shopping centres should be part of the initial plan.

All these play groups would ultimately be an integral part of any finally agreed system for the care and education of the under fives. They would also be part of the unified play service, whose staff would be qualified and graded on a professional footing. In the meantime, however, the groups will have to continue to rely on voluntary and partially trained help, with the proviso that qualified and experienced overall supervision is available.[1] This should always include preliminary advice on equipment and training.

(*b*) There should be generous full-time provision of facilities for older children staffed *permanently* by play leaders. The variety of this kind of provision which already exists—adventure playgrounds, com-

1  See this chapter, section I, F.1.

munity play centres, play parks and such—should be maintained, but more research is needed to establish what features attract children to these facilities. Not enough is known, either, about why some of this kind of provision fails to maintain its attraction.

(c) A realistic approach to the question of supervision suggests that the number of full-time, permanent schemes will have to be limited for some years to come. Much, however, can be done in the meantime.

(i) The numbers of seasonal, part-time schemes can be enormously increased. These may be sited in parks, schools, housing estates, temporary sites, even streets.

They may continue to take the form of many such existing schemes which fall into two chief categories: organised games; and the variety of activity to be found in play centres and play parks—painting, modelling and games using portable equipment. Or different kinds of mobile play service may be introduced.[1] The latter are particularly suitable for temporarily closed streets and housing estates.

(ii) Provided it is used with discretion, another method is to give duties of supervision covering a number of facilities within a given area to a permanent, peripatetic full-time leader.[2] Such a leader would be assisted by part-time, temporary leaders and volunteers.

(iii) A great many fixed-equipment playgrounds are at present manned by full-time 'attendants'. All these attendants would benefit by a short course on the principles of play leadership to help them towards a better understanding of children's play and their role as supervisors.

(iv) Similarly, those individuals whose general duties include the casual supervision of children at play—park-keepers and housing estate caretakers in particular—should be enabled to attend such courses.

(v) Understanding and sympathy for children should be a prerequisite in the qualifications of a caretaker.

(vi) Older children could be imaginatively used in the running of schemes and also in initiating ideas.[3]

1 See pp. 93-4, 97.
2 The Save the Children Fund use peripatetic supervisors with nursery teachers' qualifications for their play groups.
3 Privately published interpretation of the role of older children in adventure playgrounds by a Play Leader; and see also description of Brandon Estate Playground, Allen of Hurtwood (1968); and Benjamin (1966); and Allen of Hurtwood (1964) for a description of the Crawley experiment.

(d) special groups of children.[1]

(i) The value of play for sick children is undisputed. All hospitals with children's wards should run regular play sessions under skilled supervision.
(ii) Far more should be done for physically and mentally handicapped children of all ages. Where the disability allows for intermingling with normal children, this should be encouraged, provided there is adequate supervision. But special centres for under fives, school children and school leavers are urgently needed. These should have special equipment and trained staff.

(e) There would need to be co-operation with, and possibly some co-ordination of, the services provided by children's libraries and clubs.[2]

## 2. Fixed-equipment playgrounds

These constitute by far the greatest number of play facilities in this country. We know that they are patronised by thousands of children and we would not therefore wish to see them abolished, but it is important to distinguish the ages of the children using them. For children of ten years old and over such playgrounds offer practically nothing and this is something which cannot be too much stressed.

(a) We should like to see a substantial reduction in the number of this type of playground, by conversion into multi-purpose facilities with supervision. The value of variety in provision, however, should not be underrated. Different needs may be satisfied by different means and these need not always be supplied at one place.

(b) By its nature, a conventionally equipped playground tends to make for a short stay and early boredom.[3] Ideally, therefore, such playgrounds should only be located where there are reasonable alternatives for children to go to when the swing and the slide lose their attraction. Park sites are good in this respect, housing estates only if there is nearby supervised provision with adventure play or portable equipment, or ball-games areas as alternatives (these for older children could be within a quarter-mile distance from home).[4] But it is also possible to re-design and re-model existing playgrounds and to en-

1 Both these groups have been extensively covered elsewhere. See especially: Allen of Hurtwood (1968); Noble (1967); U.K. National Committee of OMEP (1967); Oswin (1968).
2 See footnote, p. 86.
3 See pp. 196, 197.
4 See pp. 187-9.

courage longer stay and more imaginative play. In Gothenburg, Sweden, they have even succeeded in introducing some portable equipment into unsupervised playgrounds.

Sand should be provided in all equipped playgrounds—in fact, on small sites intended primarily for small children this may be all that is necessary with the addition perhaps of a swing and a slide. These small play areas for small children should always be furnished with *comfortable* seats for mothers and have shade and grass, where possible. Water should also be provided. Where a paddling pool is not feasible there can be a 'splash area' equipped with a stand pipe. This should, if possible, be near the sand pit, as damp sand is a much more attractive play material than dry sand.

### 3. *Ball-games or kick-around areas*

The need for these was quite clearly shown in our study. Because only comparatively few children, and mostly only boys, can use a kick-around area at any one time and in spite of the fact that they stay there for a considerable time, some people feel that space is too valuable to allocate for this purpose alone. We have already suggested that such areas should be incorporated into multi-purpose playgrounds but in some instances the distribution of space may make it more convenient to have a separate kick-around area. In either case they should be hard-surfaced large enough to allow for a good game.[1] Every consideration should be given to the possibility of floodlighting where the areas are large enough for 'five-a-side' games.

### 4. *Toilet facilities*

All play facilities, whether situated in parks, recreation grounds or housing estates should have adequate provision of w.c.s and wash basins. If it is not possible to make room in the playground they should be at a distance of not further than approximately 50 yeards. On housing estates they should always be at ground level. Mobile and temporary play provision should also be equipped with toilet facilities.

There should always be clear indication in the playground of the direction of the toilet facilities.

### 5. *Some aspects of safety*

(*a*) Even with an increase in the number of play spaces and the amount of public recreational space generally, just as many children will be at risk in the streets in those areas unprotected by pedestrian

1 Not less than 325 square yards.

segregation, for although fewer will be playing in the streets they will have to cross them to reach the play areas. Strategically-sited pedestrian crossings, therefore, become more than ever urgent, particularly at the entrances to all playgrounds and public recreational spaces. Consideration should be given to the providing of guarded crossings at such places at appropriate times, wherever possible.

(*b*) There should be 'No parking' signs outside play facilities as there are now outside schools in most areas.

### 6. *Informing children and parents*

Attention should be given to the question of informing children and their parents about play facilities in their neighbourhood. The Inner London Education Authority practice, for example, of giving the children leaflets about school play centre provision to take home from school could be adopted for all supervised play provision. Welfare clinics could be used more widely for spreading information about under-fives provision. Local papers are quick to report local action-group activities and seem, on the whole, to be interested in play. More direct use could be made of their columns for information; similarly with local cinema advertising.

Continuous personal contact between playground staff and local residents[1] is probably the best means of all—house-to-house, in pubs, in the streets. This is important also before the installation of a playground, not only to publicise its coming, but to prepare people for possible inconvenience and noise and thus help them to tolerate it when it comes.

## III—POINTS MAINLY FOR PLANNERS, ARCHITECTS AND LANDSCAPE ARCHITECTS

### A.  Play and the Environment

1. The general question of housing density in all its complexity has been discussed earlier. Here we suggest only that from the childrens' point of view every effort should be made to achieve a maximum number of dwellings with immediate access to safe, adjacent space at ground level. Gardens, as well as communal space, are of great importance.

2. In residential areas and on housing estates, to enable the maximum opportunity for safe doorstep play and street play:

1  Currently being tried with success by the Camden community play centres staff.

(*a*) The policy of pedestrian segregation should be continued and developed.

(*b*) The separated pathways should be so planned as to carry a regular flow of pedestrians.

(*c*) Space, whether pathways, courtyards or what is commonly called incidental space, should be, as far as possible, visible from windows.

3. If pathways and gathering places are continuously frequented by children, care should be taken, as some architects and landscape architects already do, to ensure that features such as railings, bollards, steps[1] are usable and not abusable by children.

### B.   Special Space for Play

1. Play provision should be thought of as an essential service and as such be planned along with the rest of the neighbourhood.

This means that space, both outdoor and indoor, should be allocated in the initial planning stages by planners and architects in consultation with those responsible for running the play service, with other relevant departments and with representatives of the eventual users, i.e. parents. Where feasible, the offering of alternatives at this preliminary stage would seem to be an excellent idea.[2]

2. The location of this play space can now be determined by reference to a set of considerations which, it is hoped, will help planners and architects to work out standards applicable to their own needs. Some of our conclusions are tentative, but facts and figures can be filled in by local research on the lines indicated by our survey of children and playgrounds in ten boroughs.[3]

These considerations are as follows[4]:

(*a*) distance to be travelled;
(*b*) size and density of the child population;
(*c*) accessibility of the facility;
(*d*) size of the facility;
(*e*) characteristics of the neighbourhood, in particular the amount and location of public recreational space;
(*f*) the diverse requirements of a comprehensive play service.

1   These need not include expensive pieces of play sculpture.
2   Crick and Green (1968).
3   See Chapter 10.
4   The main discussion of these considerations may be found in the following Chapters: 4, 6, 10.

*A space in which to play*

Southwark

*A play square*

Stevenage

Southwark

*Children in the shopping area*

Stevenage

It is essential that the above suggestions should be considered together.

3. Although we have advocated large, multi-purpose playgrounds, it may be more suitable, in areas designed with a generous amount of accessible open space, to site certain play features (a large sand pit, for example) within a stretch of communal open space rather than within a playground.

4. Ideally, the design and layout of the play space should be the responsibility of a landscape architect working in association with the architect and should, of course, be dependent upon the purposes for which the space is intended.

A considerable amount of expertise on the design and layout of playgrounds has been amassed. Some has been documented and is available for study.[1] A central bureau of information would be able to give advice on particular problems. In the meantime much of this advice can be obtained from different sources.[2]

The suggestions for a policy for play put forward in this chapter do not purport to be comprehensive. Some of the gaps could usefully be filled by further research but in our view enough is now known upon which to build a service for play. Details may change according to new research findings or may vary and be modified according to local conditions or future social development. But nothing should affect the basic consideration that provision should be thought of as something intrinsic to the lives and development of children—as something to stretch the imagination, open up horizons, as somewhere to establish and extend relationships—and not just in terms of 'a place to play'.

1   See e.g. Allen of Hurtwood (1962, 1964, 1968); Butler (1947); Ledermann and Trachsel (1959); Lynch (1962); Mays (1957); National Playing Fields Association (1963); Sigsgaard (1965); Schwagenscheidt (1964).
2   See Appendix V.

# The Research

## Part I
## The Contrasting Neighbourhood Study

# 8

## Survey of Mothers and their Children in the Two Neighbourhoods

### Introduction

The choice of the two particular neighbourhoods was governed by the desire to compare two contrasting areas, particularly 'the old' and 'the new'. A considerable proportion of the neighbourhoods of urban England were built before or at the turn of the century. Since that time urban growth has developed and swallowed up much of the open countryside that was immediately adjacent to these old neighbourhoods. This development has produced what are now called conurbations, vast continuous built up areas. Within these conurbations old neighbourhoods may survive, but new ones are being built, as in the new towns, which are designed and planned with some knowledge of the problems associated with congested urban living.

It was hoped that by comparing two contrasting neighbourhoods it would be possible to reveal which urban environmental factors inhibited or encouraged the promotion of children's play. It was also assumed that such a comparison might show something of the nature of the emerging problems, if any, related to children's play in newly developed areas; there was also the question of how far play difficulties associated with overcrowding, dense population and poor housing had been eliminated by the neighbourhood planning typical of new town development.

Accordingly the two neighbourhoods chosen were in Stevenage New Town and in the London Borough of Southwark. A random sample was drawn from the election register for the streets included in the survey areas.[1] The interviewers were instructed to interview only the families with children over the age of two years. Mothers were asked some forty questions about such items as local playgrounds, open

1  For a description of this sample see Appendix II.

space, where their children played at different times, and difficulties that arose from their children playing in the neighbourhood. If a mother had more than one child over the age of two years she was asked to give the necessary information for each child. In the Stevenage neighbourhood, 116 mothers were interviewed giving information on 223 children between the ages of two years and fourteen years. In the Southwark area 108 mothers were interviewed giving information on 211 children.

## The Contrasting Environment

The neighbourhood chosen in Stevenage New Town was planned as a self-contained unit within the 'Chells' area with the typical features of a neighbourhood unit design: a primary school, a sub-post office, a small cluster of local shops and a public house. None of the present residents, of whom 58 per cent came from London, had lived in the area for more than five years. The Stevenage neighbourhood was a new one, having what the planners call a 'Radburn layout', characterised by the separation of pedestrian ways from motor traffic, to the extent that three-quarters of the residents need not cross a road for their local shopping.

The pedestrian pathways are combined with a great deal of incidental green space; and sited in the middle of the pathway complex are also three hard-surfaced play spaces, one of which has a piece of climbing sculpture. The neighbourhood has five culs-de-sac where there is sufficient space for children's play besides eleven garage access spaces where children were seen playing. The open space facilities in the immediate neighbourhood are generous and as it lies on the north-easterly outskirts of the new town, the adjoining countryside is easily accessible. Immediately beside the neighbourhood is a large meadow with a small, sparsely equipped playground (two sets of swings and a climbing frame); the two are separated by a row of trees and a hedge. The playground, called the 'Rocket' by the children because of its rocket shaped climbing frame, is set in ground with numerous bushes and trees scattered around. The playground is not much more than half a mile from the furthest point in the neighbourhood.

In the northern part of the neighbourhood there is a small wooded area, 'Sixacres Wood', which joins the grounds of one of the local schools, and in the summer, after school, small boys troop into it. The eastern side of the neighbourhood is flanked by one of the local main roads. It is a bus route and extremely busy at lunch time and when people are travelling to and from work. No building in this area is over three storeys high, though the population of the neighbourhood is slightly more dense than in the older parts of the new town.

In complete contrast is the chosen neighbourhood in Southwark. This is an area near the Elephant and Castle which originated as a residential neighbourhood about 1780. About a hundred years later many new buildings were added, which were 'designed to provide convenient and healthy dwellings at moderate rents to enable those of a grade higher in the social scale than working class to live near their work'.[1]

The area has now, however, fallen on hard times and many of the buildings need replacing. For some time the whole area has been subject to a redevelopment plan and after the survey began a start was also made on the demolition of part of the neighbourhood. If government housing policies do not change radically it is reasonable to assume that the neighbourhood's physical character and condition will remain as they are for some years to come.

Most of the eighteenth-century houses have gone, and the existing houses were mostly built before the turn of the century. There are a number of old Peabody-type blocks of buildings as well as large terraced houses converted into flats. The vacant sites that are scattered through the neighbourhood are used as dumping grounds for old furniture. The rubbish, however, does not accumulate for, as soon as it has been dumped, hordes of boys descend upon it and carry away the various pieces for their own use. A few of these sites are unfenced and so are used as playgrounds by the children. Abandoned cars scattered throughout the neighbourhood are also used by the children in their play. The local shopping centre is a busy thoroughfare used by lorries as a short route to the main roads of the south-east.

The contrast between the two areas is most noticeable in the two shopping centres on a Sunday. In Stevenage the local shops are closed; the whole neighbourhood is quiet, with the exception of the activity in the garage access spaces and a few children on the streets. In Southwark, Sunday seems like a busy holiday with most of the shops open. Whelk and shrimp stalls stand outside the pubs. This, of course, is typical of a number of neighbourhoods in South London where there are Sunday markets.

The west side of the area is flanked by the Walworth Road which is one of the main roads through South London. On the east side is another noisy through road, Brandon Street, with Deacon Street

1   South London Press (1876).

acting as a busy connecting route to the Walworth Road. The rest of the area is relatively free of traffic congestion, but it does have the problem of parked cars lining the side streets during the day. Since the survey, as a temporary expedient, a small hard-surfaced playground with two pieces of equipment has been built within the area. This is the culmination of nearly five years' agitation on the part of a local tenants' association. Other amenities nearby but outside the area are the playgrounds, which are all hard-surfaced, with the exception of the Geraldine Mary Harmsworth Park (known locally as War Memorial Park) which has a reasonable area of green grass. The physical conditions of the neighbourhood are typical of the wider district of the old Borough of Southwark. To the south a large area is being redeveloped and immediately next to this is an area that has been scheduled for open space.

# The Contrasting Social Characteristics of the Two Neighbourhoods

## Social class

We know that social class is an important variable influencing the way of life within different social groups. In the two areas under review there were significant differences in the social class distribution.

TABLE I

*Social class distribution of Southwark and Stevenage children*

| Social Class[1] | Stevenage | Southwark |
|---|---|---|
| 1 | 8 | 7 |
| 2 | 76 | 58 |
| 3 | 15 | 35 |
| Total number of children (100%) | 223 | 221 |

The children were classified according to their father's occupation into three groups derived by condensing the Registrar-General's five social class classifications.

The essential difference in the occupation of fathers in the two areas

1  The first group is made up of the Registrar-General's classes I and II, the professional and intermediate occupations; the second group of class III, clerical and skilled manual occupations; and the third group classes IV and V, the semi-skilled and unskilled occupations.

was that three-quarters of the fathers of the Stevenage children were doing clerical or skilled manual work compared with under three-fifths of the Southwark fathers; whereas more than one-third of the Southwark children come from semi-skilled or unskilled manual workers' homes compared with one in seven of the Stevenage children. These differences, in part, arise because some new towns give occupational opportunities more frequently to skilled than to unskilled workers.

The Southwark area has hardly any post-war housing and appears to present a pre-war occupational structure with a majority of the workers in semi- or unskilled occupations. On the other hand in Stevenage we see perhaps a model of the post-war affluent working class with a majority of the workers being employed in the new light technological industries.

The real difference, therefore, appears to be one of relative affluence, with Stevenage having a greater share of skilled workers and Southwark a greater share of the semi-skilled and unskilled workers.

## Types of residence

The Stevenage children, as was expected, are better housed than their Southwark contemporaries. Ninety-two per cent of the Stevenage sample lived in houses with four or more rooms besides a kitchen and bathroom, whereas this was true for only one-third (34 per cent) of the Southwark sample. The majority of Southwark families had very limited accommodation space. In many cases kitchens and bedrooms sometimes served as living rooms during the day or the one room might be used alternately as all three.

## Duration of residence

Another difference between the two samples was the length of time particular families had been living in the neighbourhood. Although Stevenage was one of the first post-war new towns the area chosen had only been developed for five years at the time of the survey, so 91 per cent had been complete strangers to the town of Stevenage when they moved there, and the other 9 per cent had moved in from another part of the new town or had come from Old Stevenage. In Southwark, 69 per cent of the children's families had been in the area for six or more years, indeed many of the mothers said their families had always lived in the neighbourhood.

## Children with working mothers

Whether a mother works or not can be an important factor influencing the use of, and demand for, facilities for school children outside the home and the school. In Southwark there were almost twice as many children (over two-fifths) with working mothers as there were in Stevenage (over one-fifth); the proportions of full-time and part-time work in the two areas, however, was similar. In view of these differences, it seems reasonable to assume either that Southwark mothers are finding it necessary to supplement the wages of semi- and unskilled workers, or that there are more employment opportunities available in Southwark.

Mothers who worked were also asked if they received any help with their children and, if so, from whom. Only a small proportion of mothers in each area (not more than three in ten) said they received any form of help with their children. But of these, a far higher proportion of Southwark mothers were helped by grandmothers and other relatives (nearly three-quarters) than were Stevenage mothers who were more often helped by neighbours or friends. In the older neighbourhood of Southwark, help from relatives is more frequently available because the two generations are likely to live near one another. What happens to this kinship help from relatives when the generations separate geographically is demonstrated in Stevenage where it is replaced by help from friends or neighbours. The mothers who received help were not all out at work; only a quarter of the working mothers of Southwark received help with their children as against one-third of the Stevenage working mothers. Children of Southwark then have twice the number of working mothers as Stevenage children and only a small minority of mothers in both areas received any form of help with their children.

## Bed times

One interesting difference between the two areas in the way children were treated was shown by the times they were expected to go to bed. A majority of Stevenage children (85 per cent) had to be in bed before nine o'clock in the summer whereas this was so for only 58 per cent of the Southwark sample of children. Although the mean age of the Southwark sample of children was one year older than that of the Stevenage children it did not account for the differences in bed times. In each of the different age groups a majority of the children of Southwark went to bed later than the children of Stevenage. These differences were even greater for winter bed times. Nearly three-quarters (74 per cent) of the Stevenage children had to be in bed before eight o'clock; of the Southwark children under a half (40 per cent) would be in bed at that time.

# Where Children Play

We can now compare the places where children play in each area, including formal and improvised playgrounds. We examine some of the factors that seem to encourage or inhibit the use of space and consider some of the opinions of mothers about play amenities.

In the greater part of the Stevenage area the front gardens and public footpaths blend together because there are no separating hedges and walls. This is so particularly within the pathway complex. It is possible for a child to play with model cars in the middle of a pavement and cause little or no obstruction. In Southwark most of the pavements are walled on one side and face busy streets, and even quiet streets are lined with parked cars. There are, however, a number of demolition sites, some of war-time origin, which are used by the Southwark children as improvised play sites. The Stevenage children have immediate access to a considerable amount of safe open space. It is quite the contrary for the Southwark children.

## Usual play places

These environmental differences would seem to be reflected in the replies of the mothers in each area to the question for each child: 'Where do they usually play out of doors?' (See Table 2.) Most of the children in Stevenage have their gardens for outdoor play and only a minority use the streets; in contrast, the majority of Southwark children (two in three) play in the street and only a few have a 'back-yard'. Perhaps surprisingly, not one Stevenage mother mentioned the 'Rocket' playground.

The term 'street' in Southwark, however, was frequently used to describe the area just outside the house or flat where there is no enclosed yard, and in some cases it included a demolition site opposite the home. A minority of Southwark children (one in seven) who usually played in a park had a 15–20 minute walk to the nearest park. Some mothers also mentioned a park 10–15 minutes away by bus. One half of the few children who were not allowed out to play were under school age and more than half of these were girls. This type of restriction is often related to the fears that mothers have about the neighbourhood. In contrast, Stevenage presents what might be

TABLE 2

## Where children usually play out of doors: Stevenage and Southwark

| | Neighbourhood | |
| | Stevenage | Southwark |
| Where children play | % | % |
|---|---|---|
| Garden | 64 | — |
| Street | 21 | 64 |
| Park | — | 15 |
| Yard at back | — | 6 |
| Recreation Ground | 5 | — |
| Green space between houses | 5 | — |
| Does not play outside | — | 6 |
| Other | 5 | 9 |
| Total | 100 | 100 |
| (Number of children) | (223) | (211) |

assumed to be an ideal picture. The 'street' in Stevenage is rather different from the street in Southwark. In many cases mothers called the pedestrian ways 'streets'; and these were free from the danger of traffic. Moreover the recreation ground mentioned is within ten minutes' walk of every home in the neighbourhood surveyed.

## Alternatives

It would appear then, according to mothers, that in neither area do the majority of children usually seek out a playground near their homes for their play. In the Southwark area, this would seem to be due to there being no genuine alternative to the street within the immediate neighbourhood. Seventy-eight per cent of the Southwark sample of mothers said there was no place in the immediate neighbourhood that was suitable for their children's play. Of the few mothers in Southwark who thought there was an alternative place to play close enough to home for the children to use, half mentioned the park, though their nearest was 15–20 minutes' walk away. Fewer mothers still, perhaps the more realistic ones, mentioned the yard at the back of the flats. A number of the flats in Southwark have communal yards across which the washing is hung out to dry. It is in these yards that a lot of the younger children play. Although the yards are rather sombre and let in very little of the sun, they are safe from traffic and can be looked down upon by the mothers from their windows.

The majority of Stevenage mothers, however, considered their children had alternatives to their gardens: the 'Rocket' playground and the recreational playing field were mentioned by most and a small minority mentioned the Play Squares. But surprisingly, few mothers cited any of the numerous plots of incidental green space between the houses and pathways, which are used by the children on fine summer evenings. The actual situation in Stevenage is that all children, except the very young, have a chance of using a recognised play site. Even so, 21 per cent of the mothers were either unaware of the facilities or did not consider them as suitable.

## Proximity of playgrounds to home

On the question of whether there was a playground near the home, 78 per cent of Stevenage mothers acknowledged that there was one whereas in Southwark only 8 per cent of the mothers knew of one, This is a reasonably accurate assessment of each neighbourhood situation. At the time of the survey Stevenage children had the comparatively wide choice of five alternatives to their gardens. Quite the opposite was true for the Southwark children for whom there was no provision within the immediate neighbourhood; a few could play in yards, some on the demolition sites if their mothers and the owners permit it. Going to the park requires for the child more organisation and time than he is allowed or prepared to give. It would appear that the children of Southwark find themselves playing on the streets out of necessity while the Stevenage children play in and around their gardens from choice.

Factors other than the immediate physical characteristics of the neighbourhood may have intervened in the children's use of designed play sites in Stevenage. Mothers may have insisted on a number of conditions before they allowed their children to use certain playgrounds. A majority of mothers would not let their children go alone and either themselves took them or arranged for someone (usually older children) to accompany them to a particular play site (71 per cent of those using playgrounds).

Though most Stevenage mothers considered the roads to be safe, 37 per cent of the children who had to cross roads to reach the play site had, in the opinion of their mothers, to cross roads that were dangerous. (The main service road runs round the periphery of the neighbourhood and cuts off the 'Rocket' playground and Ferriers Field[1] from the pedestrian pathway system.)

1  The large meadow mentioned on p. 134.

## Playground supervision

Mothers were also asked two questions about the local playground: whether there was someone at the playground to look after the children, and whether they thought it important for someone to be at the playground. The vast majority of the children in the Stevenage area used playgrounds where there was no one to keep an eye on them, whereas in Southwark the few who used a playground were supervised by a play leader or attendant. Most mothers felt it essential for someone to be at the playground, the danger of older boys bullying the younger ones and the chance of accidents occurring in the playground being the most frequently mentioned fears. One Stevenage mother expressed what was evidently a general feeling by saying 'because of injury and bigger boys'.

But in both neighbourhoods the fears mothers had for their children spread beyond accidents and bullying. They really wanted the reassurance that some responsible adult was watching over the children.

## Facilities further from home

Mothers were then asked if there was any park or playground in their district as opposed to their immediate neighbourhood that was suitable for all ages, as children have more opportunity at the weekend and during the holidays to travel beyond the immediate neighbourhood in search of entertainment. Parks are frequently a source of attraction and so are other playgrounds. It has been shown[1] that most children go to parks and playgrounds accompanied by either their siblings or friends. This frequently means that older children accompany younger ones and thus, where there are facilities for all age groups, family and friendship groups are encouraged and mothers reassured.

Though fewer mothers in Stevenage (26 per cent) compared with Southwark (42 per cent) thought there was a suitable park or playground in their district that was suitable for children of all ages the actual choice of amenities was wider in Stevenage. The Stevenage mothers were critical of the type of provision and tended to feel that facilities were inadequate for certain of the age groups, thus rejecting as unsuitable facilities that existed. Most of the mothers in Southwark had the War Memorial Park and playground in mind when they said there was a place that was suitable for children of all ages. The fact that Stevenage mothers complained that parks and playgrounds were

1 See p. 191.

inadequate in regard to the needs of children of all ages suggests that the need for extended facilities applies generally.

## Reasons for non-use of facilities

There were a number of reasons given by mothers as to why parks or playgrounds were considered unsuitable. For example, one Stevenage mother said: 'It's too far away, it's not enclosed, there are too many trees and bushes, I'm worried that a girl might wander off and meet a sex maniac in the bushes.' A Southwark mother said: 'It's quite a walk and there are too many layabouts there.' Two of the most common responses in Stevenage—'not enough equipment' and 'not suitable for younger children'—were frequently given together.

Because of the continual traffic it is no surprise to learn that in Southwark having to cross roads was the biggest single inhibition of park or playground use. This is consistent with findings of other work in the field.[1] The second most common item in the Southwark replies was that the provision was not suitable for older children. This complaint seemed justified in view of the fact that existing playgrounds which lie beyond the immediate neighbourhood are small and equipped for young children only; there is certainly little space for the older children. The older child has to go even farther afield to find bigger open spaces for ball games or adventure type activities.

## Distance children are permitted to travel alone

Underlying the use of all outside play provision is the question of how far a mother will allow her children to go on their own. Southwark children were more restricted in the distances they were allowed to travel alone. The restrictions applied particularly to the under-ten-year-olds. In Southwark one-half were not allowed out on their own; there were fewer in Stevenage, less than two-fifths. But two out of three of the 10–14-year group in Stevenage were permitted to travel alone; in Southwark only just over one in three of the 10–14-year-old: were allowed to travel more than one mile alone. These differences reflect the contrasting environmental features of the two areass Stevenage is a small light industrial town with which most inhabitants could become familiar. This cannot be said of the Southwark area which is a very small part of a vast metropolis. The parents of Southwark are more likely to restrict their children's wanderings outside the neighbourhood. Mothers may be familiar with the immediate environ-

1 Hole (1966); White (1950); Sheppard (1964).

ment, but beyond it they are aware that even they themselves may get lost. It is not surprising that Southwark mothers were more frequently restrictive than Stevenage parents. In Stevenage it is perhaps surprising that the over-tens are not allowed to make more frequent use of the wider environment, for the whole of Stevenage New Town is covered with a network of cycle paths. A substantial minority, of both sexes, were not allowed out on their own except within the immediate neighbourhood. Even then, the children played in the garage access space, a place which some mothers disliked because of the danger from motor cars, and because the children interfered with the outside water taps.

## Mothers' opinion on facilities

In spite of the planned and favourable environment of Stevenage, the majority of mothers, in Stevenage as in Southwark (over four-fifths), felt that there were not enough play facilities in their area. Differences in environment would seem and have been reflected, however, in the respective replies of each group of mothers, to the question of what improvements they would like to see. One-third of the mothers in Stevenage wanted more equipment in the playgrounds, nearly half the Southwark mothers wanted a park or open space. Perhaps most significant of all, just over a quarter of the Southwark mothers just wanted to move away. One mother responded to the question by saying:

> 'The lot should be pulled down and re-built—some decent little houses with front and back gardens so children don't have to annoy other people. I'd like my children to have a bedroom, there's four of us in one room, my husband and I and the children. Being of different sexes I don't like them sleeping together. I'd like to move miles away from here altogether.'

Forty-eight per cent of the improvements suggested by Stevenage mothers were 'more equipment' and 'a playground attendant', whereas in Southwark only 1 per cent mentioned more equipment and none specified playground attendants. For the Southwark mothers the priorities were more basic.

# Problems Related to Children's Play in the Neighbourhood

Children out-of-doors and unaccompanied can present certain problems to adult society because they do not always behave as adults feel they should. Their seemingly irrepressible urge to be active without the usual adult caution or care can bring them quite often into conflict with adults.

Mothers of the two areas were asked questions on a number of difficulties that arise through children playing in the neighbourhood.

## Keeping an eye on children

One of the natural anxieties of mothers was what their children were doing when they were out of sight and not being watched over by some responsible person. Most mothers tried to keep their children, particularly the younger ones, where they could see them. This was not always easy to manage because domestic duties brought conflicting demands and, as we have already noted, a lot of mothers preferred to know that their children were in a safe place under supervision. Mothers in both areas were asked if they were able to keep an eye on their children. Just over three-quarters (76 per cent) of the Stevenage mothers and over two-thirds (68 per cent) of the Southwark mothers said that they were. The mothers' comments reveal that although they may have said they could keep an eye on their children the task was a difficult one and in some cases the mothers preferred to keep their children indoors. Even when mothers had said they could not always supervise their children's outdoor activities they still attempted to do so. The following comments of mothers illustrate their difficulties.

Southwark mothers:

'I usually slip out now and again if I don't hear her or see her passing the door.'

'Yes, I certainly do, I get nothing done. I pray for rain every day on holiday so they can stay indoors.'

'Usually from the window—being at the top, by the time I get down if they're going to hurt themselves they've done it.'

Stevenage mothers:

'I ignore the work and keep on going to check them.'

'Not really, the kitchen is at the back and they are in the street in front.'

'So many alleyways.'

Much depended upon the age of a child and the degree of confidence that a mother had in the child's ability to look after itself. Older children were more frequently allowed to travel further away from home for a restricted time or if they were accompanied by friends.

## Traffic

When asked what they considered to be the greatest danger to their children in the neighbourhood, over three-fifths of the Stevenage mothers and three-quarters of the Southwark mothers said traffic. It is perhaps surprising that so many Stevenage mothers considered traffic a danger to their children in view of the pedestrian environment in which most of them play. However, if the other possible dangers are considered, it may be that traffic will always be the greatest single hazard that children have to face. Even in Stevenage most of the children in the area investigated have right of entry to the garage access spaces and have to cross at least one road to get to the nearest playing-field or equipped playground. What did emerge, however, was that mothers in Stevenage who admitted that traffic was a danger tended to be those with younger children only. In Southwark this was not so—mothers there, who said traffic was a danger when their children were playing out of doors, sometimes had older children as well as younger children.

## Play and neighbourly relations

Mothers were asked if people ever complained about children playing in any particular place in the neighbourhood; over two-fifths (44 per cent) of the Stevenage mothers and one-half of the Southwark mothers said they did. In Stevenage most of the complaints were made because children played in the garage access spaces and on the green in front of the houses. A few of the mothers said that people living around the play squares complained when children played there. In Southwark the main complaints were about children playing in the blocks of flats and on the streets. Complaints about children playing on the stairs in blocks of flats were frequently made by residents of housing estates, but as other research has shown these can be reduced by giving the children more attractive alternatives.[1] In Southwark, however, there are no socially approved alternatives.

Complaints were sometimes made because of the damage children did. Nearly one-half (49 per cent) of the mothers in Stevenage and just under one-half (46 per cent) of the mothers in Southwark gave examples of local damage they knew had been done by children. The most frequently mentioned items of damage in Stevenage were young trees, cars, and windows; in Southwark they were cars, abandoned cars,

1  Hole, *op. cit.*; and Sheppard, *op. cit.*

dust-bins (by setting them on fire), and windows. The mothers who said they knew of damage in the neighbourhood were also asked what they thought should be done about it; most of the mothers in both areas said parents should exercise more control over their children. Some of the Southwark mothers thought the solution was a simple and obvious one—namely that the authorities should clear up the old building sites, get rid of the cars and provide play amenities. Stevenage mothers found it more difficult to be so positive and a number even mentioned more police patrols.

## Children and noise

Parents are just as, and in some cases more, likely to be disturbed by children's noise as childless adults.[1] But it is important that children should be allowed to make a noise in their play. Since noise is the natural accompaniment for so many of children's play activities, if they are constantly told not to make a noise certain types of play activity are automatically proscribed.

All mothers in the sample were asked if the noise that children made outside bothered them. Just under a quarter of the mothers in both areas admitted that it did (Stevenage 22 per cent and Southwark 23 per cent). In Stevenage the mothers of younger children were not so bothered by the noise as the mothers of older children. This was not so in Southwark; mothers with children of all ages disliked the noise. Mothers who said the noise bothered them were asked what they did about it: most mothers in Stevenage told their children to be quiet, whereas in Southwark most mothers said it was not worth the bother to do anything. The mothers who did nothing about the noise seemed to stress endurance or tolerance. One Stevenage mother thought it was not worth the effort to complain. She replied: 'I would only get abuse'; and a Southwark mother said: 'The children have to play somewhere.'

But the mothers were also under pressure from neighbours who complained. When asked if neighbours ever complained about the children's noise either inside or outside the flat or house, over one-quarter (28 per cent) of the Southwark sample of mothers said they did, whereas in Stevenage only just over one-tenth (11 per cent) had received complaints. A number of Southwark mothers responded by trying to keep their children quiet, telling them to go further away or taking them indoors. Similar action was taken by Stevenage mothers although none went so far as to call her children indoors.

1 Sheppard, *op. cit.*

It is perhaps to be expected that crowded housing conditions mean that adults are less tolerant towards children and their noise; twice as many mothers responded to neighbours' complaints in Southwark as did those in Stevenage, although even these constituted a small minority of the sample.

## Mothers' doubts about neighbourhood safety

Various comments made during the interview showed that mothers had some general reservations about children being free to use the neighbourhood for their play. Most mothers saw traffic as the greatest danger; however, one-fifth of the mothers in both areas were worried about the possibilities of child molestation. In Southwark it was the local problem of the 'meth' drinkers, and the transient daytime population that worried mothers most; in Stevenage it was the close proximity of the fields and bushes. In both areas it was the mothers of older children (10–14 years) rather than those of younger children who tended to express their concern about molestation.

## More frequent out-of-doors play

Mothers were also asked whether they would like to see their children play more frequently than was the case. Just under one-quarter (24 per cent) of Stevenage mothers and over one-half of the Southwark mothers (53 per cent) said they would like their children to play more. The differences between the two areas may be attributed to Southwark mothers being made more aware of their children's need for better facilities than Stevenage mothers by the lack of play space and formal playgrounds in their neighbourhood. There were differences within the areas, however, between the wives of manual and non-manual workers, the former group being more inclined than the latter to say that they would like their children to play more often out-of-doors, thus reflecting the tendency for working-class children to make more use of public play provision than middle-class children.[1] A majority of the Southwark mothers who would have liked their children to play more said that the children did not do so because there were *no* facilities for them; the Stevenage mothers made the point that present facilities were inadequate. Typical of the two types of response were: 'There's not enough equipment' (a Stevenage mother), and 'Just somewhere safe to play' (a Southwark mother).

1 Central Advisory Council for Education (1967), II, para. 255.

## Summary

The obvious differences between the two areas in the places where children play would seem to arise from the difference in their respective physical environments. The majority of the children of Southwark have no play amenities other than the streets, which they use out of necessity. In Stevenage the children play in their gardens and also have the choice of a number of play sites though these are poorly equipped. Throughout the neighbourhood there are many open spaces where the children can play. When asked, the Southwark mothers just wanted more open space for the children, whereas the Stevenage mothers wanted more equipment for the playgrounds and someone to be watching over the children when they were there.

Southwark mothers restricted their children's movement; a half of the younger children were not allowed out on their own, and a half of the older children were prohibited from going distances of not more than half a mile from their homes. Mothers in Stevenage were not so restrictive, though they were still reluctant to let their children cross, unaccompanied, the one or two roads on the way to the playgrounds. Clearly, the Stevenage children have more freedom in terms of open space for their general play than do the children of Southwark.

There were important underlying differences between the two areas. The first was to be found in employment structure, as shown by the fathers' occupation. As was to be expected of one of the New Towns near London, the Stevenage neighbourhood had a significantly higher proportion of skilled workers than had the Southwark neighbourhood which in turn had a disproportionate share of semi- and unskilled workers. Over two-fifths of Southwark mothers go out to work as against only one-fifth of the Stevenage mothers. There is little difference in the amount of help parents received with their children, though in Southwark the help takes a more traditional form in the figure of grandmother. Stevenage families are much better housed than Southwark families. The children in the Stevenage area go to bed earlier than their Southwark counterparts; this difference is shown to have a social bias in another study.[1]

Most mothers in the two areas want to be able to see their children when they are out-of-doors playing. Indeed there were a few mothers who preferred to keep their children indoors rather than have them outside where they could not see them. Despite the differences in traffic arrangements, a majority of the mothers in both areas considered

1 Himmelweit, Oppenheim and Vince (1958), Table 67.

traffic to be the greatest danger to their children when they were playing outside the home. A small proportion of mothers in the two areas were also worried about the possibility of their children being molested.

Sometimes the noise children made and the particular places they chose for play led to complaints being made to mothers; this was more of a problem in Southwark than in Stevenage. These complaints led some mothers to restrain their children from playing or making a noise.

Twice as many mothers in Southwark, compared with mothers in Stevenage, wanted their children to play more frequently out-of-doors. Southwark mothers thought their children would do so if facilities were provided for them; Stevenage mothers thought their children would be out to play more often if additions and improvements were made to the existing facilities.

# 9

## A Comparison of Children's Activities in the Two Areas

### Introduction

One of the difficulties in comparing two contrasting areas was how to determine whether there was any real difference in the play of children in the two areas. We certainly did not consider that information gained from mothers during the neighbourhood survey would be adequate. This is largely because mothers find it difficult to be specific about their children's play activities. One of the obvious ways of acquiring precise information on children's play habits in an area would be to blanket the area with observers. Although we did carry out limited observations they were not of sufficient intensity or duration to make useful comparisons.

What was needed was a list of activities that was reasonably comprehensive in scope and would give some measure of type and range. Children could then be asked how often they indulged in particular activities and the responses of the two areas could then be compared. To prepare such a list of activities that is relevant to children's experience is a piece of research in itself; fortunately such a list already existed in the work of Witty.[1] Some 78 items were taken out of a list of 200 activities appearing in the Witty Play Quiz. The abstracted list was then expanded by school children adding items that they thought should be included. The inventory was then tried out in a primary and a secondary school. The activities that received either a low score or no score at all, thus indicating a low level of interest in the activity, were abandoned. We now had two inventories, a junior inventory with activities relevant to the experience of 9- to 11-year-old boys and girls, and a senior inventory relevant to the experience of 11- to 14-year-old boys and girls. The Junior Play Inventory had 134 activities and the Senior Play Inventory had 101 activities. This does not mean that the list is

1 Witty (1931).

exhaustive or that our seemingly comprehensive inventory would be a true measure of all types of play activity. It is however a measure of the extent to which those activities appearing in the inventory are engaged in in the two areas concerned. An important intervening variable is the season of the year which would favour some activities more than others.[1] An examination of the inventory[2] will show that only six activities are distinctly seasonal, though others might be marginally affected. Perhaps more important is the variation in type of space available to children both inside and out of the home. In the Neighbourhood Survey[3] details of the contrasting environments give an idea of the variation, and this was one of our principal interests.

The children in the sampled schools[4] were able to score the inventories by simply placing a tick against activities under one of the three columns headed: 'Yesterday', 'Within the last week' and 'More than a week ago', and where they could not remember or had not engaged in a particular activity to leave it blank. Thus we have a frequency scale where ticks under the 'Yesterday' or 'Within the last week' column are considered to indicate that the activities occur more often than do activities with ticks under the 'More than a week ago' column or blanks. In presenting the scoring of the inventories by the boys and girls, we have divided the four alternatives into two parts; 'Yesterday' and 'Within the last week' scores have been combined, and 'More than a week ago' and blanks were combined. Only the first two categories are shown as a percentage in the ensuing tables of this section. So in Table 3[5] 'watching television' in the first column shows 95 per cent. This means that 95 per cent of the 247 total of Stevenage junior girls marked 'watching television' as a 'Yesterday' or 'Within the last week' activity and only the remaining 5 per cent marked 'More than a week ago' or left it blank. In this way presentation is simplified.

One of the immediate differences that may be expected in any range of children's activities is that between the sexes. Some will depend on innate, others on environmental causes. The natural superiority of boys over girls in muscular strength, vital capacity and motor speeds and skills, gives them a vested interest in physically active pursuits.[6] The cultural influence encourages girls to take an interest in domestic,

---

1 It was not possible to get all the schools to administer the inventories on the same day, in fact there is a variation of summer to early winter.
2 See Appendix II for items included in both Play Inventories.
3 See Chapter 8.
4 For details of sample see Appendix II.
5 See p. 154
6 Mussen, Conger and Kagan (1964).

sedentary-type activities in contrast to the energetic-type activities that boys are expected to pursue. In more simple societies the activities that children indulge in are quite often formalised, particularly at puberty, with the boys having to emulate and join in the male adult tasks and in the same way the girls the female adult tasks.[1]

We are all aware that as children develop with age their interests become more intense and specialised, their increased abilities, mentally, physically and socially, give them a greater choice in leisure activities than was possible when they were very young. In our study there are differences between the boys' and girls' activities and between the older and younger children's activities, but there are also remarkable similarities. In the same way there are differences, although not so dramatic, in the popularity of certain activities between the two areas.

## Area Differences

In discussing the Play Inventory findings we have concentrated our attention on the differences that are shown between the two areas. First we look at those activities that are engaged in most frequently by a majority of the boys and girls both junior and senior in both areas. Then we examine activities that show statistically significant differences between the areas, regardless of whether they are indulged in by the majority or not. Later we look at the results of a factor analysis carried out on the Play Inventory items to see if any conclusions can be drawn from the correlations that result.

In Table 3 are all the activities that were engaged in by a half or more of the boys or girls in any one of the groups of either area within a week of scoring the inventory. So in terms of the actual frequency of participating in any freely chosen activity that appears in the inventory, by far the most common activity is watching television. There were eight activities that at least one half of all the children had in common. With variations of emphasis between boys and girls, and between the two areas, they were:

Watching television
Looking at comics
Reading books
Reading jokes or funny sayings
Listening to the radio
Walking

1  Whiting (1941).

Drawing with a pencil
Reading newspapers

These activities are a confirmation of other work on children's activities.[1] Television viewing seems to be an everyday pastime for a large majority of children of all ages in both areas. Although we had no indication of duration of viewing it seems reasonable to conclude

## TABLE 3

### *Activities by age group, sex and area*

(Percentages show proportions of children who engaged in an activity either 'Yesterday' or 'Within the last week')

| | Girls | | | | Boys | | | |
| | Stevenage | | Southwark | | Stevenage | | Southwark | |
| JUNIOR Activities | % | Rank Order | % | Rank Order | % | Rank Order | % | Rank Order |
|---|---|---|---|---|---|---|---|---|
| Watching television | 94 | 1 | 95 | 1 | 94 | 1 | 96 | 1 |
| Reading books | 85 | 2 | 73 | 5 | 71 | 5 | 62 | 8½ |
| Drawing with pencil, crayon or chalk | 78 | 3 | 74 | 4 | 75 | 3 | 68 | 4 |
| Listening to the radio | 77 | 4 | 68 | 6 | 72 | 4 | 64 | 7 |
| Looking at comics | 76 | 5 | 82 | 2 | 81 | 2 | 82 | 3 |
| Just sitting about | 74 | 6 | 47 | 18 | 67 | 8 | 47 | 12 |
| Walking | 68 | 7 | 76 | 3 | 69 | 6 | 64 | 5 |
| Just running about | 66 | 8½ | 58 | 9 | 68 | 7 | 62 | 8½ |
| Shopping | 66 | 8½ | 61 | 7 | 48 | 15½ | 32 | 20 |
| Reading newspapers | 63 | 10 | 56 | 10 | 61 | 11 | 58 | 10 |
| Playing with pets | 62 | 11 | 53 | 11½ | 48 | 15½ | 46 | 14 |
| Riding in a car | 57 | 12 | 33 | 20 | 55 | 13 | 43 | 16 |
| Swimming | 55 | 13 | 46 | 19 | 56 | 12 | 48 | 11 |
| Reading or looking at magazines | 53 | 14 | 50 | 15½ | 46 | 18 | 35 | 18½ |
| Reading jokes or funny sayings | 50 | 15 | 53 | 11½ | 66 | 9 | 64 | 6 |
| Playing with a ball against a wall | 28 | 20 | 60 | 8 | 37 | 20 | 46 | 14 |
| Dancing | 35 | 19 | 51 | 13 | 24 | 21 | 16 | 21 |
| Listening to records | 49 | 16 | 50 | 15½ | 47 | 17 | 46 | 14 |
| Sewing, knitting or crocheting | 47 | 17 | 50 | 15½ | 10 | 22 | 7 | 22 |
| Playing 'Chase' or 'He' | 43 | 18 | 50 | 15½ | 44 | 19 | 36 | 17 |
| Football | 3 | 22 | 16 | 21 | 62 | 10 | 87 | 2 |
| Wrestling | 13 | 21 | 14 | 22 | 50 | 14 | 35 | 18½ |
| Total number of children (100%) | 249 | | 217 | | 216 | | 213 | |

1 Ward (1948); Himmelweit *et al.* (1958); Stewart (1960); Bynner (1969).

# A COMPARISON OF CHILDREN'S ACTIVITIES IN THE TWO AREAS

| SENIOR Activities | Girls Stevenage % | Rank Order | Girls Southwark % | Rank Order | Boys Stevenage % | Rank Order | Boys Southwark % | Rank Order |
|---|---|---|---|---|---|---|---|---|
| Watching television | 96 | 1 | 95 | 1 | 95 | 1 | 96 | 1 |
| Listening to the radio | 78 | 2 | 84 | 2 | 71 | 4 | 73 | 6 |
| Reading newspapers | 77 | 3 | 67 | 5 | 76 | 2 | 81 | 4 |
| Drawing with pencil | 75 | 4 | 61 | 8½ | 69 | 5 | 72 | 7 |
| Cooking | 73 | 5 | 58 | 10 | 19 | 20 | 23 | 20 |
| Shopping | 72 | 6 | 66 | 6½ | 46 | 18 | 46 | 18 |
| Walking | 68 | 7 | 55 | 12 | 64 | 9 | 70 | 8 |
| Looking at comics | 64 | 8½ | 66 | 6½ | 73 | 3 | 82 | 3 |
| Reading books | 64 | 8½ | 61 | 8½ | 55 | 11½ | 53 | 13½ |
| Just sitting about | 60 | 10½ | 37 | 16 | 66 | 7 | 53 | 13½ |
| Playing with pets | 60 | 10½ | 50 | 14 | 53 | 14 | 52 | 16½ |
| Reading or looking at magazines | 59 | 12 | 72 | 4 | 44 | 19 | 57 | 11 |
| Listening to records | 58 | 13 | 80 | 3 | 52 | 15 | 62 | 10 |
| Riding in a car | 57 | 14 | 46 | 15 | 54 | 13 | 53 | 13½ |
| Reading jokes or funny sayings | 50 | 15½ | 52 | 13 | 65 | 8 | 75 | 5 |
| Looking at the daily comic strip | 50 | 15½ | 56 | 11 | 49 | 17 | 66 | 9 |
| Football | 4 | 20 | 13 | 20 | 60 | 10 | 83 | 2 |
| Just running about | 30 | 19 | 29 | 17½ | 51 | 16 | 53 | 13½ |
| Riding a bicycle | 34 | 18 | 17 | 19 | 67 | 6 | 52 | 16½ |
| Swimming | 42 | 17 | 29 | 17½ | 55 | 11½ | 35 | 19 |
| Total number of children (100%) | 273 | | 244 | | 231 | | 142 | |

that our children are watching television more than those surveyed thirteen years ago by Himmelweit *et al*. Our survey was carried out more in the summer than winter months so outside activities which are in competition with television viewing would be at their maximum. Again, unlike Stewart's survey our television findings show no variation in viewing with age. Bynner's survey showed that a majority of secondary school boys chose 'watching television' as a second most desirable activity after sports and games. It can be seen in our findings that watching television is one of the most popular pastimes in terms of preference,[1] after certain outdoor activities.

In looking at the eight common activities as a group it can be seen that they are non-participant in character. Stewart in her survey of the changes in children's activities that took place between 1947 and 1958 commented on the increase in non-participant types of entertainment; she found an increase in their popularity over the period surveyed.

1 See Appendix II.

## Area differences in girls' popular activities

Table 3 shows that Stevenage girls tend to sit about, read books and ride in cars more than Southwark girls. Southwark girls tend to play with a ball against a wall, dance and go walking more than Stevenage girls. All these differences are statistically significant[1] at the 5 per cent level or above.

Clearly there is a difference in type of activity here. The activities in which the Stevenage girls show significantly greater frequencies are passive activities whereas the significant activities of the Southwark girls are physically active. The surprising difference between the two sets of activities is the greater interest and participation in 'playing with a ball against a wall' in Southwark, 60 per cent against Stevenage 28 per cent. This considerable difference in the frequency of the activity may arise out of a combination of two things, the physical environment and the tradition of children's games. Although there are plenty of walls to play against in Stevenage, there are not so many passages, alcoves and stairways, all of which are places where 'ball against the wall' games can be played. Then there is the possibility of the continuity of the traditional games being broken by the move to Stevenage. Most families moving to Stevenage are families with very young children, children who have not been imbued with traditional games. A teacher in one of the primary schools in Stevenage said she had noticed a lack of the traditional games, so much so that they are now endeavouring to instil some of these games at school. But perhaps as important is the greater choice that a child gets through living in the new environment. Being better housed means there is more space in the home and equally there is more space outside the home.

'Sitting about' also seems to stress another aspect of the environment. Girls in Stevenage can sit about out of free choice because they have the space to do so whether it is indoors or out of doors. In Southwark one could well see that a child just sitting about would be in the way with all the competing demands of an overcrowded house. Equally, outside there is little space to sit about in; some of the streets have low walls where this is possible but they are directly on the pavement with all the attendant interferences and interruptions. And from what we already know about mothers' worries in Southwark they are hardly likely to encourage their 9- and 10-year-old daughters to sit about outside.

1    Tests of statistical significance of differences between percentages appearing in this section have been 'read' off the nomographs appearing in A. N. Oppenheim's *Questionnaire Design and Attitude Measurement* (1966).

## Area differences in minority activities of Junior Girls

Looking at other activities that are not so frequently engaged in we can make similar comparisons. In Table 4 are all the other activities that show significant differences (at 0·1 per cent level) in the frequency with which girls engage in them. Again there is a greater emphasis on physical activity in Southwark against more passive activity in Stevenage.

TABLE 4

## Other Junior Girls' activities showing significant differences[1] between the areas

|  | Junior Girls | |
|---|---|---|
|  | Stevenage | Southwark |
|  | % | % |
| Just playing catch and throwing | 29 | 49 |
| Skipping | 24 | 49 |
| Dolls, dolls' carriage, dolls' clothes | 47 | 32 |
| Playing other musical instruments | 45 | 18 |
| Just imagining things | 42 | 20 |
| Turning handsprings or cartwheels | 33 | 14 |
| Roller skating | 15 | 31 |
| Going to social clubs | 16 | 30 |
| Playing the piano | 29 | 11 |
| Playing horses | 28 | 11 |
| Running races | 12 | 27 |
| Climbing trees | 26 | 12 |
| Going to the pictures | 7 | 25 |
| Plasticine modelling | 24 | 12 |
| Wading in water | 20 | 9 |
| Rounders | 3 | 15 |
| Playing in the sand | 2 | 10 |
| Toy trains, ships, cars or lorries | 10 | 1 |
| Total number of children (100%) | 249 | 217 |

With one exception all the activities of the Southwark girls in Table 4 are physically active and none are home oriented. The majority of the Stevenage activities are home oriented, a fact that suggests, as mentioned earlier, that the influence of better housing conditions may determine the frequency with which certain activities are done. It is also quite reasonable to assume that a mother of a family that is badly housed may push the children out of the house whenever she can. Another aspect of the items in Table 4 is that the Stevenage activities tend to be informal in that they are governed by 'free play'. The Southwark activities tend to be formal in the sense that they are governed by the rules of the group game. The Stevenage activities also tend to be

See note on p. 156.

more individualistic than the Southwark activities. None of the Stevenage activities are necessarily group activities whereas at least four of the Southwark activities are ('rounders', 'running races', 'netball' and 'going to social clubs'). It is highly probable that 'skipping' and 'just playing catch' in Southwark are group activities, particularly many of the traditional rhyming skipping games that are played.

## Changes in girls' activities with age

It is to be expected that a number of pastimes that are popular with younger children will not be so with older children. The decline in the frequency of some of these activities is shown in Table 3. 'Looking at comics' and 'reading books' have declined, whereas 'listening to records' has increased its following. This is hardly surprising since the girls would be more under the influence of their older sisters and friends and by copying them begin the process of their immersion into the teenage milieu. Indeed some of the changes in activities reflect a change in maturing both social as well as physiological. Typical of two inversely related activities with regard to age are 'swinging' and 'having dates'. In Figure 1 we can see that the minority who use swings gradually decreases with age.

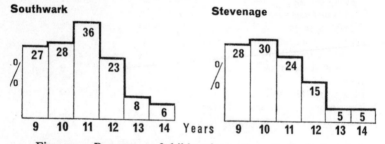

Figure 1.—Percentage of children by age groups who had used swings within the last week.

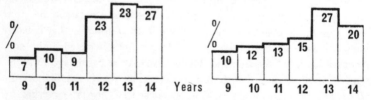

Figure 2.—Percentage of children by age groups who had a 'date' within the last week.

158

In Figure 2 the reverse process is in operation, there being a gradual increase in the proportion of children who have dates as they get older. Other activities such as 'just sitting about', 'running', 'playing with trains', 'playing catch', 'jumping' and even 'swimming' decline as the children get older. Conversely activities such as 'cooking' and 'shopping' for girls, 'reading magazines and newspapers', 'smoking', 'having dates', 'listening to records' and 'telephoning friends' increase as the children grow older through the years of nine to fourteen.

## Area differences in Senior Girls' activities

Some difference between the areas in the proportions of children indulging in certain activities remained even with the older children in secondary schools. The significant differences that remain can be observed in Table 5.

TABLE 5

*Activities of Senior Girls showing significant differences between the areas*

| | Senior Girls | |
| | *Stevenage* | *Southwark* |
| | % | % |
| Sewing, knitting or crocheting | 38 | 29 |
| Looking at pictures | 36 | 25 |
| Writing letters | 32 | 20 |
| Painting with water colours | 32 | 21 |
| Cutting paper things with scissors | 30 | 14 |
| Listening to stories | 27 | 18 |
| Cartwheels | 20 | 10 |
| Dressing up | 11 | 6 |
| | | |
| Telephoning friends | 29 | 39 |
| Going to social clubs | 18 | 29 |
| Skipping | 8 | 29 |
| Going to the pictures | 11 | 25 |
| Playing with a ball against a wall | 13 | 21 |
| Making a scrapbook | 7 | 16 |
| Hopscotch | 5 | 13 |
| Ice skating | 2 | 12 |
| Total number of children (100%) | 273 | 244 |

(All differences in this Table are statistically significant.)

The differences between the two areas show similar contrasts in types of activity as was found in the activities of the younger girls.

The activities of the older Stevenage girls shown in Table 5 tend to be home oriented whereas the Southwark older girls' activities tend to be out of or away from home.

All the activities where Stevenage girls show greater participation are activities that decrease with age whereas this is so for only three of the favoured Southwark girls' activities. The Stevenage activities may perhaps illustrate a lingering immaturity, with the exception of sewing, that is still encouraged in the home. 'Telephoning friends' and 'going to social clubs' prove to be statistically related in the factor analysis, so that what appears to be a home activity turns out to be closely linked with an out-of-home pastime. 'Skipping', 'playing with a ball against a wall' and 'hopscotch', all traditional games, are activities that diminish as the girls increase in age. These immature activities soon disappear, as is shown in Figure 3.

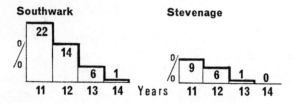

Figure 3.—Percentage of senior girls by age group who had played 'hopscotch' within the last week.

## Area differences in boys' popular activities

Of the junior boys' activities appearing in Table 3 only five items of the Stevenage boys and one of the Southwark boys show significant differences in participation. 'Sitting about', 'wrestling', riding in a car', 'listening to the radio' and 'reading books' are pastimes engaged in more by Stevenage than by Southwark juniors. In Southwark it is 'football' that has a significantly different following and is ranked in Table 3 second only to 'watching television' by both the younger and older boys. The five Stevenage items are all home or family centred. 'Wrestling', which appears to be the odd one out, is a typical boyish activity that can and does take place in the internal setting of a garden or home that has the space to permit it. This view is perhaps supported by the fact that it was boys with brothers who showed a greater tendency to 'wrestle' than did other boys.

As with the older girls, the older boys show in Table 3 a slightly different order of preference in the activities in which they have partici-

Southwark

*Incidental space*

Stevenage

Southwark

*Somewhere for mothers to sit*

A One O'Clock Club in South London

pated recently. Like the girls and the younger children, 'television watching' is at the top of the table. In Stevenage, 'reading newspapers' has jumped from twelfth place in the junior boys' activities to second place in the senior boys' activities; and in Southwark, from eleventh to fourth place. Like the girls they read less books and more newspapers than the younger boys. Stevenage boys show few changes in taste as measured by the Play Inventory. Apart from the two activities already mentioned, 'riding a bicycle' is the only big difference shown in the preferences of the older boys when their more frequent activities are compared with the younger boys. The Southwark older boys seem generally more active than their younger counterparts. They show seventeen activities that are engaged in by more than 50 per cent of the older boys. This compares with only ten such activities of the younger boys. 'Looking at magazines', 'listening to the radio', 'riding bicycles' and 'listening to records' are all activities that have increased in participation with older boys.

Only two activities that were outstandingly more popular in Table 3 with the junior boys of either Stevenage or Southwark continue to show the same difference between the areas. 'Sitting about' is significantly more popular with Stevenage boys than with Southwark boys. 'Swimming' continues to have a strong appeal to Stevenage children, and 'riding a bicycle' has emerged as an activity that has a significantly greater following in Stevenage when compared with Southwark. What now emerges in the Southwark older boys' activities seems to be a cultural difference of emphasis. Significant differences in activities between areas appearing in Table 3 show Southwark to have more participants in 'football', 'looking at comics', 'looking at a daily comic strip', 'reading jokes or funny sayings', 'listening to records' and 'reading and looking at magazines'.

## Area differences in minority activities of Junior Boys

The tendency of the Stevenage junior boys to prefer passive, home- or family-oriented activities is also shown in other items that are not so generally popular. In Table 6 we can see the proportion of boys from the two areas who engaged in such activities that show significant differences. The contrasts in the activities are again similar to those found in the junior girls.

However, a number of the activities seem to show differences that would naturally arise because of differences in environment, 'wading in water' and 'gardening' being more likely and accessible in Stevenage.

TABLE 6

*Other Junior Boys' activities showing significant differences between the areas*

| | Junior Boys | |
| | Stevenage | Southwark |
| --- | --- | --- |
| | % | % |
| Shopping | 48 | 32 |
| Listening to stories | 41 | 25 |
| Excursions to woods and countryside | 31 | 17 |
| Chess | 31 | 18 |
| Telling stories | 30 | 14 |
| Cartwheels | 28 | 12 |
| Wading in water | 21 | 7 |
| Playing the piano | 20 | 9 |
| Dressing up | 17 | 7 |
| Gardening | 12 | 7 |
| | | |
| Going to the pictures | 14 | 39 |
| Running races | 22 | 35 |
| Draughts | 24 | 32 |
| High jump | 11 | 18 |
| Flying kites | 2 | 10 |
| Total number of children (100%) | 216 | 213 |

Perhaps what is remarkable is that more children in Southwark fly kites, particularly so when we take into account the effort involved in finding space in Southwark as compared with that of Stevenage.

In Table 7 the Stevenage items 'shopping', 'gardening' and 'wading in water' show a continuity with the activities of the younger boys. With 'wading in water' as the exception these items again appear to be home and family centred. The Southwark items are more mixed with one group showing a following for activities that decrease with children getting older, such as 'playing with a ball against a wall', 'chase or he', 'digging holes', 'follow-your-leader', 'fivestones' and 'skipping', all active but rather immature pastimes for senior boys. 'Having dates' and 'telephoning friends' are activities that increase as children grow older and so probably indicate a significant mature group.

The Southwark boys then show the same type of tendencies in their activities that are significantly different in participation when compared with Stevenage boys, as do the Southwark girls. There is the tendency for Stevenage children to participate more in home- and family-centred activities than Southwark children. And there is also the tendency for Southwark children to participate more in certain traditional games and activities that are out of or away from home.

TABLE 7

*Other activities of Senior Boys showing significant differences between the areas*

| | Senior Boys | |
| | Stevenage | Southwark |
| --- | --- | --- |
| | % | % |
| Shopping | 46 | 36 |
| Stamp collecting | 30 | 19 |
| Gardening | 25 | 14 |
| Picture puzzles | 23 | 14 |
| Toy trains, cars, etc. | 21 | 12 |
| Wading in water | 13 | 6 |
| Playing with a ball against a wall | 21 | 46 |
| 'Chase' and 'He' | 24 | 34 |
| Having dates | 18 | 29 |
| Telephoning friends | 16 | 28 |
| Building or watching bonfires | 7 | 14 |
| Digging holes and caves | 6 | 14 |
| Roller skating | 5 | 13 |
| High jump | 4 | 12 |
| Skipping | 4 | 11 |
| Follow-your-leader | 3 | 10 |
| Fivestones | 3 | 9 |
| | --- | --- |
| Total number of children (100%) | 231 | 142 |

Why should there be these differences across the areas? There is a strong hint from the type of location that the activities require. The Stevenage activities emphasise the family and the home, whereas the Southwark activities emphasise an away-from-home location. We also know that Southwark's population tends towards a bias of semi-skilled and unskilled occupations and that Stevenage is biased towards skilled and clerical occupations. When we put the choice of play site together with the tendencies of the social class distribution of the two areas we have similar findings to a survey carried out by the Government Social Survey.[1] This showed that manual workers' children tended to use open space away from home more than the non-manual workers' children. Stevenage children tend like Stewart's children towards non-participant activities and these are the emerging pastimes. If this is so Southwark children with their tendency towards traditional participant activities may be reflecting the old and dying activities of children in the old working-class urban areas.

1  Central Advisory Council for Education (1967), Vol. II.

# Factor Analysis of Play Inventory Activities

With so any different items to consider, it was thought necessary to reduce the number of activities by clustering them into meaningful groups. One way this can be done is by inspecting all the activities and then placing them into categories classified by the type of activity, for example passive, active, individual, or group activities. Inevitably by this system arbitrary decisions are made about the groups and which activities go into them.

Another method, therefore, was chosen. This is a technique known as Factor Analysis whereby groups of items are formed on the basis of their statistical correlation with each other. So the activities would then be grouped into clusters of items that were mathematically related. Each cluster of inter-correlated activities is assumed to contain a factor and all the activities related to each factor give a measure of an underlying dimension. This underlying dimension has to be named according to the type of activities that appear in the factor cluster. Each item appearing in the cluster has a relationship to the factor shown by 'factor loading' and the items (activities) with the highest loadings are those which are used to define the dimension underlying the items.

In our study two factor analyses[1] were carried out, one on the Junior Play Inventory and the other on the Senior Play Inventory. Each analysis produced twelve factors. Seven for the Junior Play Inventory and eight for the Senior Play Inventory have been used in this study.

# Junior Play Inventory

Some clusters tended to have activities that had significant differences between areas, others showed few differences. In this section we have presented the clusters that tend to discriminate between the areas first.

## Active outdoor activities

The activities in Table 8 seemed to be interrelated purely by the fact that they are athletic outdoor pursuits. The one activity that does not fit into the 'athletic' mould is 'going to social clubs'.[1] In this case it could quite well be that going to a club increased the opportunity of engaging in the other activities shown in this cluster.

1   See Appendix II.

TABLE 8

*Junior active outdoor activities cluster*

| | Girls | | Boys | |
| | Stevenage | Southwark | Stevenage | Southwark |
| | % | % | % | % |
| Long jump | 5 | 12 | 11 | 16 |
| High jump | 6 | 12 | 11 | 18 |
| Running races | 12 | 27 | 22 | 35 |
| Leap frog | 13 | 21 | 17 | 15 |
| Hop, skip and jump | 16 | 22 | 13 | 7 |
| Going to social clubs | 16 | 30 | 26 | 29 |
| Total number of children (100%) | 249 | 217 | 216 | 213 |

Both the boys and girls of Southwark had a tendency to engage in this group of activities more than the Stevenage boys and girls. None of these activities are home oriented. What is perhaps surprising is that the Southwark girls are more likely to pursue these activities than Stevenage boys. This seems to go against the idea that boys tend to go in for the more physically active pursuits. As it happens the Stevenage boys do go in for more athletic activities than the Stevenage girls. 'Long jump', 'high jump' and 'running races' on the inventory must not be thought of only in the formal sense but also as informal activities that children enjoy doing in the school playground or on their way home from school, or in any open space where children congregate. It is perhaps unexpected that the Southwark children should be more active in these pursuits when we consider what facilities the immediate neighbourhood of the two areas provide.

## Indoor sedentary activities

Perhaps surprisingly, the classical indoor games as shown in Table 9 are not so overwhelmingly popular as one might expect. There is, however, a significant minority of children who are attracted to all these indoor pastimes. Children who like playing draughts and dominoes also like collecting stamps and doing crossword puzzles. The difference between the two areas is most marked with those who play draughts and chess.

Draughts was more popular with the Southwark boys (sig. diff. 5 per cent level) and the Stevenage girls, whereas chess was more popular with the Stevenage boys and girls (sig. diff. 0·1 per cent level). Again there was a difference between the sexes, with the boys engaging

TABLE 9

## Junior indoor sedentary activities cluster

| | Girls | | Boys | |
| | Stevenage | Southwark | Stevenage | Southwark |
|---|---|---|---|---|
| | % | % | % | % |
| Draughts | 22 | 16 | 24 | 32 |
| Dominoes | 10 | 12 | 16 | 17 |
| Card games | 37 | 38 | 48 | 45 |
| Collecting stamps | 14 | 15 | 30 | 25 |
| Doing crossword puzzles | 40 | 38 | 29 | 38 |
| Chess | 14 | 5 | 31 | 18 |
| Total number of children (100%) | 249 | 217 | 216 | 213 |

more in these activities than the girls and the Southwark girls being the least interested. The real difference here lies in the contrast of the two environments. In an education and home study better housing conditions proved to be important in educational attainment.[1] It would be reasonable to suppose that such accepted indoor pastimes would also thrive better in the superior housed town of Stevenage than that of the Southwark area; surprisingly this is not so.

## Feminine activities

There are a group of activities within the Play Inventory that are favoured more by the girls than the boys. This does not mean that these activities are the exclusive domain of the girls—there is an overlap, but the central tendency is for these activities to be engaged in by them. Our society tends to encourage a few activities for the exclusive use of one or other of the sexes. Playing with dolls is a typical example of this type of prescribed activity. So is boxing for boys.

Terman[2] in a study of gifted and control-group children, constructed a 'masculinity index' of the children's activities. The index consisted of a 24 classification of children's activities. At one end were the most masculine activities (i.e. those most favoured by the boys) and at the other end the least masculine (i.e. those activities favoured more by the girls). Doll-playing was the last classification at the least masculine end of the scale.

In Table 10 are the six most important activities discriminating boys from girls, and giving the percentage who indicated that they had engaged in the activities within the last week.

1 Douglas (1964).
2 Terman (1926).

TABLE 10

## *Junior feminine activities cluster*

| | Girls | | Boys | |
| | Stevenage | Southwark | Stevenage | Southwark |
|---|---|---|---|---|
| | % | % | % | % |
| Playing nurse | 13 | 15 | 1 | 0 |
| Playing shop | 18 | 18 | 7 | 2 |
| Playing house | 18 | 17 | 4 | 2 |
| Playing school | 25 | 24 | 8 | 3 |
| Playing Sunday school | 9 | 6 | 5 | 1 |
| Dolls, dolls' carriage, dolls' clothes | 47 | 32 | 1 | 1 |
| Total number of children (100%) | 249 | 217 | 216 | 213 |

What emerges from this table is that the Stevenage boys tend to engage more in girl-type activities than Southwark boys and that Stevenage girls show a significantly greater interest in playing with dolls than the Southwark girls.

In all probability the greater frequency with which girls in Stevenage will play with dolls may simply be attributed to better housing. The activity is pre-eminently a home-oriented activity, an activity that takes place either in the home or just outside, within sight or hearing of the child's mother. The contrasting physical conditions within which a majority of the girls of the two areas would live would either enhance such activities as in Stevenage or discourage them as in Southwark. Many girls in Southwark would be living in blocks of old flats where the ideal place for such play would be the stairs rather than in an over-crowded home. We know from our survey that this would be a typical example of the clash of the children's play would with adult society.

Taking into account all the activities in this group[1] the Southwark girls tended to be less active than the Stevenage girls. All the activities in Table 10 recede in popularity as the children get older; this was particularly so for Southwark girls. This is consistent with the work of Witty who found that in this age group the differences between the activities of boys and girls were maximised and that later their interests narrowed and the sexes had more interests in common.

## *Masculine activities*

In Table 11 we have activities that are interrelated or associated by being activities that boys tend to do rather than girls.

1 See Appendix II.

TABLE 11

*Junior masculine activities cluster*

|  | Girls | | Boys | |
|  | Stevenage | Southwark | Stevenage | Southwark |
|---|---|---|---|---|
|  | % | % | % | % |
| Playing soldiers | 5 | 1 | 26 | 22 |
| Toy trains, ships, cars or lorries | 10 | 1 | 36 | 28 |
| Sword-fighting | 6 | 2 | 27 | 20 |
| Boxing | 9 | 5 | 31 | 25 |
| Flying model aircraft | 3 | 0 | 12 | 21 |
| Bows and arrows | 2 | 2 | 15 | 11 |
| Total number of children (100%) | 249 | 217 | 216 | 213 |

They are the typical boys' activities in that they involve participation in vigorous aggressive play. Some of them call for typical tests of prowess that young boys are so fond of. In the more complete group list of items,[1] well over half the items were outdoor. This contrasts with the feminine factor where only three out of sixteen activities were outdoor. Terman's masculinity scale included a number of the items appearing in Table 11 at the masculine end of his scale.

There is a tendency for Stevenage boys to favour these activities more than the Southwark boys. Again the sexes are more sharply differentiated in Southwark than in Stevenage. It may be that the peer group relations in Southwark discourage activities that are nominally girl or boy pastimes, whereas in Stevenage the peer group relationships in many of the activities would not be so powerful because of the closer proximity of the home.

There is a significant difference (1 per cent level) between the two areas in the activity of 'flying model aircraft'. This is a pastime that requires open space and yet it is in this activity that, like football, there is a greater following in Southwark than in Stevenage. It is the one activity that could not be engaged in adjacent to the home, even in Stevenage. One can only conclude that the incentives for such activities as football and flying model aircraft are greater in Southwark for some reason than they are in Stevenage. In Southwark it would seem that the masculine role is more clearly defined than in Stevenage at this age. There is a tendency for Stevenage girls to be more involved in these boy-like activities than Southwark girls.

1   See Appendix II.

## Mature activities

The cluster of activities shown in Table 12 seems to be distinguished by having more mature-type sophisticated activities, when taking into account the age of the children. Most of the activities could easily be associated with normal adult pastimes; in fact they contain little of the play element.

TABLE 12

### Junior mature activities cluster

| | Girls | | Boys | |
| | Stevenage | Southwark | Stevenage | Southwark |
|---|---|---|---|---|
| | % | % | % | % |
| Telephoning friends | 14 | 24 | 10 | 14 |
| Taking photographs | 5 | 7 | 7 | 9 |
| Listening to records | 49 | 50 | 47 | 46 |
| Cooking | 41 | 40 | 19 | 21 |
| Ten-pin bowling | 3 | 2 | 5 | 9 |
| Tape recorder | 15 | 16 | 15 | 16 |
| Going to parties and picnics | 8 | 12 | 9 | 8 |
| Total number of children (100%) | 249 | 217 | 216 | 213 |

Most of the items in Table 12 increase in popularity with age which again suggests that the items are drawn together by a common factor associated with maturity.

Looking at the items overall, Southwark girls and boys tend to participate in them more than Stevenage children, and the girls of both areas show greater participation than the boys. With the exception of 'listening to records' and 'cooking' for girls, the activities in Table 12 are very much minority activities. For some reason the Southwark girls are slightly more involved with some of the activities than the Stevenage girls. ('Telephoning friends' sig. diff. 1 per cent level.)

It is perhaps to be expected that the boys in both areas would be behind the girls in participating in these activities if only because they tend to be less socially mature at this age.

## Non-conformist activities

There was a very small cluster of activities that seemed strangely associated and only a small minority of boys and girls participated. These activities (see Table 13) have been labelled non-conformist because 'having dates' and 'smoking' for 9- and 10-year-olds is not normally accepted behaviour in our society. Other studies[1] of boys' and girls'

1 McKennel and Bynner (1969).

smoking habits suggest that by smoking the boys see themselves as belonging to an older age group. Dating may equally be associated by them with older boys and girls, the group they aspire to join. 'Reading books' was negatively associated with these activities showing that these boys and girls do not like reading books.

TABLE 13

*Junior non-conformist activities cluster*

| | Girls | | Boys | |
| | Stevenage | Southwark | Stevenage | Southwark |
|---|---|---|---|---|
| | % | % | % | % |
| Having dates | 8 | 7 | 14 | 11 |
| Smoking | 0 | 3 | 4 | 3 |
| Boxing | 9 | 5 | 31 | 25 |
| Reading books (negatively associated) | 85 | 73 | 71 | 62 |
| Wrestling | 13 | 14 | 50 | 35 |
| Total number of children (100%) | —— | —— | —— | —— |
| | 249 | 217 | 216 | 213 |

The only differences in participation are between the sexes, the boys being more involved than the girls.

## General outdoor play activities

The activities associated in this cluster are all fairly general activities of boys and girls and they are all outdoor. There is a tendency for the boys to engage in these activities more than the girls. One activity—'roller skating'—was, however, more popular with the girls of both areas. With 'roller skating', 'climbing trees' and 'wading in water' there were significant differences between the girls' participation in the two areas at a 0·1 per cent level. The former of the three activities was more popular with the Southwark girls and the latter two more popular with Stevenage girls.

'Wading in water' also showed a significant difference (0·1 per cent level) between areas for the boys, the activity being more popular in Stevenage. Stevenage boys also rode about on their bicycles more than Southwark boys. Most of the differences between areas in the individual activities can be accounted for by the differences in the actual physical environments the two sets of children play in. So Stevenage girls are able to climb more trees and the Southwark girls to exploit their environment by roller skating more. There are a number of small streams in and around Stevenage, whereas Southwark boys and girls

TABLE 14

## *Junior general outdoor activities cluster*

| | Girls | | Boys | |
| | Stevenage | Southwark | Stevenage | Southwark |
| | % | % | % | % |
|---|---|---|---|---|
| Riding a bicycle | 22 | 19 | 36 | 26 |
| Playing in sand | 1 | 0 | 7 | 11 |
| Fishing | 1 | 2 | 7 | 10 |
| Swinging | 27 | 39 | 31 | 34 |
| Wading in water | 20 | 9 | 21 | 7 |
| Boating | 0 | 2 | 1 | 5 |
| Roller skating | 15 | 31 | 9 | 12 |
| Bonfires | 8 | 5 | 7 | 8 |
| Climbing trees | 26 | 12 | 35 | 30 |
| Swimming | 55 | 46 | 55 | 48 |
| Total number of children (100%) | 249 | 217 | 216 | 213 |

would have to travel to the nearest well-equipped playground to find a paddling pool to wade in. The difference in the popularity of flying kites[1] (0·1 per cent level) between the boys of the two areas is typical of many of the activities indulged in. Southwark children seem to exploit this semi-formal type of activity more than Stevenage children, whereas the Stevenage children indulge more readily in the freer, less structured activities. Overall the Stevenage boys engage more in the general outdoor activities than the Southwark boys because the different environment favours some activities more than others, though there are exceptions. Stevenage girls are slightly more active in these activities than the Southwark girls.

# Senior Play Inventory

## *Mature activities*

All the items appearing in Table 15 are activities that have increased in popularity with the older children. There are no obvious play activities among them; all of them might well be activities that older teenagers would be engaging in.

The activities then are associated by the fact that they are mature pastimes. They reflect the tendency of seeking leisure independent of the family. The first four activities are all more popular in Southwark than in Stevenage. The Southwark girls are the most active in these pursuits and the Stevenage boys the least active. The differences

1 See Appendix for complete list.

## TABLE 15
### Senior mature activities cluster

| | Girls | | Boys | |
| | Stevenage | Southwark | Stevenage | Southwark |
| --- | --- | --- | --- | --- |
| | % | % | % | % |
| Listening to records | 58 | 80 | 52 | 62 |
| Telephoning friends | 29 | 39 | 16 | 28 |
| Ice skating | 2 | 12 | 3 | 4 |
| Going to the pictures | 11 | 25 | 18 | 34 |
| Going to parties or picnics | 13 | 11 | 9 | 8 |
| Dancing | 41 | 49 | 10 | 7 |
| Reading or looking at magazines | 59 | 68 | 44 | 57 |
| Having dates | 18 | 20 | 18 | 29 |
| Total number of children (100%) | 273 | 244 | 231 | 142 |

between the two areas here are consistent with other differences already found, they underline the tendency of Stevenage to engage more in home-centred activities and Southwark children to engage more in away-from-home pastimes.

## Younger outdoor activities

The first three items that appear in Table 16 are all activities that have declined in popularity as the children have grown older. Indeed all the items have declined in popularity with the older children.

## TABLE 16
### Senior younger outdoor activities cluster

| | Girls | | Boys | |
| | Stevenage | Southwark | Stevenage | Southwark |
| --- | --- | --- | --- | --- |
| | % | % | % | % |
| Playing with a ball against a wall | 13 | 21 | 21 | 46 |
| Swinging | 9 | 15 | 17 | 15 |
| Just playing catch | 24 | 29 | 21 | 24 |
| Sliding on playground slide | 8 | 5 | 13 | 12 |
| Skipping | 8 | 29 | 4 | 11 |
| Total number of children (100%) | 273 | 244 | 231 | 142 |

Besides being activities of younger children they are all outdoor pastimes. The real differences here lie between the Stevenage girls and the rest. As boys tend to pursue outdoor activities more than girls, particularly the more immature activities, this might account for the difference between the Stevenage girls and boys. That there is little difference overall between the Southwark boys and girls must be explained by the tendency of Southwark children to be more out of, or away from home. The activities are typical, traditional play activities which might account for Southwark children being slightly more involved than the Stevenage boys.

## Inactive pastimes

In the Junior Play Inventory a similar group of activities also included some of the more obvious inactive pastimes like 'sitting about'. With the older children such items have ceased to show differences; it can also be observed that they have declined in popularity with an increase in age. The items that remain (see Table 17) are more positively associated than they were with the younger children.

TABLE 17

*Senior inactive pastimes cluster*

|  | Girls | | Boys | |
|---|---|---|---|---|
|  | Stevenage | Southwark | Stevenage | Southwark |
|  | % | % | % | % |
| Reading jokes or funny stories | 50 | 52 | 65 | 75 |
| Looking at daily comic strip | 50 | 56 | 49 | 66 |
| Looking at comics | 66 | 66 | 73 | 82 |
| Reading the newspapers | 77 | 67 | 76 | 81 |
| Teasing somebody | 32 | 27 | 41 | 47 |
| Telling or guessing riddles | 22 | 21 | 20 | 23 |
| Total number of children (100%) | 273 | 244 | 231 | 142 |

Two obvious features in this group are the element of ready-made non-participant entertainment and also a lack of social interaction. Himmelweit *et al.* in their television study showed that the children who read comics most were the younger, less intelligent children from working-class homes and that they also spent more time watching television. Although there is an element of stimulation in the activities shown in Table 17 they tend to be passive and rather idle. Indeed children who go in for this group of activities tend not to go in for the purposeful group activities. Southwark boys go in for these pastimes significantly more than Stevenage boys, and the boys of both areas more than the girls of both areas. Part of the difference in intensity of activity may be accounted for by the differences in the occupational grouping of the two areas.[1]

## Non-conformist activities

Both 'smoking' and 'having dates' are grouped together along with 'reading books' which is negatively associated, meaning that those who smoke and have dates tend not to read books. This is a similar grouping to that found in the junior activities though the items in Table 18 have a higher loading than the junior items.

TABLE 18

*Senior non-conformist activities cluster*

|  | Girls | | Boys | |
|  | Stevenage | Southwark | Stevenage | Southwark |
|  | % | % | % | % |
| Smoking | 5 | 1 | 9 | 10 |
| Having dates | 18 | 20 | 18 | 29 |
| Shooting with air rifle | 0 | 0 | 9 | 11 |
| Reading books (negatively associated) | 64 | 61 | 55 | 53 |
| Total number of children (100%) | 273 | 244 | 231 | 142 |

Again, compared with the younger children the first two items have tended to increase in incidence with the older children. Reading books has decreased for both older boys and girls; for the boys of both areas the decrease is greater than that for the girls. The boys' average percentage incidence is twice as big as that of the girls, and the Southwark boys show a slightly bigger incidence in these activities than the Stevenage boys. There appears to be a small group of older boys who read less than the others and who also smoke and have dates. This group is again reflecting the type of attitudes observed in the junior children who smoke and date.

## Purposeful activities

For some reason this group of activities as shown in Table 19 did not clearly emerge in the junior analysis.

The activities are all active, purposeful and independent. Most of them are pastimes that have sustained or increased their popularity as the

1 See p. 137.

TABLE 19

## Senior purposeful activities cluster

| | Girls | | Boys | |
| | Stevenage | Southwark | Stevenage | Southwark |
| | % | % | % | % |
|---|---|---|---|---|
| Playing with other musical instruments | 15 | 13 | 21 | 24 |
| Swimming | 42 | 29 | 55 | 35 |
| Making or assembling radios or other electrical apparatus | 5 | 2 | 17 | 17 |
| Gardening | 6 | 10 | 25 | 14 |
| Riding a bicycle | 34 | 17 | 67 | 52 |
| Total number of children (100%) | 273 | 244 | 231 | 142 |

children have grown older, particularly the boys. This is not true of swimming, for swimming as a specific activity declines as children grow older. The simple point is that older children will only pursue those pastimes in which they have attained a certain standard of proficiency.

Stevenage boys show a greater tendency to engage in these activities than Southwark boys, and Stevenage girls more than Southwark girls. It is obvious that playing musical instruments and assembling electrical apparatus requires space and the chances are that the Stevenage children will have more available, because they are better housed than the Southwark boys. Equally, most Stevenage homes have a garden and most Southwark homes do not. So if there was a tendency for Southwark boys to want to be engaged in the more purposeful activities they would be frustrated.

## Athletic activities

Although the first four activities in Table 20 are in the same order of association as they were with the junior children, all the activities have declined in popularity. With the older children they were much more highly associated. The small minority of boys involved is very likely to be engaged in all four activities.

The reason why these apparently more mature activities have declined as the children have grown older may be similar to the case of swimming. These activities were engaged in as more general pastimes by the younger children. As the children have grown older these activities have taken on their more specific athletic mould and only those who excel wish to continue.

TABLE 20

## Senior athletic activities cluster

| | Girls | | Boys | |
| | Stevenage | Southwark | Stevenage | Southwark |
|---|---|---|---|---|
| | % | % | % | % |
| Long jump | 1 | 3 | 3 | 8 |
| High jump | 1 | 2 | 4 | 12 |
| Running races | 6 | 13 | 13 | 18 |
| Leap frog | 13 | 9 | 14 | 15 |
| Total number of children (100%) | 273 | 244 | 231 | 142 |

Table 20 shows that Southwark boys seem to be slightly more athletically inclined than Stevenage boys, and Stevenage girls the least athletically interested.

## Feminine activities

The group of activities appearing in Table 21 distinguishes the girls more than the boys, although one or two of the activities show equal participation by the boys. As in the masculine activities cluster a number of the activities diminish in importance with the increase in the age of the girls. There is a tendency then for this cluster of activities to represent more the younger, immature girls than the older girls. In this factor there is little real difference between the areas and the pastimes are very much minority activities.

TABLE 21

## Senior feminine activities cluster

| | Girls | | Boys | |
| | Stevenage | Southwark | Stevenage | Southwark |
|---|---|---|---|---|
| | % | % | % | % |
| Stringing beads | 1 | 1 | 2 | 2 |
| Sewing, knitting or crocheting | 38 | 29 | 3 | 3 |
| Hopscotch | 5 | 13 | 4 | 6 |
| Playing fivestones or jinks | 11 | 11 | 3 | 9 |
| Telling fortunes | 5 | 5 | 4 | 5 |
| Skipping | 8 | 29 | 4 | 11 |
| Total number of children (100%) | 273 | 244 | 231 | 142 |

## Masculine activities

There were a group of inter-correlated activities that distinguished the older boys from the girls. These activities appear in Table 22. The activities are similar to the junior activities but they involve only minority proportions of boys.

TABLE 22

*Senior masculine activities cluster*

| | Girls | | Boys | |
| | Stevenage | Southwark | Stevenage | Southwark |
| | % | % | % | % |
| Digging caves or holes or dens | 1 | 3 | 6 | 14 |
| Wrestling | 9 | 6 | 30 | 26 |
| Toy trains, ships, cars or lorries | 3 | 1 | 21 | 12 |
| Boxing | 1 | 2 | 13 | 12 |
| Building a dam | 1 | 1 | 4 | 5 |
| Flying model aircraft | 1 | 0 | 16 | 18 |
| Total number of children (100%) | 273 | 244 | 231 | 142 |

Although the activities are sometimes tough and independent, some of them are also a little immature for boys of 11 years and older. A majority of the activities have a diminished following with the increase in age of the boys. This is particularly so of 'wrestling', 'playing with trains', 'boxing' and 'building dams'. As in the feminine factor, there is little difference between the areas.

# Summary

There appear to be important differences between the children's activities of the two areas.

More Stevenage than Southwark children tend to engage in passive or home-oriented activities. More Southwark than Stevenage children tend to engage in active and away-from-home activities; they also tend to play more traditional group games. This is so for some activities that involve more than one-half of the children in one or both areas. In some of the minority pastimes there were similar differences, but over a greater range of activities. In some of the clusters of activities these differences are emphasised.

Some of the difference may be accounted for by the contrast that exists between the two physical environments, and also by the different strengths of tradition that might be found in the two neighbourhoods. The superior housing, the abundant open space, full employment in new industries in Stevenage, might be producing different changes in the way children use their leisure time. Certainly the results of Stewart's survey, that show the tendency towards non-participant activities, are reflected in the activities of the Stevenage children. Southwark children in their tendency towards independent group activities perhaps reflect the old traditional values.

# Part II
# The Ten-Borough Survey

# IO

## Children and Playgrounds

### Introduction

As well as a look at general patterns of play behaviour[1] an investigation of children's use of playgrounds was also carried out. The main objectives in studying the playgrounds and the use made of them by children were to discover the number of children likely to attend different types of playground; the relative importance of a limited number of factors influencing children's attendance, including competition from other playgrounds in the vicinity and any particular features of the playground; the distances children travelled from their homes to the playgrounds; whether or not on their journey they had to cross any main roads; and whether or not they were accompanied on their visits to the playgrounds. It was hoped that an analysis of such information would give a reasonable basis for the locating and equipping of playgrounds in urban areas.

The selection of the cities and urban areas for this survey was made in consultation with the Town Planning Institute and also to coincide, if possible, with the areas selected for the survey of facilities.[2]

The ten participants[3] were:

> The London Borough of Brent
> Bristol
> The London Borough of Camden

---

1 See Chapter 9.
2 See Chapters 11, 12 and 13.
3 Stevenage, an original participant, had to be abandoned as the only day upon which field work could be carried out was so wet that no children came to the playgrounds.
Southwark joined the survey at their own request.
In addition, Stockholm was chosen in order to provide some measure of comparison with a European city in which the design of environment and the provision of play areas are given much attention. Unfortunately, in spite of full co-operation, the material proved insufficient for comparable analysis.

Leicester
Liverpool
Newcastle-upon-Tyne
Southampton
Southwark
Swansea
Worcester

Three broad types of playground were selected for study:

(a) having both play leaders and equipment;[1]
(b) having equipment (but no play leader);
(c) having neither equipment nor play leader.

The participating authorities were asked to select by random sample at least five playgrounds from within each of these three groups, the desirable minimum being fifteen. In the event of any local authority not having enough playgrounds in any of the three categories, they were asked to make up, where possible, the fifteen from the remaining groups, giving priority to the order shown above.

A field survey was then undertaken based on:

(i) a description of the location, size, content, etc., of each playground;
(ii) an interview with each child attending the playground.

In addition, hourly notes were made of the weather, the number of children playing in various ways and using each type of equipment (if provided). In order to record these classes of information three forms were devised.[2]

The field work was carried out in the months of July, August and September 1965. Each playground was to be surveyed during the course of one day and, as the days were sometimes different between areas and between playgrounds within the areas, the day of the week and the date of the survey were recorded so as to allow for possible variations in attendance arising from such differences.

The results were first analysed by area and individual reports were prepared for each local authority. A composite report was also made, based on this preliminary analysis.[3] The material was then submitted

1 Equipment was defined as any item, fixed or mobile, usable for the purposes of play. The exception was equipment relating to *organised* games, e.g. goal posts, as this type of provision was regarded as sports provision rather than play provision.
2 See note on p. 250.
3 See note on p. 250.

to a more complex analysis, the technical details of which are given in Appendix III. The main findings of these two analyses are presented in this chapter.

## The Playgrounds

A total of 152 playgrounds were studied but, as will be seen from the ensuing tables, there occurs a variation in the number upon which the analysis is based owing to insufficient information on some of the questions. The great majority of these playgrounds were in residential areas of varying age, density and distance from the centre. Many were in byelaw and pre-byelaw areas, some were in inter-war housing areas, and others in post-war areas of many kinds including suburban overspills of various kinds, and urban redevelopments, usually at high densities. Some are unique—at Southampton's Mayflower Park children can swing and watch the Cunarders coming in. There do not seem to be any playgrounds closely associated with predominantly middle-class residential streets.[1]

### Playground distribution

It became clear in the preliminary analysis that real distinctions could be seen between two kinds of playgrounds—those with and those without equipment.[2] (The playgrounds with play leadership were too few in number for consideration in the main analysis as a distinct group but, in view of their importance, were looked at separately.) Also, it was found that in some respects playgrounds in parks or recreation grounds were sufficiently different to need separate analytical treatment. The playgrounds, therefore, were regrouped as follows:

Type 1—Playgrounds forming part of parks and recreation grounds.
Type 2—Other playgrounds with equipment.
Type 3—Play areas with no equipment (or one piece of equipment).[3]

Table 28 shows the distribution of the 148 playgrounds (the four in Stockholm are excluded).

1   It had been intended to study the geographical location of the playgrounds in greater detail, but it was not possible to obtain the necessary information for so many areas.
2   See footnote (1), p. 182.
3   Generally if a playground contains equipment, then it contains several pieces of equipment. Three playgrounds only had one piece of equipment each, but in every other way were similar to the play streets and play areas, and were included in type 3. So 27 of the type 3 playgrounds were play streets or play areas with no equipment, while three had just one piece of equipment.

TABLE 28[1]

## Number and distribution of three main types of playground

| | Equipped Playgrounds in Parks etc. (Type 1) | Other Equipped Playgrounds (Type 2) | Unequipped Play Areas (Type 3) | Total |
|---|---|---|---|---|
| Brent | 9 | — | — | 9 |
| Camden | 2 | 6 | 2 | 10 |
| Southampton | 6 | 4 | — | 10 |
| Leicester | 3 | 4 | 7 | 14 |
| Swansea | 9 | 5 | — | 14 |
| Bristol | 12 | 3 | — | 15 |
| Liverpool | 3 | 6 | 7 | 16 |
| Worcester | 5 | 7 | 4 | 16 |
| Newcastle | 5 | 7 | 7 | 19 |
| Southwark | 10 | 12 | 3 | 25 |
| Totals | 64 | 54 | 30 | 148 |

## Playground characteristics

Most of the equipment in the playgrounds was of the conventional, manufactured kind: swings, slides, roundabouts, 'umbrellas', rocking boats and the like. The counting of such equipment was standardised in this study to result in a number of 'units' for purposes of analysis.[2] Of the ninety-six equipped playgrounds exactly half had three, four or five 'units' of formal fixed equipment; only nineteen had nine or more units. There was hardly any special provision for very young children other than a few sand pits and miniature swings; covered accommodation to be used in bad weather was more rare than the British climate seems to require. Most of the playgrounds (as distinct from play areas or streets) had lavatories adjoining or near at hand;[3] this is particularly

---

1 Because of the desire to include all types of playground and to have samples of roughly comparable size the playgrounds in the total samples are not necessarily representative of the number and distribution for each borough (for this reason comparison between the boroughs is not useful). Where *all* playgrounds in a given area, for example, were examined as in the facilities survey (see Chapter 12) the proportion of equipped playgrounds sited outside parks and recreation grounds—mostly on housing estates—was found to be greater than for those within parks. This also would seem to have had some effect on the average size of the playgrounds in the two surveys as those situated on housing estates tend to be smaller than those in parks and recreation grounds.

2 The method of measurement is described in Appendix III.

3 This contrasted with the findings of the facilities survey. See p. 230.

true of those in parks and recreation grounds. The size of the playgrounds which was to prove of significance in attracting children to certain of the playgrounds varied considerably.

# The Children

## Children's attendance

TABLE 29
*Children's attendance by type of playground*

| Type of playground | Number of playgrounds | Total attendance | Average attendance |
|---|---|---|---|
| Type 1 <br> Parks, etc. | 64 | 9,223 | 144 |
| Type 2 <br> Other—equipped | 54 | 5,848 | 108 |
| Type 3 <br> Unequipped | 30 | 1,960 | 65 |
| Totals | 148 | 17,031 | 115 |

A total of 17,031 children were recorded as attending the 148 playgrounds and there was considerable variation in attendance according to the type of playground, the unequipped play areas attracting the smallest number of children. Equipped playgrounds situated in parks and recreation grounds had the highest attendance figures. Weather appears to have noticeably affected attendance only when it was very wet. The relationship between attendance and type of playground was subsequently confirmed by further analysis.[1]

## Children's age and sex

Of the 17,031 children interviewed 83 per cent were between five and fourteen years old with the larger number amongst the lower half of the age group. Not unexpectedly children aged 15+ comprised only 2·4 per cent of the total number attending; the great majority of the playgrounds investigated had little to attract teenagers.[2] The number

---

1 See p. 196.
2 It must also be allowed that use of the equipment in some playgrounds may have been prohibited, though this is not likely to have significantly affected the figures.

of under fives attending was also proportionately low—only 14·5 per cent.

Do boys use playgrounds more than girls? Table 30 shows that the proportion of girls to boys within each age group varied quite considerably.

TABLE 30

*Playground attendance by sex and age structure*

| Age group | Children attending Ratio | | |
|---|---|---|---|
| | Girls | : | Boys |
| 0– 4 | 100 | : | 87 |
| 5– 9 | 100 | : | 105 |
| 10–14 | 100 | : | 130 |
| 0–14 | 100 (7,822) | : | 113 (8,800) |
| 15+ | 100 (87) | : | 370 (322) |
| All Children | 100 (7,909) | : | 115 (9,122) |

In the under-five age group there were more girls than boys at a ratio of 100 : 87, but for all other groups, the older the children the larger the proportion of boys. The 5 to 9 age group shows a ratio of girls to boys of 100 : 105, the 10 to 14 age group 100 : 130, and the over-14 age group 100 : 370, although this last group contains only a small number of children. There is therefore a distinct trend that as children grow older, so the playground becomes increasingly less attended by girls than it does by boys. It is possible that as girls grow older they become more home oriented, either from choice or because they are expected by their parents to help with home chores. It is also possible that the playgrounds themselves hold less attraction to older girls.[1] Table 31 shows the main variation between boys and girls to be in unequipped play areas, confirming the particular preference of boys for team games found in the study of children's activities.[2]

[1] The problem for 15- to 18-year-old girls in the youth club context has been interestingly analysed. See Hanmar (1964).
[2] See Chapter 9.

**TABLE 31**
*Proportion of children attending by sex and type of playground*

| Playground type | Children attending Ratio | | |
|---|---|---|---|
| | Girls | | Boys |
| Type 1 Parks, etc. | 100 | : | 111 |
| Type 2 Other—equipped | 100 | : | 111 |
| Type 3 Unequipped | 100 | : | 152 |

# Playground Use

## Distance travelled to the playgrounds

Table 32 shows, logically enough, that about half the children (49·2 per cent) came to the playgrounds from a distance of less than a quarter of a mile. There is a steady decrease apparent in the numbers attending as the distance from the playground increases; but as many as 30·9 per cent came from over half a mile. The differences between boys and girls are negligible.

**TABLE 32**
*The distance children travel to reach all types of playground*

| Age group | Under ¼ mile | ¼–½ mile | ½–1 mile | Over 1 mile | Total % |
|---|---|---|---|---|---|
| | % in Each Interval | | | | |
| 0–14 | 49 | 20 | 15 | 16 | 100 (16,622) |
| Boys | 50 | 20 | 14 | 16 | 100 (8,800) |
| Girls | 48 | 20 | 15 | 17 | 100 (7,822) |

It may at first appear surprising that, as revealed in Table 33, there is not more variation in distance travelled between the three age groups or indeed that the younger age group travels the furthest.

**TABLE 33**
*Median distance travelled by children*

| Age group | Median distance |
|---|---|
| 0– 4 | 494 yards |
| 5– 9 | 432 yards |
| 10–14 | 493 yards |
| All children | 461 yards |

Further analysis of this lack of variation showed that this was probably due to the fact that the younger children were likely to be accompanied by an adult or an older responsible child. This pattern was repeated in all the ten areas with the exception of Stockholm (not included in the above tables) where a noticeably shorter distance was travelled by the 0- to 4-year-olds.

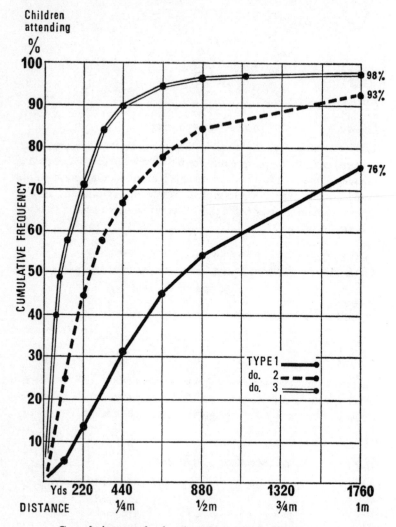

Cumulative graph showing percentage of playground attendance against distance travelled.

There were, however, variations in the median distances travelled according to the type of playground. For type 1 (equipped playgrounds in parks, etc.) it was 809 yards—just under half a mile; for type 2 (other equipped playgrounds) 296 yards, and for type 3 (unequipped play areas) 101 yards. Predictably, therefore, it may be concluded that playgrounds in parks and recreation grounds are capable of attracting children from a wide area but that play streets and play areas without equipment are local in character. This last group showed the most striking pattern. Children playing here had come only a very short distance; well over half travelled less than 110 yards (often the same street in the case of a play street), and a radius of 220 yards accounted for 75 per cent of the children.

The graph shows differences in the cumulative aspect of children's attendance at the three main types of playground. Taking the distance of a quarter of a mile, for example, only 30 per cent of the children attracted to playgrounds within parks and recreation grounds (type 1) can be accounted for, as against 66 per cent of those attending the equipped playgrounds sited elsewhere (type 2), and 90 per cent of those using play streets and other unequipped play spaces. To account for 75 per cent of the children attending type 1 playgrounds the radius has to be extended as far as one mile. Thus a quarter of the children were coming from distances over a mile away from the playground.

## Playground catchment area

A catchment area was constructed for each of the three types of playground as a circular area surrounding a playground by studying the numbers attending. Since, as has been shown, the number of children attending a playground falls off quite sharply as the distance increases, with the majority of children living relatively close to the playground, the catchment area radius was taken as the distance within which three-quarters of the children lived. For type 1 playgrounds this was one mile (1,760 yards), for type 2 660 yards, and for type 3 220 yards.

## Proportions of children attending

The advantage of an established catchment area for different types of playground is that it makes possible an assessment of the *proportions* of children attending a given playground.[1] (This might appear to be more meaningful if attendance at other playgrounds within the catchment

1 For our analysis the total number of children living within the catchment area was calculated from 1961 census data given by enumeration districts.

radius was taken into account as, in the initial examination of the material, competition from other playgrounds appeared to affect attendance. Subsequent analysis, however, showed this not to be the case, although there was a significant effect on the length of time children stay at a playground.)[1]

This attendance as a proportion of children of the appropriate age groups (ignoring that of 15+) living within the catchment area was expressed as an 'activity rate'. In the 5 to 9 age group, for example, this ranged from 3 per cent in an area of predominantly type 1 playgrounds to 27 per cent in an area where the play facilities were mostly either type 2 or type 3, thus confirming the localised character of these two types of play facility. Clearly, the reasons for variations in these activity rates are many, and do not only relate to broad categories of playground; each individual playground would have its different characteristics as would each catchment area.

## Major roads crossed

Important in connection with the question of distance travelled is, of course, the number of major roads[2] that children cross to reach a playground; 58·4 per cent of the children crossed no main road at all. This, although bearing out the pattern of short distances travelled by the majority of the children, is nevertheless a little surprising when one thinks of the network of major roads in the towns and cities of today. Probably much of this is accounted for by the playgrounds located on housing estates and the play streets. There are, nevertheless, a considerable number of children who have to cross either one or two major roads—28·4 per cent. The average number of major roads crossed for the under-five age group was 1·66, compared with 1·36 for the 5- to 9-year-olds, and 1·28 for the 10- to 14-year-olds. This follows from the fact that the young children are accompanied by adults while the other children are alone or with friends and so do not tend to travel so far. There was no significant difference in the number of roads crossed to be discovered between boys and girls.

## Method of transport

The great majority of children (79·6 per cent) walked to the playground, only 9·4 per cent using a bicycle. The remaining 11 per cent used a bus, or car, or train. Here there was a difference in the habits

1 See p. 194.
2 For definition of 'major road' see Appendix III.

of boys and girls. The proportion of girls walking was much higher, while boys made much more use of a bicycle to travel to the playground. The method of transport also varied with age. As children get older the more they use a bicycle and the less they use a bus, car, or train.

## Accompaniment of the children

Who accompanies the children to the playground varied greatly with age and sex. Nearly half (47 per cent) of the under-five-year-olds were accompanied by an adult, the proportion falling rapidly with the increase in age. A similar pattern, but far less marked, could be seen for those children accompanied by a brother or sister. This process was reversed for those going to the playground with friends. In the older age group (10–14) a majority (59 per cent) went to playgrounds with friends. And, quite naturally, the proportion going alone increased with age (only 5 per cent of the under fives were unaccompanied). As well as these age variations there were the differences between boys and girls. A higher proportion of girls were accompanied by an adult or a brother or sister, while boys were more likely to go alone or with friends.

As has already been indicated the question of who accompanies the children to the playground had a considerable effect on the distance travelled.

TABLE 34

*The distance children travel to the playground by whether they were accompanied or not*

| Who accompanied by | % in each interval | | | | | Median distance travelled (yards) |
|---|---|---|---|---|---|---|
| | Under ¼ mile | ¼–½ mile | ½–1 mile | Over 1 mile | Total % | |
| Alone | 72 | 16 | 6 | 6 | 100 (2,294) | 215 |
| Friends | 48 | 22 | 16 | 14 | 100 (6,918) | 465 |
| Brother–sister | 50 | 20 | 16 | 14 | 100 (3,975) | 453 |
| Adult | 22 | 18 | 21 | 39 | 100 (2,514) | 1,311 |

There is evident a distinct and important trend in Table 34. Children going to the playground alone travelled only short distances with 72 per cent from less than a quarter of a mile and only 12 per cent from over half a mile. On the other hand those attending with adults travelled much greater distances, 60 per cent from over half a mile and just 22 per cent from under a quarter of a mile. Between these two extremes and showing a very similar pattern were the children going with friends or with a brother or sister, where about half came from within a quarter of a mile and 30 per cent from over half a mile away.

Comparison of the median distance travelled shows that for the children travelling alone it was 215 yards, for those with a brother or sister 453, for those with friends 465, but for those accompanied by an adult it was 1,311 yards. It is because such a high proportion of the children under five years old are accompanied by an adult that these children tend to travel such a long way to the playground.

A similar pattern is evident in the number of major roads crossed by the children. For those travelling alone the mean number of roads crossed was 0·86, with 75 per cent crossing no roads at all, while for those accompanied by an adult it was 3·68, with only 28 per cent crossing no roads. For those going with a friend the mean was 1·07 and those with a brother or sister 1·10, with about 60 per cent crossing no roads in each case.

## What factors attract children to playgrounds?

The foregoing data give a general picture of the playgrounds, of the children attending them and of certain features relating to the attendance. It was thought that a more detailed study of these features might help towards an understanding of the whys and wherefores of children's use of playgrounds. Accordingly, the method of a multivariate analysis was used, which would enable all the variations in attendances at playgrounds to be looked at against the variations in playground characteristics.

Initially attendance figures only were used as the measure of attraction to the playground. This was felt to be inadequate and the additional factor of duration of stay was introduced. Each child entering the playground was interviewed and at each hour, on the hour, a count was taken of the number of children in the playground. These gave two figures which could be used as a measure of playground use, the total attendance at a playground, and the total hourly count from 10.00 a.m. to 6.00 p.m. for each playground, which gives roughly the total child-hours spent at each playground.

Playgrounds surveyed in exceptionally poor weather and playgrounds where not all the children were interviewed were neglected, leaving

Southwark

*Individual activity*

Stevenage

Liverpool

*Making the most of our open spaces*

Blackburn

110 playgrounds for analysis. Each of the three main types of play-ground was analysed separately in order to study the differing degree of influence of the various factors. Of the 110 playgrounds being analysed, 44 were of type 1 (parks, etc.), 41 of type 2 (other—equipped), and 25 of type 3 (unequipped).

The possible factors which might influence playground attendance or duration of stay were considered and nine were selected for use in the analysis.

First was the number of children living near the playground. This had been calculated on the basis of a catchment area.[1] Second was the number of other playgrounds within the catchment area. One would expect children to be attracted to a playground by the facilities that are provided, and so the remaining seven factors concerned the play-grounds themselves.

The following, then, were the nine factors on which it was hoped enough data would be available upon which to concentrate the analysis.

1. Number of competing playgrounds within catchment area.
2. Child population within catchment area.
3. Size of playground.
4. Paddling pool.
5. Team games area.
6. Sand pit.
7. Play leader.
8. Adventure facilities.
9. Units of formal equipment.[2]

A multiple regression analysis[3] was performed on each of the three types of playground and on all the playgrounds together (this gave a total of eight multiple regression analyses). Unfortunately, the repre-sentation of certain of these factors was subsequently discovered to be so slight as to invalidate their use in the regression analysis. The four factors which were considered to be too lightly represented were: the paddling pool; the sand pit; adventure facilities; the play leader. These are therefore not included in the following account.[4]

When considering all three types of playground together the number of children living in the vicinity proved to be highly significant in its

---

1  See p. 189.
2  See Appendix III.
3  As the multiple regression technique demonstrates statistical and not casual relationships, inferences should be drawn with considerable caution.
4  A full account with all the factors is given in Appendix III.

effect on total attendance but, as might be expected, not on the length of time children stay at a playground. Here the presence of a team ball-games area was the most significant factor, followed in order of significance by: the size of the playground; the presence of formal equipment; the competition from other playgrounds within the catchment radius. The first three of these—ball-games area, playground size and equipment—are not surprising; children are likely to stay longer at a larger playground which offers variety of activity, and team games require a fair amount of time to play. The fourth factor—competition from other playgrounds—is less expected, as the results[1] showed that the more playgrounds there are nearby the higher will be the total count. This is discussed in the ensuing paragraph. Still looking at all playgrounds but returning to what would seem to attract children initially (total attendance), the presence of formal equipment,[2] a ball-games area,[3] and the size of the playground (in that order, following catchment population) were all significant factors, similar to those for duration of stay, though differing in order of significance.

Taking the three types of playground separately distinct variations can be seen. The only significant factor accounting for both total attendance and duration of stay in the unequipped play areas (type 3) was the presence of a team ball-games area. This in fact appeared each time for the other two types of playground (type 1 equipped in parks, etc., and type 2 other—equipped) though in a varying degree of significance. The catchment population figured as significant for the total attendance of both types 1 and 2, and for the duration of stay for type 2, but was not significant for duration of stay for playgrounds in parks and recreation grounds (type 1). Formal equipment, on the other hand, significantly held children longer at parks playgrounds, but not at those situated elsewhere, whereas it was significant in attracting children initially to these type 2 playgrounds though not to those in parks. Playground size appears to be important for duration of stay at type 2 playgrounds.[4] A seemingly peculiar significant factor for duration of stay at type 2 playgrounds was competition from other playgrounds. This means that the more playgrounds found within the catchment area the longer children are likely to stay. This seems contradictory because it would be expected that more playgrounds would increase the likelihood of children going from one playground to another—in other words that they would be competing for children's attendance.

1   The coefficient was positive.
2 and 3   And see also Table 49 in Appendix V.
4   See Appendix III.

This obviously needs to be examined further but there may be a number of explanations. Type 2 playgrounds tend, for example, to be concentrated in high-density areas and, even where the housing development is new (in some cases particularly so, in high-rise developments), such areas tend to restrict children's mobility. These areas may also give rise to *mothers* restricting the distances their children may travel, as is shown in the contrasting neighbourhood study.[1] It is possible, too, that high density areas are lacking in other kinds of amenity—general recreational space, for example.

## Playground use by sex and age

The attendances at type 1 and type 2 playgrounds were broken down into three age groups and into boys and girls, and a multiple regression analysis was performed on each group.

For playgrounds in parks and recreation grounds (type 1 playgrounds) the catchment population was significant in attracting both boys and girls, but also, as one would expect, the presence of a team games area significantly influenced boys' attendance. In looking at the different age groups, catchment population was always significant. For the older children (10 to 14 years), a team-games area becomes important, as does the size of a playground. Formal equipment ceases to be significant for this age group.

The presence of a team-games area is again highly important in attracting boys to playgrounds equipped but situated elsewhere than in parks and recreation grounds (type 2 playgrounds). Boys' attendance also depends on the catchment population, whereas for girls the main factor is the presence of formal equipment. As at type 1 playgrounds, formal equipment is a significant factor for the 0 to 4 age group, but here it remains important for the 5 to 9 age group as well. And again it is the presence of a team games area that is the most important factor in explaining playground attendance variations of the 5- to 9- and 10- to 14-year-old age groups. For the older children (10- to 14- years-old), the size of the playground becomes important, as it did at type 1 playgrounds.

# Predicting Attendance

Obviously, where possible, playgrounds should be located and equipped so as to provide for their maximum use. It was felt that it might be helpful to planners to devise a formula for predicting

1   See Chapter 8.

attendance. This was done using relevant data from the multiple regression analysis and using also information which had been collected on the numbers of children engaged on different activities at the playgrounds (the hourly counts).

This is not to say that all factors which determine children's attendance at playgrounds have been taken into account. Such a survey would require a far more complex approach than was used in this work. Nor must it be forgotten that attendance is only one of many considerations in the provision of play facilities. Despite this, the prediction equation[1] should certainly be of great interest to those wishing to develop objective assessments in this field.

## The Playgrounds with Play Leadership

Of the 148 playgrounds only twelve had full-time, and five had part-time, play leaders present on the day of the interview. Of the playgrounds with full-time leaders only nine could be considered;[2] inaccurate or insufficient recording eliminated the other three. This latter problem was, in fact, responsible for further eliminations of certain aspects of the analysis. Thus for overall attendance comparisons only seven playgrounds could be finally considered, and for duration of stay—only six. No firm conclusions, therefore, can be drawn.

### Attendance

A comparison between the ten playgrounds with play leadership and an overall average sample of eight type 2, and two type 1, playgrounds showed about a 40 per cent higher average attendance at the former. However, when a more strictly comparable analysis was made, namely a comparison between seven play-leader playgrounds and twenty-five other playgrounds with similar equipment the difference was reduced to negligible proportions. In the nature of things the equipment in the two categories of playground cannot be exactly similar but it is interesting to note that apart from the obviously greater number of special and adventure facilities in the play-leader playgrounds over twice as many of these playgrounds had sand and a team ball-games area. It should also be pointed out that the non play-leader playgrounds

1 The equation of type 1 playgrounds is given in Appendix III for use as a model.
2 Of these, one was situated in a park and the rest were type 2 playgrounds (equipped and sited 'off street', or on housing estates).

selected for comparisons had a higher than average number of equipment units.

## Duration of stay

There were only six play-leader playgrounds with reliable total counts. A comparison with the same group of type 2 playgrounds revealed the following:

TABLE 35

*Comparison of duration of stay between playgrounds with and without play leaders*

|  | All type 2 playgrounds | Play-leader playgrounds | Similarly equipped sample of type 2 playgrounds |
|---|---|---|---|
| Total count | 200[1] | 494 | 177 |

There is evident a remarkable difference showing that children stayed well over twice as long at the playgrounds with play leaders. These figures, however, must be regarded with some caution as the difference was accounted for by exceptionally high readings in only two of the six play-leader playgrounds.

## Sex and age

A comparison was also made for sex and age.[2]

TABLE 36

*Comparison of age structure of children between playgrounds with and without play leaders*

| Age | All type 2 playgrounds % | Play-leader playgrounds % |
|---|---|---|
| 0– 4 | 13·3 | 11·8 |
| 5– 9 | 48·4 | 42·2 |
| 10–14 | 35·9 | 43·2 |
| 0–14 | 97·6 | 97·1 |
| 15+ | 2·4 | 2·9 |
| All children | 100% (5,848) | 100% (1,323) |

1 This is the equivalent of a stay of less than one hour.
2 Here, it was possible to use nine play-leader playgrounds.

Table 36 shows little difference in attendance between the play-grounds in the youngest age group, but the proportion of older children attending is higher in the play-leader playgrounds.

There is, however, a very marked difference between the playgrounds in the sex of the children attending.

TABLE 37

*Comparison of sex structure of children between playgrounds with and without play leaders*

| All type 2 playgrounds Ratio | | Play-leader playgrounds Ratio | |
|---|---|---|---|
| Girls | Boys | Girls | Boys |
| 100 : | 111 | 100 : | 134 |

A much higher proportion of boys than girls use the play-leader playgrounds. This persists throughout all age groups but is particularly noticeable amongst the 10 to 14-year-olds where the ratio of girls to boys is as high as 100 : 193 as against 100 : 130 in all type 2 playgrounds.

## Distance travelled

There was a very similar pattern between the playgrounds for distance travelled by the children, but there was a difference in whether or not the children were accompanied by an adult; only 2·3 per cent at the play-leader playgrounds as against 10·7 per cent at all type 2 play-grounds.[1] This was reflected in the smaller number of main roads crossed by the younger children attending play-leader playgrounds.

# Playground Costs

The cost to a local authority of providing a playground may be cal-culated as an annual cost including land acquisition, site preparation, equipment and running costs. A standard range of land prices, based on the proximity of the playground to the central area, may be derived in order to calculate the cost of site acquisition for each playground. All the stages of preparing the site for use as a playground may be incorporated in one standard cost per square yard of playground which

1  The shorter distances travelled to playgrounds by the Stockholm 0–4 age group may very well be accounted for by the fact that the playgrounds were supervised.

can then be used to calculate the initial cost of site preparation. The prices of the various forms of equipment will enable an estimate of the total cost of initial provision to be calculated. Allowance should be made for money borrowed at usual local authority rates of interest over sixty years for the acquisition of the site, and over thirty years for the initial cost of preparing the site and buying the equipment. This would give an annual cost, to which must be added the running costs of maintenance and depreciation of equipment, rates on the land, and also the cost of any personnel employed at the playground. Such a calculation was, in fact, made for the purposes of this analysis and it was clear that, where it existed, the principal annual expenditure was on personnel, either a play leader or an attendant. Obviously, also, the cost of providing a large playground is greater than that of providing a small one. The cost, on the other hand, of providing equipment is only a relatively small annual cost per playground. In an attempt to relate attendance figures to costs the increasing cost of equipment was seen to be outweighed by the increase in attendance. Attendance did not appear to increase, however, in anything like the same proportion to the increase in costs through employing a play leader or attendant, or providing a larger playground.

No conclusions, however, can be drawn from this for, as has already been suggested, to use attendance figures as the sole measure of benefit is clearly inadequate.

## Summary and Conclusions[1]

From the review of the 148 playgrounds play facility provision may be considered as falling broadly into three categories:

Type 1—equipped and situated in parks and recreation grounds (64).
Type 2—equipped and situated in housing estates and 'off street' (54).
Type 3—unequipped play spaces and play streets (30).

It was only possible to investigate nine playgrounds with play leadership although a special attempt had been made in the sampling to include playgrounds with this kind of supervision.

The great majority of the 17,031 children who were interviewed on the playgrounds were between the ages of five and fourteen, the numbers tailing off in the older ranks. The proportion of boys to girls using all playgrounds was higher except for the under-five age group and increased with the age of the children. This was particularly

1    The implications are discussed in Chapters 4 and 6.

marked in the unequipped areas for which the average attendance was by far the lowest of the three types of playground, those in parks and recreation grounds attracting the greatest number of children.[1] There was a marked difference in the distance travelled by children between the three types of playground; the furthest, naturally, was for those playgrounds situated in parks and recreation grounds (type 1) and the shortest was for the play streets and unequipped play areas. There was a surprising similarity in the distance travelled between the age groups, largely attributable to the fact that the younger children were accompanied by adults or older brothers or sisters. Playgrounds with play leaders appeared to attract children from roughly the same distance as did type 2 playgrounds, but with the difference that the youngest age group tended to come from shorter distances, as they did to the playgrounds in Stockholm. This can almost certainly be accounted for by the fact that children attending fully supervised playgrounds are more rarely accompanied by an adult. More boys than girls used bicycles to get to the playgrounds, but the majority of all the children walked, and over a quarter of these had to cross one or two major roads to reach a playground.

Catchment areas for the three main types of playground were constructed resulting in a radius of: 1,760 yards for type 1; 660 yards for type 2; and 220 yards for type 3. Logically the proportions of children living within the catchment areas who attended the playgrounds was in inverse ratio to the size of the catchment radius. This should not mean, however, that, because the highest percentage of children within a small radius use them, unequipped play areas should become the model for playground provision, as it will be remembered that their *total average attendance figures* were far lower than those of the other two types of playground. Rather should it suggest that type 2 playgrounds (with the important addition, where possible, of supervision) should be increased in number and improved so as to attract a greater proportion of children (the prediction of attendance equation[2] will be useful in achieving this). It would also appear to reflect a dearth of play and other amenities in the immediate neighbourhood. This was confirmed in the nineteen-borough survey which showed that play streets had usually been introduced in such areas.[3]

Various factors were found to be significant in attracting children to

---

1   The fact that the survey was carried out mostly at weekends or on week-days during the holidays is likely to have influenced these attendance figures.
2   See Appendix III.
3   See Chapter 11.

the playgrounds and in accounting for the time they stayed there. Two of these were the number of children and the number of playgrounds within a given catchment radius of the playground. A team ball-games area proved to be one of the most significant factors both in attracting children to the playgrounds and in keeping them there. Playground size and formal equipment, were two other features which figured as significant.

At playgrounds with play leadership there were indications of a longer duration of stay than at the non-supervised playgrounds. The data were insufficient to show fully the reasons for this. The proportion of boys to girls using these playgrounds considerably exceeded that for the non-supervised playgrounds.

The findings on attendance totals and on the proportions of attending children within the catchment radius suggest that advantage should be taken of existing recreational space (parks, etc.) for the provision of play facilities. At the same time there is evident a need to provide facilities as a neighbourhood service (an important note here is that children should not have to cross a main road to reach a playground).

Supervised provision, with its unconventional equipment and greater range of facilities, and with its greater holding power, should be an integral part of this neighbourhood service. The fact that children appear to stay longer at supervised playgrounds and can go to them without an adult is important.

The undoubted popularity of team ball games must be taken into account in the planning of play provision. Although on housing estates it may be more convenient to provide a ball-games area separately, the evidence suggests that there are advantages in incorporating such an area into multi-purpose playgrounds. Here, of course, size is important.

Except for the youngest age group, the ratio of girls to boys was always lower, particularly at the play-leader playgrounds. This latter point is surprising as girls are catered for at most supervised facilities. More study is needed both to establish what features, apart from formal equipment and the more obvious attractions such as cooking facilities, do or might attract girls, and also to discover whether there might not need to be a certain degree of acceptance of girls' orientation towards home.

In this study it has been assumed that, together with playground catchment population and competition from other playgrounds, the features of a playground are the sole criteria for assessing children's attendance and length of stay at playgrounds. Clearly this should not

1  See p. 273.

be so. But whatever the motivations in observed attendance at different playgrounds with varying features, consistent changes of attendance, according to type of playground, show a clear correlation between certain physical characteristics of playgrounds and the number of children using them.

# Part III

# The Survey of Existing Facilities

# Introduction

## Aims

The survey of existing facilities was carried out in nineteen selected urban areas in England and Wales. Its object was to investigate the availability of existing facilities rather than their actual use. We wished to discover how the allocation of general recreational space affected provision for children. If, for example, they live in a part of the city well served with public parks and gardens are they also well served with play spaces? Is it possible to detect a pattern in provision varying according to the region or outside environment of the city? We were interested also in the following questions: How far do or could, schools contribute to children's out-of-school activities? Are playgrounds mainly of one type or is there variety? Are they attractive to look at, interesting and exciting to play in? How well are the under fives and the over fourteens provided for? Are children restricted in their use of playgrounds? In what state of repair are these play spaces? How much supervision is there? We also wished to discover who was responsible for the administering and financing of children's play provision.

## Choice of Boroughs

Four main factors influenced the choice of boroughs for this survey: geographical location, population size, availability of local voluntary help and the willingness of the Authority to co-operate. These two latter points inevitably prevented the sample from being a random one.

A pilot study had convinced us that within the local government framework there is a great deal of the left hand not knowing what the right is doing. Thus we felt it imperative that the areas should be investigated by field workers on the spot, working in collaboration with the local authority.

In choosing the boroughs the eight newly created planning regions of the Department of Economic Affairs were adopted as being the most appropriate, for the Department's economic planning councils were to be concerned in the planning of land use and development and of the relevant services. We extracted London Administrative County from the South East Region, thus making a ninth region. Two or three boroughs of different population sizes were than selected from within each region. We decided that a population of approximately 50,000 was the optimum working unit. It allowed for a sufficient diversity of environment and range of activity and was, at the same time, of a manageable size for investigation.[1] That meant that in the larger cities the whole area was not always covered but that 'neighbourhoods' of approximately the required size were chosen for review.

We approached boroughs in each region with population ranges of 50,000–100,000; 100,000–200,000 and over 200,000 in or near which was a college of education. It was in these colleges that we hoped to find our source of voluntary field work help and we were not disappointed.

The map on the following page shows the finally agreed selection.[2] Once the regional distribution of the boroughs and the approximate size of the areas for review had been decided, it was necessary to agree a common basis for the composition of these areas (where they did not comprise the whole borough). Children, we realise, are no respecters of map boundaries; main roads, park railings, railway sidings are the kind of boundaries which they understand. Difficulties arise where administrative and social boundaries fail to coincide. It was finally decided, however, to form the review areas from a group of adjacent wards.[3]

The review areas were chosen in each case by the respective planning or borough engineer's department. It was suggested that the areas should be predominantly residential. Where one sample area only was being covered this was to be as representative of the general residential pattern of the town as possible. Where two or three sample areas were being reviewed, the aim was to achieve contrast between the areas. There were inevitable differences in population size and in acreage between the review areas. We have therefore taken as our unit of comparison 'per 1,000 population'.

1 A pilot study in St Pancras had been carried out in an area of 67,000 population.
2 Population figures and other details are given in Appendix IV.
3 The chief reason being the availability of statistical information, an important consideration in view of the extent of the survey and the limited time to spare of the officers concerned.

# Method of Work

Two questionnaires were devised;[1] one was designed for completion by the local authority and the other, relating to individual playgrounds, was for use by the field worker. Each area (with one exception) was visited and discussions were held with either the Authority or the College of Education, in most cases with both.

At the outset it became clear that the question of classification would be a problem. A number of recreation and open space surveys have been carried out in recent years[2] and from these it can be seen that common definitions are very broadly based. Differences appear with breakdowns into more precise categories. For our survey we sought advice from the Ministry of Housing and Local Government and from two of the participating Authorities, Liverpool and Camden, and the resulting questionnaire for use by the Authorities was based on this advice and on the assurance that the information asked for could be produced.

In all the nineteen boroughs it was necessary to return to various departments for clarification or reinterpretation or simply with a plea to complete a question which had been left blank—in most cases with success. Particular difficulties and discrepancies in definition and classification will be dealt with individually in the discussion of the analysis.

1  See note on p. 250.
2  See e.g. Liverpool Open Space Report (1964); County of Lancashire Report (1967); British Travel Association, University of Keele Report (1967); Regional Sports Councils' Preliminary Reports: Eastern, South Western, Wales, Yorkshire and Humberside (1967).

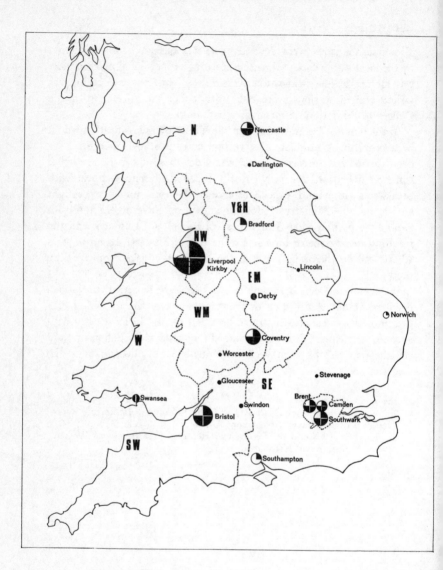

The nineteen boroughs surveyed

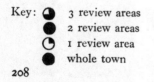

Key:  ◕  3 review areas
      ●  2 review areas
      ◔  1 review area
      ●  whole town

*Forbidden to play*

*Encouraged to play*

*A group of Sixth Form schoolboys building a children's playground*

# II

## The Boroughs Compared

### Public recreational space in the nineteen boroughs

Open space is central to our study of opportunities for children's play but we are aware that it is only one aspect of environment. What follows, therefore, is no attempt to measure environment. Where possible some social, economic, demographic and topographical features of the areas under review have been sketched in. This may help to set in perspective the picture of open space provision—in particular the recreational space and designated play space which is available for use by children. We shall consider first the picture of provision in the nineteen boroughs as a whole.

It will be remembered that the population factor determining the choice of boroughs related to size and not to density. Overall town density, the number of persons per acre, is affected by factors other than open space provision; by the amount and disposition of industrial building and commercial undertakings, for example, or by variations in type of housing. Tall blocks of flats housing a great many people take up less ground space than substantial single family houses with large gardens. But our concern is with open space, particularly public recreational space. Much classified open space—under-used allotments for instance, land awaiting development—could almost certainly be converted to temporary or permanent recreational use, as indeed is happening in certain areas, but the following analysis is limited to existing public recreational space. This includes commons, heaths, woods, parks, recreational grounds, municipal gardens, sports grounds and playing fields, amenity spaces, which are available to the public and which are to be found within the borough boundary.

Table 50 shows the nineteen boroughs in order of population size, density and amount of public recreational space per 1,000 population.

Liverpool, Southwark and Brent cluster at or near the head of all three columns: Liverpool, the largest of our review cities, a port and

## TABLE 50

*Boroughs in order of population size, overall population density and amount of public recreational space per 1,000 population*

| Population size in descending rank order (in thousands) | | Population density in descending rank order (persons per acre) | | Acreage of public recreational space in ascending rank order (per 1,000 pop.) | |
|---|---|---|---|---|---|
| 1 | Liverpool 728 | 1 | Camden 45·7 | 1 | Southwark 1·5 |
| 2 | Bristol 437 | 2 | Southwark 44·2 | 2 | Brent 2·5 |
| 3 | Coventry 330 | 3 | Brent 27·3 | 3 | Liverpool 2·6 |
| 4 | Southwark 313 | 4 | Liverpool 26·2 | 4 | Bradford 2·9 |
| 5 | Brent 296 | 5 | Newcastle 23·2 | 5 | Darlington 3·4 |
| 6 | Bradford 296 | 6 | Southampton 17·7 | 6 | Derby 3·5 |
| 7 | Newcastle 257 | 7 | Bristol 16·7 | 7 | Kirkby 3·7 |
| 8 | Camden 245 | 8 | Coventry 16·4 | 8 | Camden 3·9 |
| 9 | Southampton 205 | 9 | Derby 15·9 | 9 | Coventry 3·9 |
| 10 | Swansea 167 | 10 | Swindon 15·3 | 10 | Bristol 3·9 |
| 11 | Derby 129 | 11 | Norwich 14·6 | 11 | Southampton 4·2 |
| 12 | Norwich 119 | 12 | Gloucester 13·2 | 12 | Norwich 4·4 |
| 13 | Swindon 97 | 13 | Darlington 12·8 | 13 | Swansea 5·2 |
| 14 | Darlington 83 | 14 | Kirkby 12·2 | 14 | Swindon 5·6 |
| 15 | Lincoln 77 | 15 | Bradford 11·5 | 15 | Worcester 5·6 |
| 16 | Gloucester 69 | 16 | Worcester 10·9 | 16 | Newcastle 6·4 |
| 17 | Worcester 67 | 17 | Lincoln 10·2 | 17 | Stevenage 7·8 |
| 18 | Kirkby 57 | 18 | Stevenage 9·3 | 18 | Lincoln 8·4 |
| 19 | Stevenage 55 | 19 | Swansea 7·7 | 19 | Gloucester 9·8 |

The figures in this table as in Tables 64, 65, 66 in Appendix IV are those obtained at the time of the survey in 1965. The source of the population figures was as follows: Bradford, Bristol, Camden, Darlington, Gloucester, Norwich, Swindon, Worcester, Registrar-General's mid-year estimates, 1965.

We have been notified of two changes of more than a minor character since the completion of the table: Gloucester's population, by the extension of its boundaries in 1967, has increased by some 20,000; Southwark's, which has declined continuously since the beginning of the century, has now fallen to 296,000. This of course affects favourably the ratios in columns 2 and 3. Also to be noted is an increase in 0·6 acres per 1,000 of public recreational space in Norwich.

great industrial centre, densely populated and poorly served with public recreational space; Southwark, embedded in the metropolis, the worst provided with recreational space and of exceptionally high density, and the London Borough of Brent, nearly 4,000 acres larger than Southwark (10,927 against 7,114), smaller in population by 17,000 persons, but with the second lowest amount of public recreational space. Southwark and Liverpool as with the majority of the review boroughs anticipate considerable increase in open space provision under their respective Development Plans (both have carried out detailed open space surveys) but in Brent 'there is likely to be little change in the overall amount of open space although there may be slight improvement in the areas of the borough after redevelopment'. 'Considerable extra provision', however, is envisaged for children's play facilities.[1]

Coventry, Bristol and Southampton, all with populations over 200,000 and highish densities—Coventry an industrial centre and the latter two cities great seaboard centres of commerce with some industry —fall midway between the best and worst provided with public recreational space. Gloucester, Lincoln and Worcester were found to be exceptionally well provided with recreational space as was Stevenage— four towns with populations under 80,000.

In general the picture was as one would have expected. The larger, mainly industrial cities and the metropolitan boroughs had high densities and a paucity of recreational open space; the small mainly commercial or marketing towns had lowish densities and a more generous allowance of recreational space. In between, the gradations followed a fairly predictable pattern. There were, however, some noticeable exceptions. Newcastle was one. Like Liverpool it is a port and an industrial centre; it has a population of 257,000 and a high density and yet it was found to be the fourth best provided with public recreational space. This was accounted for mainly by the 362-acre Town Moor which falls within the city boundaries. The third of the London Boroughs—Camden—which had the highest density of all the nineteen boroughs (a population of 245,707 crammed into an area of only 5,364 acres) was found to be fairly well off for recreational space because of Hampstead Heath and Regent's Park. Bradford, on the other hand, has a large population, covers an extensive acreage (25,525) but, as can be deduced from Table 50, recreational land has in the past been sacrificed to industrial demands. By 1971, however, an increase in recreational space of 572 acres (1·9 acres per 1,000 population) is scheduled under the current Development Plan.

1   Quoted from questionnaire.

A number of ideal open space[1] standards have been calculated and set. Examples from the nineteen boroughs, calculated on the basis of their particular needs and possibilities, range from Liverpool's three acres per 1,000 population to Swansea's 8·3 acres per 1,000 population. The 1943 County of London Plan envisaged seven acres per 1,000 population, three of which would be provided in the Green Belt. Though the 1951 Administrative County of London Plan, and its 1960 Review, lowered the effective standard for the Administrative County to two-and-a-half acres per 1,000 population, the National Playing Fields Association considers that at least six acres per 1,000 population should be provided for playing fields only.[2] The recommended standard for New Towns is ten acres of open space per 1,000 population.

Thus, even in ideal standards there is considerable variation though lack of common definition may be partially responsible for this. But from the survey it is apparent that there are everywhere attempts to resolve the conflicting pressures of more housing for the increasing population and more open space for its recreation. This is particularly true of the cities with nineteenth-century legacies of overcrowding and congestion.

## Children's play space in the nineteen boroughs

The nineteen local authorities varied considerably in their definition of children's play space. Some used only the qualification of equipment. Others included specified free play or kick-around areas. Others again recognised spaces which, although not specifically designated, had been appropriated by the children as their own.

To achieve a common basis, therefore, we defined a play space as one officially designated exclusively for children's play. This virtually ruled out the third of the above categories and because of this the picture presented excludes a lot of space frequently used by children. Difficulties in defining the sizes of the play areas also sometimes arose. Here again interpretations varied but the differences related more to the type of playground than to the particular local authority. Again, therefore, for the sake of a common basis an arbitrary definition was made. Where either the field workers or the local authority officers had doubts about the size of the play area the boundary was fixed at a ten-

1  It should be noted that although information on allotments, private open space, or school playing fields was sought from the nineteen boroughs, the analysis discussed in this section refers to public recreational spaces only.
2  See Appendix V.

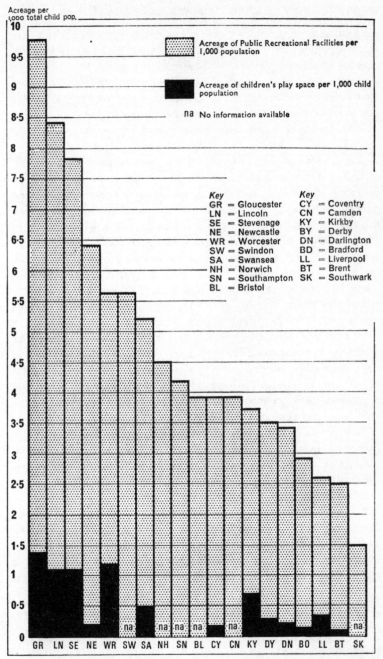

Acreage per
1,000 total child pop.

Acreage of Public Recreational Facilities per
1,000 population

Acreage of children's play space per 1,000 child
population

na No information available

Key
GR = Gloucester
LN = Lincoln
SE = Stevenage
NE = Newcastle
WR = Worcester
SW = Swindon
SA = Swansea
NH = Norwich
SN = Southampton
BL = Bristol

Key
CY = Coventry
CN = Camden
KY = Kirkby
BY = Derby
DN = Darlington
BD = Bradford
LL = Liverpool
BT = Brent
SK = Southwark

Figure 4.—Borough provision of public recreational space per 1,000
population and children's play space per 1,000 child population

yard radius from the outer pieces of equipment.[1] In most cases where the playground size had been calculated by a field worker this was checked by a Local Authority Officer but it is probable that there were inaccuracies on the part both of field workers and officials. Some sizes have been over-estimated and others under-estimated. Because of this the play space acreage should be regarded as approximate.

First, in Figure 4 children's space is related to general recreational space.[2]

It is unfortunate that at the time of the survey for six of the boroughs, including that with the highest density—Camden, and the one worst provided with public recreational space—Southwark, there was no play space acreage, available within the terms of our definition.[3] For the remaining thirteen boroughs it can be seen that, with exceptions, the best served with general recreational space—Gloucester, Lincoln, Stevenage, Worcester, Swansea—were also provided with more space for play. Newcastle and Liverpool have a great many play streets.[4] These have not been included in the acreage shown in Figure 4 but, where play streets were found within the review areas, their acreage has been included in the relevant analysis.[5]

Of those boroughs with less than four acres per 1,000 population of public recreational space Kirkby, a new development, was found to have the highest acreage of play space, 0·7 acres per 1,000 child population. This is interesting in view of its phenomenally high child population. Brent, a mixed suburban metropolitan borough, had the least, 0·1 acres per 1,000 child population.

Acreage on its own gives an incomplete picture of the amount of play space. Is the space concentrated in a few playgrounds or distributed throughout many? We attempted to discover the answer to this in a rudimentary fashion by relating the number of playgrounds to the number of children.[6]

Figure 5 shows that the four boroughs—Coventry, Darlington, Brent and Bradford—in which the play spaces considered as a whole had each to cater for 2,000 or more children, had also the smallest known total acreage per 1,000 children. Looking back to Figure 4 it can be seen that these four boroughs were also amongst the nine least

1  As in the Children and Playgrounds Survey. See Chapter 10.
2  Child populations of the boroughs may be found in Appendix IV.
3  This is available, however, for the review area analysis. See p. 217.
4  See p. Appendix I.
5  See pp. 217 and 218.
6  The total number of play spaces in each borough and the child population are given in Appendix IV.

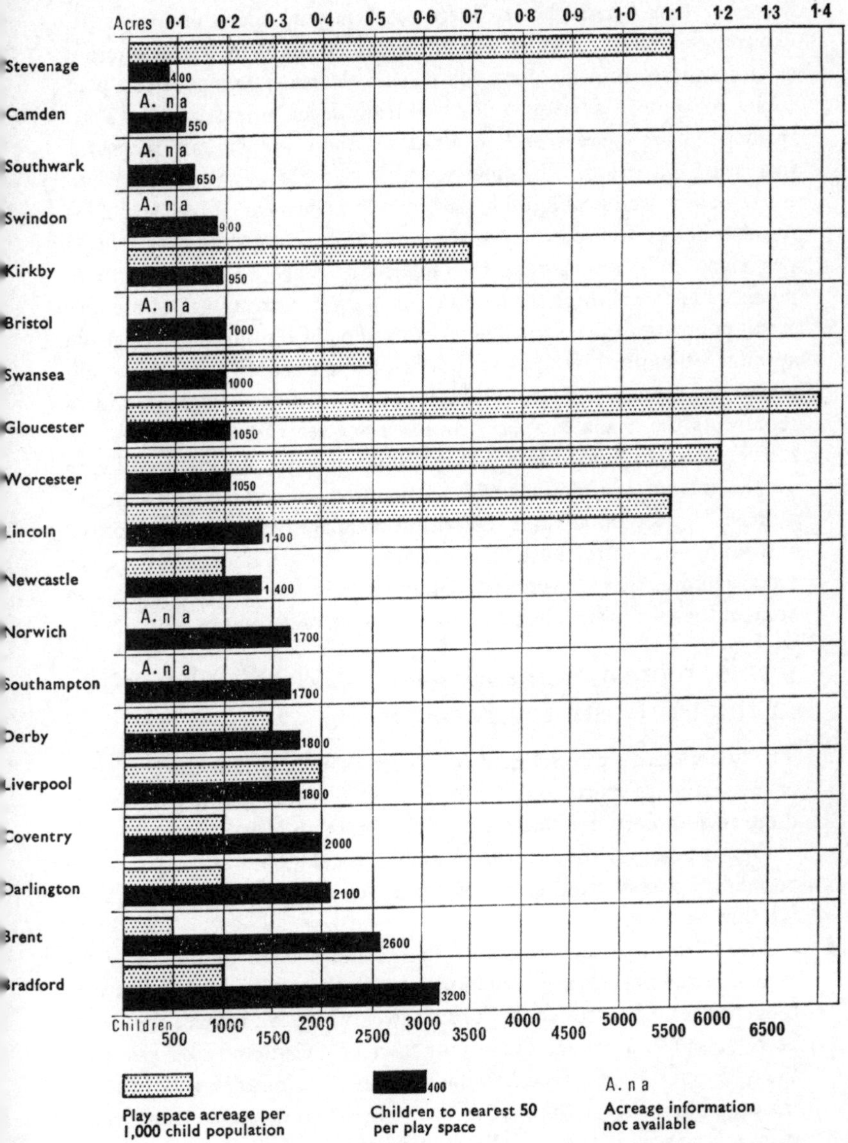

Figure 5.—Number of children per play space and play space average per 1,000 child population by borough.

215

well served with general recreational space. It has already been noted, however, that Brent plan to increase their play space provision. In Coventry children's play spaces are provided on all new Corporation estates and are insisted upon for private estates. Darlington too plan such provision in all new council housing development or redevelopment of twilight areas and in Bradford there are various plans for increasing provision. The new town in our survey, Stevenage, and Kirkby show well on Figure 5, particularly Stevenage with the smallest number of children per play space (392) and the third highest acreage per 1,000 child population, 1·1 acres. Stevenage was also found to possess the third highest amount of public recreational space per 1,000 population. Swansea was one of the eight boroughs which made specific although undesignated provision for children's free play and whose 0·5 acreage per 1,000 children, as shown on the diagram, under-represents the available space. Swansea has sea and a large extent of foreshore too, although this is not easily accessible for children living on the inland side of the town. Gloucester, Worcester and Lincoln, all below 77,000 population and within comparatively easy reach of the surrounding country, have substantial acreage of play space but over 1,000 children per playground. This suggests too few play spaces in spite of the comparatively generous allowance of acreage.

## Public recreational space and children's play space in the thirty-six review areas

Thirty-six areas[1] were selected for closer examination of the provision of recreational space and children's play space. We shall discuss these review areas irrespective of which borough they belong to.[2]

Figure 6 shows the acreage of public recreational space per 1,000 population and of children's play space per 1,000 child population for the thirty-six areas.

The thirteen review areas with five or more acres of public recreational space per 1,000 population include four (Gloucester, Lincoln, Stevenage and Worcester) of the six towns which were small enough to be reviewed as a whole. These four towns by virtue of their size have the advantage of easy access to the surrounding countryside. Of the remaining nine of these thirteen review areas seven belonged to boroughs of over 200,000 population (Brent, Bristol, Camden, Coventry, Liverpool, Newcastle, Southwark). Though some were more mixed than

1  See p. 206.
2  For reference they are listed in Appendix IV grouped by boroughs and showing their population figures, their acreage and overall density.

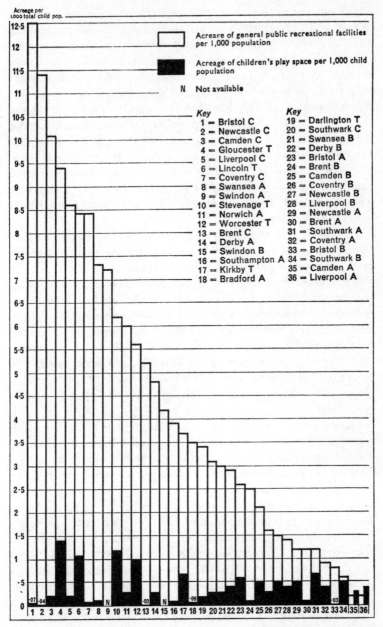

Figure 6.—Review area provision of public recreational space per 1,000 population and children's play space per 1,000 child population.

217

others and one or two had a little industry they were mostly of low density and predominantly suburban in character. Some contained the highest class residential districts in the city. Council estates tended to be post-war or inter-war and there was very little Victorian terrace housing. This type of housing was predictably more prevalent in the review areas with the least amount of public recreational space. The eleven review areas with less than two acres of public recreational space per 1,000 population all belonged to the large cities and London boroughs. But six of these cities and boroughs it will be remembered also had an area amongst those best served with recreational space. The good stretches of open space in Southwark's Dulwich and Peckham areas did not nevertheless qualify either of them for inclusion in the first thirteen review areas. (Bradford and Southampton were unfortunately only represented by one area.)

The majority of the eleven review areas worst served with public recreational space were scheduled for, or in the process of, redevelopment, with open space accorded high priority.

It is interesting to observe that the proportion of children's playing space to general recreational space tended to be higher in these eleven areas than in those which were better off for open space; in two cases the available play space per 1,000 children actually exceeded the amount of general recreational space per 1,000 total population. This contrasts noticeably with the picture for the boroughs as a whole revealed in Figure 4. This difference between the boroughs and the review areas is illustrated again by a comparison of Figure 5 with Figure 7 which is given below.

Discrepancies in provision between different parts of the city which appear in Figure 7 are evened out in the borough Figure 5. Moreover, it can be seen that the evening out covers up deficiencies rather than sufficiencies. In the borough analysis the greatest number of children per play space was just over 3,000 and in only three boroughs were there more than 2,000 children per play space. In the review areas, however, the greatest number of children per play space was nearly 6,000 and in twelve areas there were more than 2,000 children per play space. One Liverpool area, with an overall density of 90·6 (the highest of all the review areas) had attempted to alleviate the situation by providing play streets, and if these are taken into account the number of children per play space is reduced from 2,095 to 350. A similar dramatic reduction in numbers per play space by the use of play streets can be seen in a Newcastle area—where the figure 7,500 becomes 2,400 children per play space.

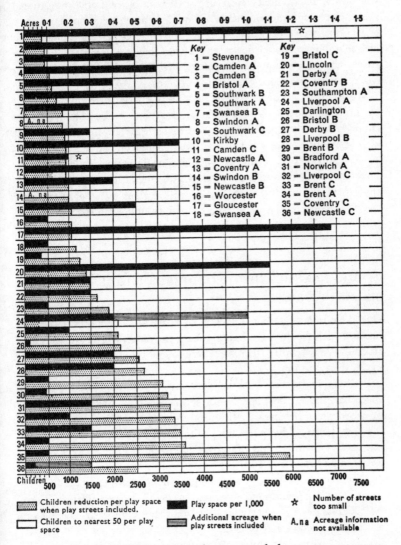

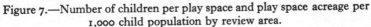

Figure 7.—Number of children per play space and play space acreage per 1,000 child population by review area.

Of the fourteen review areas with fewer than 1,000 children per play space, six were all poorly provided with other usable recreational space. Stevenage and one of the Camden areas on the other hand were exceptionally well provided with over eleven acres per 1,000 population of general recreational space and fewer than 500 children per play space. Stevenage had the advantage also of the second highest play space acreage per 1,000 children—1·1 acres.

We have already seen how the picture of space provision is changed by breaking down the boroughs into review areas. The distances children travel to play[1] relate more realistically to our smallest unit of investigation—the ward. An analysis[2] based on the 198 wards surveyed confirmed the suspected widening of discrepancies in provision. Fourteen wards comprising a total of 25,000 children, had neither play space nor general recreational space within their own boundaries. Of these fourteen, nine were in high-density neighbourhoods and situated within review areas which were generally ill-provided with public recreational space.

## Sports facilities in the boroughs and in the thirty-six review areas

Our definition of public recreational space included sports facilities because such facilities are important for the older half of the age group studied. We attempted, therefore, very roughly to assess them separately in the thirty-six areas.[3]

Predictably the areas least well served with general public recreational space had the smallest number of sports facilities. Outstandingly well provided were Swansea (both areas), Worcester, Gloucester, Kirkby, the low-density Liverpool area, with Derby (both areas), Lincoln, one area of Swindon and Stevenage following behind. Only six review areas, to be found in Coventry, Brent, Southwark, Stevenage, Swansea and Camden, reported any specific provision for athletics.

Facilites for swimming, covered in detail by the British Travel Association Report[4] were considered on a borough basis—taking into account the actual and potential opportunities afforded by schools.

In the analysis of children's preferences,[5] swimming figures pro-

---

1 See Chapter 10.
2 Not shown.
3 Borough acreage of sports provision can be found in Appendix IV, as can also an analysis of the type of provision by review area.
4 British Travel Association (1967).
5 See Appendix II.

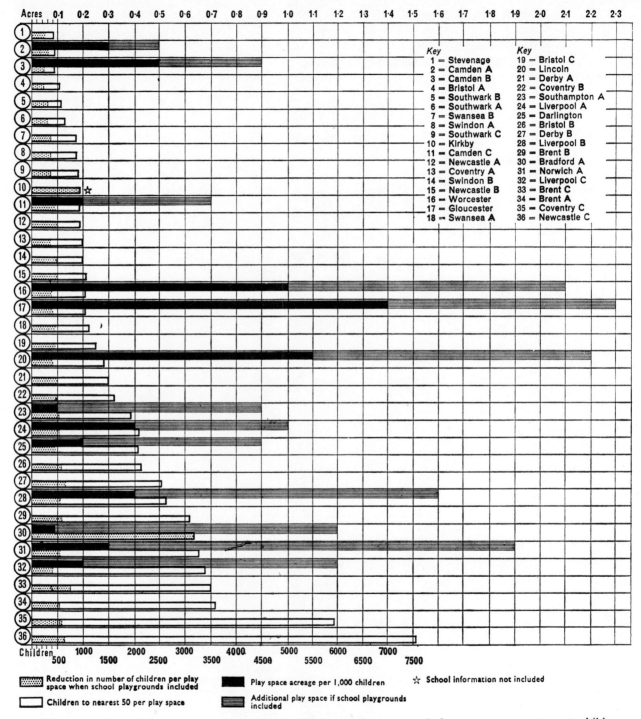

Figure 8.—School playgrounds and number of children per play space and play space acreage per 1,000 child population by review area.

minently as a popular activity. There was a marked lack of opportunity to indulge this preference in the nineteen boroughs. Most were badly provided with public baths though in a few instances, notably Southampton and Bradford, this was somewhat counteracted by better than average school provision. Swansea, Darlington, Brent and Swindon had more than 8,000 children per swimming bath (public and school). In the great majority of cases, the proportion of schools with swimming baths was less than 10 per cent. Where school baths existed, however, they were mostly used fully—out of as well as during school hours.

## School provision for out-of-school activities

In view of the possible use of schools as centres of indoor and outdoor play out of school hours, we established the number of maintained schools in each of the review areas and considered these in relation to the number of public play spaces. It happens frequently that two, sometimes three schools share the same playground on the same site. For Figure 8 the number of school sites rather than of schools has been counted so that the given numbers are, if anything, an underestimate. The Plowden Committee made the point that primary schools were more suitable for dual use than secondary. In all the review areas (except one in Newcastle where the numbers were even) the primary schools far outnumbered the secondary schools, so that even if we had restricted the numbers to primary schools only, the picture revealed in Figure 8 would not have been appreciably altered. Where possible, the acreage of the school's surrounding open space was also established. This proved difficult. In some instances the information was not available; in others only partially; some combined playing fields and playgrounds, whilst in others we were given acreages which included the school buildings. Nevertheless, we feel it is worth giving what figures we have—see Figure 8—to show how school playgrounds could affect the total acreage of available play space per 1,000 children as well as the numbers of children per play space.

The above diagram suggests that play acreage per 1,000 children could be enormously increased and numbers of children per playground drastically reduced if school playgrounds were used to their full extent. We realise that the above presents a crude picture. Much is left out of account; the school's suitability for dual use, for instance, and the quality of the service provided. Nevertheless, in terms of usable space and catchment area the picture cannot be ignored. The existing safety precautions surrounding school buildings—guarded crossings, parking restrictions and so on—are another advantage.

All the boroughs let some school premises for use by children out of school hours, usually to organisations such as scouts, guides, cubs and various recognised clubs. But play use in the sense indicated above was to be found in only four boroughs—the two London boroughs of Camden and Southwark, Newcastle and Liverpool.

These school play centres[1] were all to be found in areas with poor provision either of public recreational, or of playground, space or of both and were honourable examples[2] of an attempt to compensate for the lack of such provision.

# Club and library provision

We took only a cursory look at indoor provision for children's leisure activities, such as clubs and libraries, since this survey was primarily concerned with play space.

## Clubs and National Uniformed Organisations

Only six of the nineteen boroughs—Bradford, Brent, Bristol, Derby, Gloucester, Lincoln—supplied a limited amount of information on clubs. The pattern of provision was fairly consistent—fewer mixed groups than those for boys or for girls only, the vast majority meeting in the evening for only one day a week all the year round. There was evidence that in some of the boroughs the Youth Service was extending its service into the under-fourteen age group or into the community as a whole. In Brent, for instance, Community Associations are part of the Borough Education Service.

## Libraries

Again, for libraries our examination of the position was a superficial one. Our aim was simply to get an overall picture of provision in the boroughs. There was considerable variation. Fifteen boroughs returned information and of these the best provided had as many as nine libraries serving a 25,000 child population (2·6 thousand children per library), fourteen libraries for 39,000 children (2·8 thousand children per library), and the worst, six libraries for 70,000 children (11·8 thousand

---

1  See Appendix I.
2  In Camden and Southwark the school centres are administered by a different authority, the Inner London Education Authority, from provision in parks.

children per library). The population size of the borough appeared to have little relevance to the number per thousand children of libraries provided; some of the worst provided boroughs were the smallest both in population size and area.

## Provision for the under fives

The play needs of pre-school children are bound to differ from those of older children. Their patterns of play are special to their particular stage of development (differing within the one- to five-year period as well as between their own and older age groups); their dependence on adults, particularly on their mothers, is much greater than that of older children. This survey is particularly concerned with space and in the following chapter we shall see how much and what kind of space in the nineteen boroughs is allocated to the under fives. We were, however, interested to discover the extent of day care provision generally. Six of the nineteen boroughs were entirely without local authority day nurseries. In some cases this was a matter of deliberate policy—the old fallacy that by not providing day nurseries mothers are discouraged from going to work.[1] Looking at the thirty-six review areas, fifteen were without local authority day nurseries at all. Of the remaining twenty-one, eleven had one local authority day nursery, seven had two, two had three and one had four. Ryan, in his study of day nursery provision, analyses the situation by number of *places* per 1,000 child population under five. We used the same, somewhat cruder principle that we used for play spaces and considered the provision in terms of the number of under fives per day nursery. At worst this meant one day nursery per 7,957 children and at best one day nursery per 1,460 children. Of the fifteen review areas with no provision the highest under-fives population was 6,544 and eleven had 0–5 populations of over 4,700.

Only five of these same fifteen review areas recorded full-time private day nursery provision, and eight of the twenty-one areas with local authority nurseries also had full-time private provision.

Information was requested on play groups but this proved difficult in view of the prevalent confusion in nomenclature. Most play groups are registered with the local authority as private nurseries, as are private nursery schools—so that it was impossible from our comparatively simple questionnaire to classify exactly these three categories. Twenty-eight areas had some forms of private play group or part-time nursery

1 Ryan (1964).

provision, which is evidence of the attempt of the private sector to meet the growing demand for such provision. There were even fewer nursery schools run by the local authorities than there were day nurseries, only seventeen review areas possessing any. Twenty-three areas provided nursery classes.

## Summary

At the present time it is largely a matter of luck for a child living in one of the nineteen boroughs studied whether he is brought up within easy reach of good places for play. His chances are increased on the whole if he lives in one of the smaller towns for they are more likely to have extensive areas of general recreational space and to have reasonably quick access to surrounding countryside. There were no marked regional differences.

General public recreational space is of vital importance for children but it carries inevitable restrictions of use and should only complement space designed especially for children. Is there more of this special space in small towns than in large? In general, the answer appears to be yes in terms of acreage but because there tend to be fewer playgrounds per 1,000 children they may have to go further to get to it than in some of the larger cities.

There are parts of most of the big boroughs where there is a liberal allowance of general recreational space, in three instances, exceptionally so—more than 10 acres per 1,000 population. But in those areas designated play space is in short supply both in acreage and numbers of spaces. A dearth of special playing space is also to be found in several areas where the general recreational space is minimal. Here, several thousand children can be said to be seriously deprived of opportunities for play. These are twilight neighbourhoods for the most part, scheduled for redevelopment with play space provision included in the plans, but development plans can take a long time to materialise. In a few instances there is marked compensation for lack of general recreational space by a more than usually generous play space provision, though sometimes this is only in the form of play streets.

The older children in most of the boroughs can find little outlet in organised games. There are, with one or two exceptions, strikingly few facilities for sport and swimming. The under fives are as ill-provided with facilities for their care as one would expect from recent disclosures.[1] Only four boroughs are making any attempt to utilise fully school space out of school hours.

1  See Yudkin (1968).

# 12

# The 467 Playgrounds

This chapter presents an analysis of playground characteristics—situation, size, design, equipment, supervision—based on the total number (467) of playgrounds investigated within the nineteen boroughs.

## The situation of the playgrounds

Table 51 shows where the 467 playgrounds were situated and whether or not they had any form of equipment.

TABLE 51

*Equipped and unequipped playgrounds according to situation[1]*

| | Playgrounds situated in: | | | | | | | |
|---|---|---|---|---|---|---|---|---|
| Type of | Parks, etc. | | H'sing estates | | Other | | Total | |
| | No. | % | No. | % | No. | % | No. | % |
| Equipped | 171 | 95 | 179 | 70 | 34 | 100 | 384 | 82 |
| Unequipped | 9 | 5 | 74 | 30 | — | — | 83 | 18 |
| Total | 180 | 100 | 253 | 100 | 34 | 100 | 467 | 100 |

The majority of the playgrounds were to be found on housing estates. Two problems in classification arose for this category; first, defining a housing estate and second, deciding whether a playground was in fact part of the housing estate. Thirty-eight of Stevenage's forty-eight playgrounds, for example, have been classed as housing

1 Two further tables in Appendix IV give a breakdown of the first ('Parks, etc.) and third ('Other') categories.

estate playgrounds. This is correct if one regards a New Town as a collection of housing estates but as such it differs from estates commonly found in the redevelopment areas of boroughs such as Liverpool or Southwark.[1]

The fact that more playgrounds were to be found on housing estates than within the other two categories is in part a reflection of the amount of post-war building in the areas under review (playgrounds on pre-war housing estates were exceedingly rare), but it must also be pointed out that the number would have been even greater had space for play been incorporated into all the new estates. Four-fifths of the housing estate playgrounds were to be found in only fifteen of the thirty-six review areas and these in turn belonged to fewer than half the boroughs (nine). This can be partially explained by the non-existence of new housing development in certain of the remaining twenty-one review areas but there were, within these areas, many example of new estates without playgrounds as there were also in the better provided areas.

Several field workers mentioned the attractiveness of playgrounds situated in parks and on commons and referred to the obvious intention that space outside the playground should be used for play. In Lincoln, one playground 'had been sunk below the level of the park, being thus separated from it by grassy slopes'. Roughly 50 per cent of all the public recreational facilities in the thirty-six review areas had provision of some kind specifically designed for children. This proportion would not appear to reflect the demand for special children's space within larger recreational areas suggested by the results of the Playgrounds and Children Survey.[2]

Only 7 per cent of the 467 playgrounds were sited in places other than public recreational space or housing estates.

## The size of the playgrounds

In Table 52 the acreage for playgrounds in parks and similar open spaces could have been a higher figure if the 'playing areas' surrounding a number of playgrounds had been taken into account. But counteracting this is the fact that, in spite of emphasis on our rigid definition, these surrounding areas have undoubtedly been included in some play space sizes.

---

1 It can be strongly argued that playgrounds within municipal housing estates should be classified as private but for this survey it was agreed that the distinction would be too difficult to maintain.
2 See Chapter 10.

TABLE 52
*Size range of all playgrounds*[1]

| Size range (in square yards) | Playgrounds situated in: Parks, etc | H'sing estates | Other | Total |
|---|---|---|---|---|
| | % | % | % | % |
| Under 484 | 17 | 31 | 15 | 25 |
| 484–1,210 | 32 | 28 | 29 | 30 |
| 1,210–3,630 | 32 | 24 | 41 | 28 |
| 3,630–7,260 | 12 | 12 | 12 | 12 |
| Over 7,260 | 7 | 5 | 3 | 5 |
| | 100 | 100 | 100 | 100 |
| Total number of playgrounds | (170) | (236) | (34) | (440) |

On housing estates 31 per cent of the playgrounds fell into the smallest size range—under a tenth of an acre—and 28 per cent into the next largest. Thus over half of all the housing estate playgrounds were under a quarter of an acre. It should be pointed out, however, that more than one playground was provided on at least twenty-two of the housing estates surveyed. Where there was multiple provision it was on the basis of either different age groups or of the type of activity provided but sometimes, apparently, for purely architectural or aesthetic reasons. Of the seventy-four playgrounds in the smallest size group a quarter were under 165 square yards which is roughly the size of half a tennis court. Most of these had one or two pieces of fixed equipment, usually for the younger age groups. For playgrounds situated elsewhere—in parks, recreation grounds, bomb sites and so on—the middle size range—less than three-quarters of an acre—predominated.

There was a marked falling off in the number of playgrounds within the larger size ranges irrespective of where they were located. Twelve per cent of all the playgrounds were between three-quarters of an acre and one and a half acres and only 5 per cent were over one and a half acres.[2] (A football pitch is only a little over one and a half acres in size.)

## Physical characteristics of the playgrounds surfaces

Table 53 shows the surfaces in the 467 playgrounds under review.

1 The twenty-seven playgrounds in Swindon are excluded as sizes were not available.
2 These figures should be considered in relation to the findings on size in the Children and Playgrounds Survey, Chapter 10.

TABLE 53
*Playground surfaces*

| Surface | Playgrounds situated in: | | | Total |
|---|---|---|---|---|
| | Parks, etc | H'sing estates | Other | |
| | % | % | % | % |
| Hard | 29 | 43 | 41 | 38 |
| Grass | 12 | 25 | 9 | 20 |
| Others | 1 | 1 | 6 | 1 |
| Mixed | 58 | 31 | 44 | 41 |
| | 100 | 100 | 100 | 100 |
| Total number of playgrounds | (180) | (253) | (34) | (467) |

The position here shown is slightly better than might have been expected. Forty-one per cent of the 467 playgrounds had mixed surfaces and 20 per cent had grass only. Over a third, however, were exclusively hard-surfaced—mostly the familiar asphalt. In a few cases the surface was difficult to classify for, whatever it may have started as, it had deteriorated into a mass of rubble, usually strewn with broken glass and bits of old iron. In adventure playgrounds a piece of ground is deliberately left in its natural state to allow for digging and the kind of activity that goes with 'natural' surroundings. But of these there were only three in our survey. As many as 75 per cent of the exclusively hard-surfaced playgrounds and 26 per cent of the grassed spaces had equipment. Almost all these were situated in housing estates. Grass alone, apart from the problem of its over-use, has weather limitations—frost and wet make it unsatisfactory, particularly for the younger child. Thirteen per cent of all the playgrounds were paved, either wholly or in part. Cobbles and cinders were two other surfaces mentioned (only twice in each case) and for a playground on Swansea's foreshore children were lucky enough to have the entire surface covered with sand.

## Design features of the playgrounds

Table 54 summarises the design features to be found in the 467 playgrounds.

Thirty-eight per cent of all the playgrounds had not been 'designed' at all. They had just been built and, in most cases, conventionally equipped. A further 22 per cent were redeemed by some form of planting which has, as already pointed out, the additional advantage of

TABLE 54
*Design features*

| Features | Parks | H'sing estates | Other | Total |
|---|---|---|---|---|
| *Playgrounds situated in:* | | | | |
| | % | % | % | % |
| Trees/planting | 31 | 17 | 12 | 22 |
| Slopes/shaping | 4 | 12 | 3 | 8 |
| Wall | 2 | 10 | 3 | 7 |
| Combination | 34 | 16 | 41 | 25 |
| Nil | 29 | 45 | 41 | 38 |
| | 100 | 100 | 100 | 100 |
| Total number of playgrounds | (180) | (253) | (34) | (467) |

acting as a sound barrier. Fewer than a quarter of the 467 playgrounds under review had any form of slope, either artificial or natural. Only sixty playgrounds had a wall which could be used as a 'prop' for play.

The following field workers' comments aptly describe the two extremes in playground design to be found in our survey: 'a most imaginatively laid out area for small children, at different levels, separated by wood fencing partly and partly by walls, with many different kinds of architectural features. The secretary of the tenants' association said this was very much used and appreciated'; 'just the usual grim square'. There were a number of field workers' reports of the bad conditions of the playgrounds—broken equipment, dirt and litter.

## Hygiene in the playgrounds

How good was the provision of w.c.s and washbasins on the 467 playgrounds?

Just under half the playgrounds shown in Table 55, which excludes all unequipped playgrounds and all playgrounds on housing estates, had w.c.s. If allowance is made for the twenty-three playgrounds within easy reach of alternative lavatory facilities, which is reasonable, then the figure can be raised to just over half, 56 per cent. By any standards this is shocking but when two further factors are taken into account, the position worsens.

First, only forty-one of the ninety-three playgrounds with w.c.s had washbasins. Thus, 44 per cent of all equipped playgrounds (other than those on housing estates) had no w.c.s and no means of reaching one easily, and of those with w.c.s 66 per cent were without washbasins.

TABLE 55

*W.C. provision in equipped playgrounds excluding those on housing estates*

| Provision | Playgrounds situated in: | | | | | |
| | Parks | | Other | | Total | |
| | % | % | % | % | % | % |
| With w.c.s and washbasins | 21 ⎫ | | 15 ⎫ | | 20 ⎫ | |
| | | 47 | | 35 | | 45 |
| W.c.s and *no* washbasins | 26 ⎭ | | 20 ⎭ | | 25 ⎭ | |
| None | 40 ⎫ | | 62 ⎫ | | 44 ⎫ | |
| | | 53 | | 65 | | 55 |
| None but some within easy reach[1] | 13 ⎭ | | 3 ⎭ | | 11 ⎭ | |
| | 100 | 100 | 100 | 100 | 100 | 100 |
| Total number of playgrounds | (171) | (171) | (34) | (34) | (205) | (205) |

The second factor aggravating the position was the condition of some of the w.c.s on the playgrounds surveyed. 'The toilets were in a filthy condition. One was inoperative. No paper was supplied.' 'Toilets in a fouled condition.' These two comments, quoted from the field workers' questionnaires, typified many.

It was not surprising to find that unequipped playgrounds were with three exceptions without w.c.s. Housing estate playgrounds do not appear in Table 55 either because they too with three exceptions had no lavatory facilities as an integral part of the playground. The three exceptions were all playgrounds with play leaders.

On some of the larger estates surveyed w.c.s were provided for general use at ground level but it was unusual for these to be sited with any obvious relevance to the position of the playground. Even where they had been so sited they had frequently either been damaged or were found to be locked. On some estates, such as in Stevenage, the play spaces were situated so that children could easily get to their homes when necessary, but these were the exceptions.

## The range of activities on the playgrounds

What were children able to do on these 467 playgrounds? Was there

1 I.e. not further than 50 yards away with no roads to cross.

equipment and what kind was it? Were they inhibited from running about either by the danger of unguarded moving equipment or by restrictions resulting from playground size or arising from rules and regulations? Were they allowed to kick a ball about? Was there someone present to guide and stimulate their play or merely someone to watch over the equipment or bandage a scraped knee? Or was there no adult in charge at all? What were the hours of opening and might children of any age use the playground? Was there anywhere for them to play indoors?

## The broad picture

In the first table (56) we have made a threefold division to give a broad picture of the activity range on all the playgrounds and have added two further types of provision.

A brief word is necessary about the definitions. Under 'fixed' equipment we have included anything—swings, slides, play sculpture, climbing frames, 'forts'—which were a permanent, fixed feature of the playground. Later, we shall consider this category in greater detail.

'Ball games' defines an area which was large and empty enough for the playing of spontaneous ball games. A marked out pitch on a sports ground intended for use by clubs did not qualify.

'Free play' for this survey of facilities has been limited to cover the running about games, roller skating, playing catch, etc., in other words, general freedom to move.

'Additional activities' refers to those playgrounds which provided facilities dependent on the presence of a play leader.

'Indoor provision' in this table covers only accommodation large enough and suitable for children to play in during bad weather.

A most important aspect of children's play, it will be noticed, has not been included in these definitions, namely the various forms of 'inactive play'—sitting, standing, watching others, lying down, talking and those imaginative and fantasy games which are carried on with the minimum of physical activity. These together occupied the children of Vere Hole's survey for a considerably greater time than any single more energetic activity.[1] Inactive play is not necessarily dependent on special space and equipment and for this survey which was concerned with *facilities* it was not practicable to include it as a specific area of activity within the playground. This does not mean that the importance of

1   Hole (1966), pp. 21-4.

quiet corners, somewhere to sit and chat or play houses, should not be seriously taken into account in playground design.

The first thing one may observe from Table 56 is the minute proportion of the 467 playgrounds in which there were opportunities for play other than those provided either by conventional equipment or by

TABLE 56
*Activity range in all playgrounds*

| Type of facility | Playgrounds situated in: | | | |
| | Parks, etc. | Housing estates | Other | Total |
|---|---|---|---|---|
| | % | % | % | % |
| Fixed equipment only | 13 | 14 | 26 | 15 |
| Fixed equipment and/or ball games and free play | 82 | 57 | 74 | 68 |
| Ball games and/or free play | 5 | 29 | — | 17 |
| | 100 | 100 | 100 | 100 |
| Total | (180) | (253) | (34) | (467) |
| | No. | No. | No. | % |
| Additional activities | (7) | (3) | (4) | 3 |
| | | | | (14) |
| Indoor provision for play | (4) | (2) | (4) | 2 |
| | | | | (10) |

unequipped spaces: fourteen out of the 467 (3 per cent) catered for additional activities and in only ten (2 per cent) could children play indoors.

By far the largest number of playgrounds, 68 per cent, gave scope for more than one of the three major groups of activity, the most (175) combining two—fixed equipment and free play: 122 playgrounds catered for ball games as well as the other two groups.[1] But in a few instances the field workers had apparently interpreted the requirements for a ball-games area a little generously. Separate comparison of the activity range with the size range of the playgrounds has shown some of these mixed-activity playgrounds to be too small to accommodate the variety for which they were supposed to cater. Against this, however, it must be said that for the playgrounds situated within general recreational open space considerably more space must be reckoned for free play and to a lesser extent for ball games than is shown in the above figures. Swansea was a case in point. Twenty-two out of their thirty-five equipped playgrounds were surrounded by grass areas on

1  Taken from untabulated material.

which the children were free to play. But, according to our definition, the acreage of these areas could not strictly be counted as exclusive children's space. Free play for children living on housing estates is also certainly not confined to the official play spaces.

It will be noticed that most of the unequipped play spaces were to be found on housing estates. Some were fenced off ball-games areas, some were little spaces intended for toddlers. Fifty-six per cent of these were less than a quarter of an acre in size. It is also perhaps of interest that these unequipped estate spaces were to be found in the review areas of only nine of the boroughs. Of these Camden, Southwark and Stevenage contained the great majority.

Seventy per cent of all mixed-activity playgrounds had no form of division between the various activity areas. Of those mixed-activity playgrounds which included fixed equipment, 68 per cent were without artificial or natural barriers. Of those playgrounds which had divisions, metal or wood fencing was used on far the greater number. Six had a wall; different levels functioned as a division on five; on four there was some form of planting and on twenty-seven there was a combination of one or more of these methods.

Looking back for a moment to the surfacing of the playgrounds an analysis has shown that two-thirds of the sixty playgrounds which catered exclusively for play with fixed equipment were hard-surfaced and a third of the mixed-activity playgrounds had no corresponding mixture of surfaces.

## Kinds of equipment

Since, in Table 56, the term 'fixed equipment' covers everything from traditional, old-fashioned items to the concrete toadstools so dearly loved by housing estate architects, it is necessary to break down this general classification.

In Table 57 therefore the term 'traditional' refers to those pieces of equipment whose origins can be traced to pre-war days and their post-war variations—swings, slides, roundabouts, maypoles, ocean waves, see-saws, etc. Also included under this heading are sand pits and paddling pools, but these will be discussed separately later on. 'Gymnastic' speaks for itself—climbing frames, parallel bars and the like. 'Architectural, improvised and special' includes such items as pieces of play sculpture, concrete pipes, tree trunks, old cars and constructions. In the fifth category, 'Additional', we find pieces of mobile equipment such as bicycles, stilts and building blocks, painting

233

and modelling materials; hammers and nails and bits of junk; dressing-up clothes and 'quiet' games—chess, ludo, etc.

## TABLE 57
### *Types of equipment*

| Types of equipment for permanent use | Playgrounds situated in: | | | |
| --- | --- | --- | --- | --- |
| | Parks, etc. | Housing estates | Other | Total |
| | % | % | % | % |
| Traditional only | 77 | 47 | 59 | 61 |
| Gymnastic only | — | 2 | — | 1 |
| Architectural, improvised, special only | — | 10 | 6 | 5 |
| Combination | 23 | 41 | 35 | 33 |
| | 100 | 100 | 100 | 100 |
| Total number of playgrounds | (171) | (179) | (34) | (384) |
| | No. | No. | No. | No. |
| Additional | (7) | (3) | (4) | (14) |

It can be seen that the vast majority of the 384 playgrounds were traditionally equipped, either exclusively so—61 per cent—or in combination with other items. Most of the items of equipment appeared to be 'straight from the catalogue'. Tubular steel is gradually replacing iron, and plastic instead of wooden seats can now sometimes be found on swings.

Table 57 also shows what a small proportion, fourteen out of 384, of the playgrounds were furnished with any form of mobile equipment or material for constructive play, indoor or outdoor. Building blocks are a perennial source of pleasure to children—no Stockholm play park is without them. In only a handful of the playgrounds surveyed were they recorded as an item of equipment.

## Sand and water

In Table 58 we show how many of the 384 equipped playgrounds possessed provision for sand and water play.

Eighty-seven per cent of all the equipped playgrounds were without the two features considered by the experts and known by many parents to be of especial importance in the development of the young child and to give immense pleasure. One in ten playgrounds had sand; one in

TABLE 58

*Sand and water provision in equipped playgrounds*

| Provision | Playgrounds situated in: | | | |
| --- | --- | --- | --- | --- |
| | Parks, etc. | Housing estates | Other | Total |
| | % | % | % | % |
| Sand only | 6 | 6 | 6 | 6 |
| Water only (paddling pool, tap for play use or both) | 5 | 1 | 6 | 3 |
| Sand and water | 6 | 1 | 9 | 4 |
| Nil | 83 | 92 | 79 | 87 |
| | 100 | 100 | 100 | 100 |
| Total number of playgrounds | (171) | (179) | (34) | (384) |

fourteen provided some kind of water for play; one in twenty-seven had both. The picture worsens when the emptiness and conditions of some pits and pools is taken into account (seasonal emptiness of paddling pools has been disregarded). The filling-in of sand pits as a result of misuse is common and was found to have occurred several times in this survey.

## Provision for the under fives

The question of sand and water leads naturally to the provision of play facilities generally for the under fives. Since this survey was concerned with *space* for play rather than with care as a social or as an educational service play groups do not figure in the following table unless they are on a permament, full-time basis with designated outdoor space. Unless there was a notice specifying ages or a play leader present who could inform the field worker, the criterion for judging whether or not a playground, or part of a playground was intended for use by pre-school children was the type of equipment to be found there. Some housing estates were provided with very small, unequipped spaces which could have been intended for infants but which might also have been used by older children for playing marbles or for sitting and talking. Similarly some types of non-mobile equipment such as a piece of play sculpture could have been happily climbed over by eight- or nine-year-olds. Where there was any doubt, therefore, these playgrounds have not been included in Table 59.

As shown in Table 59, out of a total of 384 playgrounds only 193 had any special features for infants.

TABLE 59

*Proportion of equipped playgrounds containing specific provision for under fives*

| Provision for under-fives | Playgrounds situated in: | | | |
| --- | --- | --- | --- | --- |
| | Parks, etc. | Housing estates | Other | Total |
| | % | % | % | % |
| With supervision | 17 | 3 | 23 | 11 |
| Without supervision | 40 | 40 | 30 | 40 |
| *No* provision for under fives | 43 | 57 | 47 | 49 |
| | 100 | 100 | 100 | 100 |
| Total number of playgrounds | (171) | (179) | (34) | (384) |

The 'specific' in the table's heading amounted to little more than chair swings. There were the odd few little spaces, chiefly on housing estates, adorned with a piece of miniature play sculpture or with a collection of architecturally designed items such as stepping stones or little logs. Twenty per cent of 198 playgrounds with provision for under fives had sand, and 15 per cent had some kind of water. Seats for accompanying mothers were fairly plentiful, although too often uncomfortable. An afternoon spent on a backless bench after a hard morning's housework is hardly relaxing.

Following the general pattern a negligible proportion of these playgrounds for under fives had play leaders and the equipment associated with play leadership.

## Supervision

### The total picture

Table 60 gives the total picture of supervision on the 384 equipped playgrounds.

In the questionnaire there were three separate categories for 'unattended', 'keepers/gardeners' and 'caretakers'. There were obvious ambiguities in the completion of these categories. In some boroughs, for instance, housing estate playgrounds were listed as 'unattended' whilst in others they were said to be supervised by caretakers.

For the majority of playgrounds without permanent supervision it would be true to say that some form of intermittent overlooking occurs. One category—'casual supervision or unattended'—therefore has been formed out of the three.

The distinction between attendant and play leader must be emphasised.

TABLE 60

*Supervision of equipped playgrounds*

| Supervision | Playgrounds situated in: | | | Total |
| | Parks, etc. | Housing estates | Other | |
|---|---|---|---|---|
| | % | % | % | % |
| Permanent | | | | |
| F.t. play leader | 1 | 1 | 11 | 2 |
| P.t. play leader | 1 | | | |
| F.t. attendant | 18 | 2 | 9 | 10 |
| Casual supervision or unattended | 80 | 97 | 80 | 88 |
| | 100 | 100 | 100 | 100 |
| Total number of playgrounds | (171) | (179) | (34) | (384) |
| | No. | No. | No. | No. |
| Temporary, part-time play leaders | (6) | (1) | (3) | (10) |

The play leader's primary concern is with the children; the attendant's with the playground. Only 2 per cent of the 384 playgrounds were supervised by play leaders. A further 10 per cent had full-time attendants. Thus, for roughly only an eighth of the total number of playgrounds was there someone whose duties kept him on the playground for all the time it was open. The rest, nearly nine out of every ten playgrounds, were without the benefit of such a person. This meant at best the occasional but regular 'eye' of a park ranger or a caretaker; at worst, a total lack of official adult interest and concern.

## Play-leadership schemes

We shall now examine in greater detail those facilities for which some form of trained or experienced supervision is used and fourteen of which have already appeared under the heading 'Additional Activities' on Table 56.

It will be seen from Table 61 that the five main types of play-leadership schemes—adventure playgrounds; play parks and play centres; community play centres; organised games; school play centres were to be found in our survey, though not necessarily in sharply definable categories. The numbers are greater than those that appear under the heading 'Additional Activities' in Table 56 owing to the inclusion of schemes organised on sites other than playgrounds and of school play centres.

TABLE 61

*Number of play-leadership schemes*

| Type of facility | Schemes located in: | | | | |
| | Parks | Housing estates | Schools | Other | Total |
| | No. | No. | No. | No. | No. |
| Permanent, full-time schemes | | | | | |
|     Play centres | — | 2[1] | — | 2 | 4 |
|     Play centres with adventure facilities | 1 | — | — | 2 | 3 |
| Holiday and/or part-time term-time schemes | | | | — | — |
|     Play centres | 2 | 1 | | | 3 |
|     Play centres with adventure facilities | 1 | — | — | — | 1 |
|     Play parks and One o'clock clubs | 3 | — | — | — | 3 |
|     Organised games | 4 | — | — | 3 | 7 |
|     School-based facilities | — | — | 43 | — | 43 |
| Total | 11 | 3 | 43 | 7 | 64 |

It is necessary here to draw attention to the problem of defining full-time and part-time in discussing play-leadership schemes. In its fullest sense full-time implies that a facility is open every day of the year from the morning to the evening. This is the ideal and to our knowledge at the time of writing only occurs in the Camden community play centres. It is reasonable also to include those schemes which have one day a week closing or which have a limited, or even no evening attendance. There are a number of permanent schemes which only open at midday or at 4 p.m. during term time and these have been counted as part-time. The seasonal and holiday schemes have also been counted as part-time.

The seven play centres and two of the play parks had indoor play facilities although the huts belonging to two of them had been burnt down by vandals. Three of the holiday schemes had storage provision of their own on site, the others having to make do with nearby storage facilities. The permanent centres and play parks had full-time leaders in charge for the respective periods of opening, the larger ones having both full-time and part-time help. A similar pattern on a part-time basis was evident for the holiday schemes.

1   One for under fives only.

Only four—three full-time and one part-time—catered for the full range of 'adventure activities': lighting fires, making things out of old bits of junk and scrap, digging, making a thorough mess both of themselves and of a part of the playground.

One of the play centres which had the greatest variety of equipment was furnished with an elaborate road system complete with traffic lights, zebra crossing, go-carts, bicycles and tricycles. Some of the play-leader playgrounds were more slanted to the arts and crafts than others, one even possessing a pottery wheel and kiln. In most the under fives were catered for with special care. In none of these playgrounds at the time of the survey were there any pets.[1]

All the facilities of Table 61 were to be found in twelve of the thirty-five review areas: the three areas each of Southwark, Camden and Liverpool; two areas of Newcastle; and in Stevenage. Newcastle, Camden, Southwark and Liverpool were the only boroughs (four out of nineteen) with school play centre facilities. In Newcastle there were no other play-leadership schemes. The only other borough to claim play leadership (which has not appeared on the table because the scheme was operating outside the review areas) was Bradford which organised three centres in parks and one at a Youth Centre and swimming classes for a period of three weeks during the summer holidays.[2]

The Greater London Council are rapidly increasing their provision of play parks and one o'clock clubs. At the time of the survey one of these situated in Camden was temporarily closed and hence has not been included.

## Hours of opening and regulations

There remain to consider two further aspects of the survey: the question of hours of opening of the playgrounds and whether or not there were restrictions on their use.

Every playground was open all the year round although a few on housing estates were found locked and in one area the equipment was removed for the winter months. Most playgrounds were open on all days of the week. The exceptions usually had Sunday closing. One entire borough fell into this group, which also included a few of the

1 Pets have since been successfully reintroduced into one of the Camden community play centres.
2 Since the survey was carried out, Coventry have appointed a play leadership organiser under the Director of Education with special holiday duties and a proposed extension of duties at a later stage; and adventure playgrounds have been started in Newcastle, Stevenage and Southwark.

play-leader playgrounds. A great number of the playgrounds had no lockable gate; many were unfenced. Of those which were fenced and lockable the great majority were open during daylight hours. Thus it can be said that in most cases children wishing to use the playgrounds under review could do so at any reasonable hour. It is very important to remember, however, that the lack of indoor accommodation, our climate and our long winter evenings seriously reduce the number of these 'reasonable' hours.

Finally, were children restricted in their use of playgrounds? Where restrictions existed they were usually concerned with one of two things: the ages of the children or the question of housing estate private rights. Occasionally they were the result of red tape. Several playgrounds excluded boys over ten and girls over fourteen, for instance, but unless there was an attendant the regulation was often evaded. There are arguments on both sides over the use by non-residents of housing estate playgrounds. Much depends both on the siting of the playgrounds and on the number of other playgrounds in the district which could be used by children not living on the estate. One large estate in Southwark has compromised by restricting the use of three of its playgrounds, sited on inner courtyards, to estate children only and allowing children from the surrounding area to play on the fourth playground which is sited on one of the estate boundaries with both an internal and an external entrance.

One absurd example of red tape which restricted use of space was discovered from a field worker's comments: 'A playground was sited next door to a nursery school but the infants were not allowed to use the outdoor space for insurance reasons!'

## Summary

Analysis of the 467 playgrounds in the nineteen boroughs has confirmed a preconceived picture of play facility provision in this country.

The majority of playgrounds are flat, uninteresting and unimaginative in design and too small for a wide range of activities. Whilst there are more with mixed surfaces than had been expected, over a third are wholly hard-surfaced and these are almost all asphalted. Traditional equipment predominates; other kinds of fixed equipment—gymnastic items, play sculpture and so on—are to be found on just under 40 per cent of the equipped playgrounds and are more prevalent on housing estates than elsewhere. The reverse is true of mobile, portable and adventure play equipment. This is altogether strikingly absent. Only three housing estate playgrounds possess any; it is to be found in eleven playgrounds situated elsewhere.

Sand and water, two immensely important play materials, are in exceedingly poor supply. They are present on only 13 per cent of the equipped playgrounds—10 per cent of the total number of playgrounds surveyed. About half are either specially for toddlers or include a limited number of items of equipment for their use.

There are more playgrounds situated in housing estates than in parks, public gardens, recreation grounds and so on. The great majority of all the playgrounds—82 per cent—have some form of equipment. Most of those without equipment are situated in housing estates and are usually either very small spaces for under fives or designated ball-games areas. It therefore is no surprise that children continue to use undesignated space for much of their play.

Very little advantage is taken of sites awaiting development—only 5 per cent of all the playgrounds are to be found on this kind of site.

Standards in upkeep vary considerably. The majority of the playgrounds are in reasonably good condition—some particularly so—but where they are bad, they are very bad.

Only half the equipped playgrounds—not counting those on housing estates—have w.c.s and of these two-thirds are without washbasins. Lavatory facilities are particularly vulnerable to vandalism and even without this are liable to be ill-kept. Most playgrounds are open at times when children would want to use them during the summer months but the extreme lack of indoor facilities cuts out a great many winter hours and innumerable days throughout the year when the weather is bad.

For the great majority of playgrounds supervision in the full meaning of the word is non-existent. A few, 10 per cent, are looked after by a full-time attendant but only 2 per cent boast a full-time play leader. A further 2 per cent have temporary holiday schemes. All those with play leaders have a varied and imaginative range of activity.

# *13*

## *Responsibility for the Provision of Play Facilities in the Nineteen Boroughs*

### Statutory and Voluntary Provision of Play Facilities

Our survey confirmed that local authorities are the principal providers of play facilities in this country. In only three of the nineteen boroughs —Camden, Southwark and Liverpool—at the time of the survey was there additional provision by voluntary organisations,[1] either within or outside the review areas. In each case the provision was grant-aided by the Authority. It will be remembered that, for the larger boroughs, sample areas were selected for review. Within these review areas of Camden, Southwark and Liverpool, only one voluntarily organised play centre was to be found and this was run by the London Council of Social Service on a large South London housing estate. Two other voluntary playgrounds were investigated in the Children and Playgrounds Survey.[2]

### Local Authorities and Play Provision

#### *Local government structure*

A brief description of local government structure may help towards an understanding of the pattern of responsibility.

Two forces operate within the local framework. These are the unpaid administrators or councillors and the paid officers or officials.

The councillors, who are elected to represent us, with varying degrees of interest and enthusiasm, are concerned with policy. They function

---

1　We are not talking here of special provision for the under-fives, and see footnote 2, p. 239.
2　See Chapter 10.

through committees and sub-committees. They may have expert knowledge of the subject under their control but not necessarily so. The real experts are the paid officers who, these days, both help to formulate policy and are responsible for its implementation.[1]

In recent years central government has played an increasingly significant part in local affairs. Grants from the appropriate Ministry have become an integral part of local government; local rates are simply not enough to pay for the present enormous range of local government activities. A single central authority also has a vitally important role in ensuring that standards are set and maintained. The balance of power between local and central government may change, however, in the coming years. A great deal of both local and central government thinking is along regional lines as can be seen from much of the evidence before the Redcliffe-Maude Commission on Local Government.[2]

Local authority structure has grown more complicated with the enormously increased complexity and size of our towns and cities. This urban growth has led to the creation of self-contained authorities— the powerful, all-purpose county boroughs. Within the county council hierarchy the county, like the county borough, is charged with the major functions of education, health and welfare, children's service, police, roads and traffic, town and country planning, and so on. The smaller boroughs and the urban and rural districts are responsible for only certain services, some of which, such as housing, they may share with the county. Parish councils have inevitably lost most of their old functions to the larger authorities but still, for instance, retain exclusive control over allotments and may share with their county council and any intervening councils the responsibility for public open space within their boundaries.

## Local council responsibility

Open space in a given area, as stated above, may be the responsibility of one or more authorities. So already it can be seen that one aspect of play provision—the space which enables its existence—has multiple possibilities of administration and finance. The same is true for the

1  It is interesting, when one considers the size and power of many local government departments, to realise that payment to officers in local government is comparatively recent. It did not occur until well into the nineteenth century, when the vastly increased pressure of work from urban and population growth gave rise to the need for paid assistants to help the existing voluntary officers. Hasluck (1948), p. 18.
Royal Commission on Local Government in England (1966).

other main aspect of play provision—the type of service. This may be the responsibility of a variety of different departments. These departments may either be found exclusively in different grades of authority—education, for example, belongs to counties or county boroughs only—or, as is the case for open spaces and leisure activities, they may be duplicated in several different grades of authority.

This confusion in responsibility at Council level was only partially revealed in our survey of existing facilities as the great majority (fourteen) of the towns investigated were county boroughs which are responsible for virtually all the services within their boundaries.

All fourteen, therefore, had sole responsibility for play facilities (other than those run by voluntary organisations in the three referred to on page 242).

Two towns, Stevenage and Kirkby, were administered by urban district councils. Kirkby U.D.C. held sole responsibility for children's play provision. In Stevenage, however, Hertfordshire County Council was involved in its capacity of local education authority. The situation here was further complicated by the fact that, as a designated New Town, initial responsibility for many of its services had been vested in its Development Corporation. Play facility responsibilities at the time of our survey were in the process of being handed over to the District Council.

The remaining three boroughs were all in the County of London and as such presented the most complex picture. In Camden and Southwark three separate Authorities administered and financed children's play facilities. The Greater London Council was concerned through its Parks Department and Housing Department. The respective borough councils were the second responsible Authority and the third was the Inner London Education Authority. In addition, in Camden, a central government agency, the Ministry of Public Building and Works, which has direct responsibility for London's Royal Parks, was therefore, in Regent's Park, concerned with playgrounds. Brent, an outer London Borough and its own Education Authority, was in exclusive control of all children's play provision except for one anomaly. The City of London Corporation, which owns a great deal of property outside its boundaries, controlled one facility.

## Departmental responsibility

What determined the allocation of responsibility to one department or another?

The analysis of the position in the nineteen boroughs has resolved itself into one main tabulation and this is based on the only factor which appeared to have any influence on the allocation of responsibility—the location of the play facility.

TABLE 62

*Departmental responsibility for play facilities by situation of facility*

| Responsible departments[1] | Playgrounds situated in: | | | |
| | Parks, etc | Housing estates | Other incl. play streets | Schools |
|---|---|---|---|---|
| Parks only | 11 | 3 | 5 | — |
| Eng./Surveyor's only | 6 | 3 | 6 | — |
| Housing only | — | 6 | — | — |
| Parks and Eng./Surveyor's | — | — | 1 | — |
| Parks and Housing | — | 4 | — | — |
| Parks and Education | 1 | — | — | — |
| Parks, Housing and Education | — | — | 1 | — |
| Parks, Surveyor's | 1 | — | — | — |
| Clerk's, Eng./Surveyor's and Housing | — | 2 | — | — |
| Education only | — | — | — | 4 |
| Development Corporation | — | — | 1 | — |

From Table 62 it can be seen that the majority of facilities situated in parks, public gardens, etc., were under the control of Parks Departments, either solely or in conjunction with other departments. A similar pattern can be seen for the housing estate playgrounds—these were predominantly run by Housing Departments. In spite of this bias, a closer look reveals a certain degree of inconsistency. In three boroughs, for instance, housing estate playgrounds were the sole responsibility of Parks Departments. Engineers' and Surveyors' Departments figured in all three situation columns, mostly as the single controlling body.

In three boroughs the Education Department joined forces with either the Parks Department, or with Parks and Housing together, for playgrounds in parks and similar public open spaces, in housing estates

1  (a) In two of the boroughs the Parks Department belonged to a different Authority from the Controlling Council.
   (b) In two of the boroughs the Education Department belonged to a different Authority from the Controlling Council.
   (c) In two of the boroughs, Housing was under the control of two separate councils.
   (d) Although Architects' and Planning Departments in no case held direct responsibility, their influence was apparent in certain boroughs.

and on off-street sites; otherwise its responsibility was confined to school premises in the four boroughs which provided play facilities in schools out of school hours.

In a separate analysis an attempt was made to discover if the prominence of Engineers' and Surveyors' Departments in Table 62 could be attributed to maintenance duties. This was found not to be the case. Engineers' and Surveyors' Departments must certainly be concerned in some maintenance duties but according to replies to our questionnaire the actual financial and administrative responsibility for maintenance with three exceptions was consistently held by those departments who were responsible for provision. Responsibility for supervision also belonged to the 'providing' departments except in three instances where it belonged to the Education Departments.

A further analysis showed that there was no apparent relation between the type of play facility and the type of department. Thus, for example, a Borough Engineer's Department was found to be solely responsible for play leadership schemes which in another borough were the joint concern of the Parks, Education and Housing Departments.

Table 63 shows how many departments within each borough were concerned in play provision.

## TABLE 63
### Number of responsible departments

| No. of boroughs | No. of departments |
|---|---|
| 6 | 1 |
| 4 | 2 |
| 5 | 3 |
| 3 | 4 |
| 1 | 5 |

On the whole, the larger Authorities tended to use a greater number of departments for children's play provision though Bristol and Southampton, with only two departments (Engineer's and Housing) involved, and Swansea with only one (Parks), were exceptions. Conversely, Stevenage, which was the smallest of the towns, used the greatest number of departments—five.

At the time of the survey only three boroughs held regular inter-departmental meetings on the subject of children's play provision. One or two others referred to 'informal' inter-departmental contact.

Since the survey took play one of the Authorities, to our knowledge, has made positive advances towards full and meaningful co-operative measures. The Parks Department of the Greater London Council is formally involved in the provision of play facilities on housing estates at the planning stage. Moreover, a special working party has been set up under the auspices of the Parks Department whose function is to co-ordinate the various facilities for children and young people provided by the various departments.

## Committee responsibility

In the nineteen boroughs direct Committee responsibility at Councillor level for children's play facilities usually lay with the full Committee of the relevant department, though occasionally with sub-committees. These Committees bore titles which were appropriate to the subject in varying degrees. A random selection will indicate the range: Planning and Public Works; Estates and Properties; Highways and Public Works; Parks, Baths, Cemeteries and Garden Allotments; Town Improvement and Streets; Housing; Parks and Entertainment; Education; Libraries and Amenities.

The quality and the amount of play facility provision for children appeared to bear no relation to the nature of the responsible Committees' titles nor to the function of the controlling departments.

# General conclusion

Our survey would seem to confirm the impression that at the moment the necessary drive to get good play facilities installed depends largely on individual Councillors and Departmental Officers with the help and inspiration of outside pressure groups. It is these individuals who, irrespective of the nature of their ostensible duties—drains, cemeteries, highways, housing—will use their initiative to persuade their fellow councillors or officers of the importance of children's play provision.

# Appendices

NOTE

It has not been possible to include in this publication the considerable amount of documentation relating to the three surveys. Copies of the questionnaires, etc., are, however, available as listed below on request from:

> The Council for Children's Welfare,
> 183/189 Finchley Road,
> London, N.W.3.

*The Contrasting Neighbourhood Study*
1  Interview Schedule.
2  Junior Play Inventory.
3  Senior Play Inventory.
4  Instruction Sheet and Operation Sheet.

*The Children and Playground Survey*
1  Playground Use and Record Sheet.
2  Interview Field Sheet.
3  Relevant Instruction Sheets and Notes.
4  Preliminary Reports for:
> Brent, Bristol, Camden, Leicester, Liverpool,
> Newcastle-upon-Tyne, Southampton, Swansea, Worcester
> and the Composite Report.

*The Survey of Existing Facilities*
1  Local Authority Questionnaire.
2  Playground Questionnaire.
3  Relevant Instruction Sheets and Notes.

# Appendix I

## *Play Facility Definitions*

The problem of nomenclature in the field of children's play applies as much to the question of describing places where children play as to that of describing the activity itself. There are, at the time of writing, no universally accepted definitions, but those given below attempt to cover all the major kinds of provision to be found in this country.

For the purposes of this study a *play facility* is defined as an area which is officially designated for chidren's play. It may be provided and run by statutory bodies or by voluntary organisations. It may be equipped, supervised or unsupervised. It may include indoor accommodation but not necessarily so—in fact, not usually so. The facility may be situated in any place to which a reasonable number of children have access. It may be open all day and in the evenings all the year round, or it may only be open for a limited number of hours or days. Children of all ages may be permitted to use it or it may be available only to certain specified age groups. Clubs or organisations which require membership are not included in this definition.

PLAYGROUNDS

'Playground' is the word most commonly used to describe an area for children's play. For this reason it is the one we ourselves use as an umbrella term in the study chapters rather than play facility, play space, play area, or even child space. More precisely, however, a *playground* may be defined as an area for children's play containing fixed equipment. The equipment may be traditional or specially designed; it may be static or moving, but must be fixed. The area may be rectangular, flat and asphalted or it may be landscaped with different levels and surfaces. It may be sited in parks and recreation grounds, in housing estates, or within residential areas, when it may be known as a *neighbourhood playground*. There may or may not be an *attendant*. Attendants have been employed by many local authorities at some of their larger conventional playgrounds for a number of years.

Their duties include the keeping of order, watching over use of the equipment, looking after the w.c. and washing facilities and, perhaps, tending minor injuries. The vast majority of conventional playgrounds are provided by local authorities but some are privately or commercially run.

## UNEQUIPPED PLAY SPACES

These, also mostly provided by local authorities, are intended for the most part as *kick-around areas* and are usually hard-surfaced. Goalposts are occasionally provided, in which case, and according to their size, they would be known as *five-a-side pitches*. Very rarely they are floodlit at night. Quite often, these unequipped spaces form part of a playground. They are also usually provided in supervised play facilities. There are also unequipped spaces, usually grassed, intended for use by toddlers.

## PLAY STREETS

Play streets were introduced under the Street Playgrounds Act of 1938. They are ordinary streets, closed to traffic (except nowadays for residents' vehicles or visiting trade vans) during daylight hours. Recently, some other streets have been closed to traffic and seasonal supervised schemes have been introduced.

## SUPERVISED PLAY FACILITIES

Supervision implies the presence of an adult whose duties are directly concerned with the children and their play. This adult is most commonly known as the play leader.[1] The facilities may be permanent or seasonal and the staff full-time or part-time.

There is a wide range of supervised provision:

### Adventure playgrounds

Very often playgrounds which have more adventurous and unusual types of fixed equipment are called adventure playgrounds by both local authorities and public. It is very important that this confusion in nomenclature should be cleared up for the real adventure playgrounds are totally different places.[2] The latter are often known as *junk playgrounds*, but for various reasons this title has lately gone into disrepute. They have been described as 'perhaps the most revolutionary experiment we know for absorbing the interest and releasing the energies of young people from two to eighteen years of age. Their deep

1   Details about the qualifications of play leaders in this and other countries and a discussion of their role may be found in Chapters 3 and 6.
2   The origins of the movement are described in Chapter 2.

urge to experiment with earth, fire, water and timber, to work with real tools without fear of criticism or censure, and their love of freedom to take calculated risks are recognised in these playgrounds and are met under tolerant and sympathetic guidance.'[1] All *adventure playgrounds*, besides providing the wherewithal for the 'basic activities' suggested above—digging, building and lighting fires—include facilities for arts and crafts. There is often a ping-pong table or a similar piece of equipment. Conventional fixed equipment is taboo but some form of rope pulley or slide is usually improvised. Some kind of indoor play area, usually a hut, is considered an essential part of these playgrounds. There may also be opportunities for gardening, keeping pets, cooking, playing records and so on.

The great majority of *adventure playgrounds* are run by voluntary committees.[2]

*Play parks and play centres*
Closely akin to the adventure playgrounds are the Greater London Council *play parks* which are organised from within the Parks Department by a former adventure playground leader. Here, where possible, natural sites within parks are exploited and by placing them next door to existing conventional playgrounds money is saved, as toilet facilities and so on can be shared.

Notices at the gates of many of these parks ask parents to keep out. The full range of adventure activity cannot usually be indulged in. There are restrictions, for instance, on lighting fires. The term *play park* has now been adopted in this country for an *un*supervised area with special design features—following the pattern of those to be found in some countries abroad.[3]

In the supervised facilities commonly called *play centres* the bias tends to be towards the arts and crafts, water play, drama and dressing up, though free play and improvised games are encouraged. These may be run by voluntary committees or by a local authority department. The Liverpool Education Authority, for instance, organises, in co-operation with other departments, such play centres during the Easter and summer holidays, and during the summer term. They may be in parks or within residential areas, but they should not be confused with *school play centres*.[4]

1  Allen of Hurtwood (1964), p. 5.
2  See Chapters 6 and 7.
3  See Allen of Hurtwood (1968), pp. 96–102.
4  See p. 255.

## Community play centres

*Community play centres*, at the time of writing, are to be found in their fullest realisation in one borough—the London Borough of Camden where, again, a former adventure playground leader has been given remarkably free rein to experiment with his ideas on integrating the child into the community. For this is the fundamental difference between these centres and the kind of provision described in the two preceding sections. The ingredients for play do not differ all that much, though the Camden centres tend to be more elaborate and some formal equipment is allowed, but in Camden there is a deliberate attempt to attract the whole family. Most play leaders, if pressed, see themselves as social workers. In Camden, however, the schemes are conceived consciously as a social service for young and old. Ultimately they would like to see Family Advice Centres based on the play centres.

Other areas are experimenting in community leisure, with children's play as the focal point, notably the Sparkbrook Association in Birmingham, the North Kensington Trust and Manchester University Settlement.[1]

## Provision for the under fives

*Community play centres* embrace in concept the whole community and in practice this has emphatically included the youngest members.

The Greater London Council are as famed for their *one o'clock clubs* as for their play parks, and for these the policy of excluding adults is reversed and mothers are expected to stay with their toddlers. Most *adventure playgrounds* and *play centres* cater deliberately for the under fives, sometimes organising their own groups and sometimes throwing open their premises for use by other organisations.

The Save the Children Fund have enormously expanded their *play group* service during the last few years. They operate almost exclusively in deprived areas, employing trained staff with voluntary assistance. Local Authorities are slowly beginning to give concrete recognition to the significance of this service through grants and the provision of premises.

The Pre-School Playgroups Association performs an important function in co-ordinating the work of hundreds of *play groups* throughout the country and inspiring the formation of new ones. Here it is usually the parents who are the originators and the organisers. In most cases too they run the groups and the Association is particularly

---

1   For a discussion of community participation in play provision see Chapters 6 and 7.

conscious at the moment of the need to maintain, and in some cases to raise, standards.

*Play groups* are almost invariably run on a part-time basis, often only for two or three hours a day for two or three days a week. They are not always initiated by parents. Churches, local and national organisations and associations are becoming more and more concerned in this kind of provision. Sometimes one individual may spark off a movement; more rarely a local authority takes the initiative and provides a group attached, for example, to a welfare clinic.

### Other play-leadership schemes

Apart from the schemes outlined above there are those, very much greater in number, in which the emphasis is more on organised games and activities. There is the minimum of equipment, they usually occur only during the summer and Easter holidays and either make use of existing play facilities or of public recreational open space. They are to be found in rural districts as well as in larger Authorities, though some of the latter—Lewisham, for instance—have developed their schemes far beyond their simple beginnings so that they approximate more to the play centre schemes outlined above.

An important feature of most supervised play schemes is that of the outings and expeditions organised either by the play leaders or by the children themselves with or without their parents. These outings include afternoon visits to the Zoo, day trips to the seaside, camping expeditions lasting for a week or a fortnight, and regular visits to swimming baths.

### School play centres

Education authorities in a limited number of areas have assumed responsibility for children's out-of-school hours. Essentially, the *school play centre* provides a service for those families in which there is no parent or parent substitute in the home during the holidays and from 4 to 6 p.m. on school days, usually because the mother is out at work, but sometimes because she is ill. The centres are located in primary schools on an alternating basis within the chosen districts. The range of activity varies but caters, on the whole, for children below the age of 11. The staff are usually, but not always, ancillary to the school staff and the equipment is kept separate from that of the school.

### Community schools

Here, the school, secondary as well as primary, is used as a base for community leisure activities. There are very few such schools in this country at the moment.

### Provision for handicapped children

Current thinking is opposed, on the whole, to the segregation of children with physical disabilities. Nevertheless, for some types of disability, if it is particularly severe, for instance, or where special equipment or transport are needed, it may be more suitable to provide a special facility. Also, play as therapy is of particular relevance to physical or mental handicap and opportunities for this may be more easily realised in specialised groups where professional skills can be concentrated. A few such groups exist, very occasionally supported by local authorities but more usually by voluntary societies or, more simply, organised by the children's parents.

### Hospital play provision

Organised play for children in hospital is only just beginning to take hold in this country. Some hospitals provide their own staff and equipment; others seek help from outside organisations. For really ill children facilities for play are created in their beds and cots. Play corners or, where possible, play rooms are provided for those children who are able to leave their beds.

# Appendix II

## A. Material relating to the Survey of Mothers in the Two Areas (Chapter 8)

### 1 Sampling

A 'quasi-random' sample was drawn from the list of the electors of the Elm Green area of Stevenage and of the area called Heygate in Southwark. As we wished to interview only mothers with children between the ages of two and fourteen years all single names were erased off the list on the assumption that the vast majority of mothers would be living with their husbands. In Stevenage sixty-five names were crossed off, leaving 600 households to sample from; in Southwark 629 names were crossed off, leaving 750 households to sample from. The sample in Stevenage was drawn from one in five of the households remaining on the list, and in Southwark from one in two. The higher fraction for Southwark was in anticipation of a much higher loss of possible interviewees, because of childless households and removals from existing addresses. The following table gives the response breakdown.

### TABLE 23
*Sample response of mothers*

|  | Stevenage | Southwark |
|---|---|---|
| No children households | 52 | 167 |
| Children over age | 5 | 20 |
| Children under age | 13 | 16 |
| Moved | 2 | 38 |
| No contact made with person at address | 56 | 25 |
| Refused to be interviewed | 37 | 4 |
| Interviews discarded | 3 | 2 |
| Total | 168 | 272 |
| Successful interviews (sample) | 115 | 107 |

The considerable difference between the refusal rates of the two areas is attributable to two basic factors. First, in Southwark professional market research interviewers were used, whereas in Stevenage mature students taking a social work diploma at the local Further Education College did the interviewing. Second, part of the interviewing stretched into the holiday period; in Southwark few of the families went away on holiday, whereas in Stevenage it appears that most take a holiday. The most common excuse given for not being interviewed was that the family was preparing to go away on holiday; for the inexperienced interviewers this was an insurmountable problem.

# 2 Weekend activities

## TABLE 24

*Weekend activities as given by mothers for morning, afternoon and evening on Saturday and Sunday, grouped within areas*

| | Stevenage | | | | | | Southwark | | | | | |
| | Saturday | | | Sunday | | | Saturday | | | Sunday | | |
| | a.m. | p.m. | eve. | a.m. | p.m. | eve. | a.m. | p.m. | eve. | a.m. | p.m. | eve. |
|---|---|---|---|---|---|---|---|---|---|---|---|---|
| Field, rocket, park, play square | 3 | 8 | 4 | 6 | 8 | 2 | 5 | 9 | — | 6 | 18 | 1 |
| Street or bombed site | 4 | 4 | — | 7 | 4 | 1 | 11 | 21 | 4 | 17 | 11 | 3 |
| Garden/yard | 17 | 17 | 4 | 15 | 14 | 7 | 3 | 3 | 1 | — | — | 1 |
| Specific activities | 7 | 2 | 1 | 4 | 4 | — | 6 | 5 | 1 | 1 | 2 | 1 |
| Away/out visiting | 16 | 29 | 18 | 25 | 36 | 18 | 18 | 23 | 10 | 22 | 41 | 19 |
| Shopping/church | 35 | 18 | — | 19 | 4 | — | 26 | 18 | — | 29 | — | 1 |
| Watching T.V. | — | 3 | 45 | — | 7 | 32 | — | 3 | 45 | — | 12 | 37 |
| Indoors | 10 | 6 | 19 | 15 | 14 | 27 | 19 | 12 | 30 | 20 | 9 | 34 |
| Other | 6 | 12 | 6 | 9 | 7 | 10 | 12 | 6 | 7 | 4 | 6 | 3 |
| Don't know | 1 | 1 | 2 | — | 1 | 1 | — | — | 1 | — | — | — |
| | 100 | 100 | 100 | 100 | 100 | 100 | 100 | 100 | 100 | 100 | 100 | 100 |
| Number of children | 223 | 223 | 223 | 223 | 223 | 223 | 211 | 211 | 211 | 211 | 211 | 211 |

# B. Material relating to a comparison of children's activities in the two areas (Chapter 9)

## 1 Preferred activities

At the end of the Play Inventory the children were asked the question 'Looking back at all the activities you lke doing in your spare time: which three do you like doing most?' The following table shows the order of preferences.

TABLE 25

*Preferred activities in the two areas*

| Stevenage | | Southwark | |
|---|---|---|---|
| *Junior Girls* | % | *Junior Girls* | % |
| Swimming | 37 | Swimming | 31 |
| Reading | 20 | Reading | 22 |
| Playing with pets | 12 | Netball | 17 |
| Watching T.V. | 11 | Watching T.V. | 16 |
| | | | |
| *Junior Boys* | % | *Junior Boys* | % |
| Football | 43 | Football | 64 |
| Swimming | 32 | Swimming | 23 |
| Watching T.V. | 14 | Watching T.V. | 12 |
| Cricket | 10 | Cricket | 11 |
| | | | |
| *Senior Boys* | % | *Senior Boys* | % |
| Football | 43 | Football | 55 |
| Swimming | 34 | Swimming | 32 |
| Cycling | 16 | Dating | 14 |
| Fishing | 10 | Table tennis | 10 |
| | | | |
| *Senior Girls* | % | *Senior Girls* | % |
| Swimming | 27 | Swimming | 22 |
| Dancing | 23 | Listening to radio and | |
| Reading | 19 | records | 22 |
| Listening to radio and | | Dating | 14 |
| records | 18 | Ice skating | 14 |

Note: Percentages show totals of first, second and third preferences.

## 2  Factor analysis

The factor analyses were carried out with a computer programme.[1] The first was of the 137 items of the Junior Play Inventory. It produced twelve factors, only seven of which were interpretable for the purposes of the study. The second factor analysis was of the 107 items in the Senior Play Inventory. Twelve factors were produced; only eight were interpretable. Factor loadings above 0·3 are shown in the tables below.

TABLES 26 (a), (b), (c), (d), (e), (f), (g)
*Junior play inventory factors*

(a) *Junior outdoor activities*

| Factor | Factor loadings |
|---|---|
| Long jump | −0·78 |
| High jump | −0·75 |
| Running races | −0·59 |
| Leap frog | −0·52 |
| Hop, skip and jump | −0·51 |
| Going to social clubs | −0·35 |
| Skipping | −0·33 |
| Just running about | −0·30 |

(b) *Junior indoor sedentary activities*

| Factor | Factor loadings |
|---|---|
| Draughts | −0·49 |
| Dominoes | −0·47 |
| Card games | −0·46 |
| Collecting stamps | −0·42 |
| Doing crossword puzzles | −0·39 |
| Chess | −0·36 |
| Marbles | −0·31 |

(c) *Junior feminine activities*

| Factor | Factor loadings |
|---|---|
| Playing nurse | −0·86 |
| Playing shop | −0·83 |
| Playing house | −0·80 |
| Playing school | −0·77 |
| Playing Sunday school | −0·71 |
| Dolls, doll carriage, doll clothes | −0·68 |
| Playing horse | −0·63 |
| Playing circus | −0·62 |
| Stringing beads | −0·61 |

(c)—*continued*

| Factor | Factor loadings |
|---|---|
| Dressing up | −0·54 |
| Playing actor and actress | −0·53 |
| Playing other make-believe games | −0·38 |
| Spinning tops | −0·38 |
| Hop, skip and jump | −0·37 |
| Combing a friend's hair | −0·35 |
| Other hopping games played on the pavement | −0·31 |

(d) *Junior masculine activities*

| Factor | Factor loadings |
|---|---|
| Playing soldiers | −0·73 |
| Toy trains, ships, cars or lorries | −0·73 |
| Sword fighting | −0·65 |
| Boxing | −0·62 |
| Flying model aircraft | −0·62 |
| Bow and arrows | −0·57 |
| Playing robbers and police | −0·57 |
| Shooting with air rifle | −0·55 |
| Wrestling | −0·54 |
| Using a hammer, saw or nails | −0·54 |
| Playing cowboys and Indians | −0·53 |
| Train conductor, engineer or brakeman | −0·51 |
| Building a dam | −0·50 |
| Building dens | −0·50 |
| Football | −0·50 |

1  Hendricksen and White (1964).

| TABLE 26 (d)—continued | Factor | (f)—continued | Factor |
|---|---|---|---|
| Factor | loadings | Factor | loadings |
| Digging caves or holes | −0·49 | Boxing | 0·33 |
| Toy horn or toy drum | −0·44 | Reading books | −0·32 |
| Making or assembling radio/electrical equipment | −0·43 | Wrestling | 0·30 |

(e) Junior mature activities

| Factor | Factor loadings |
|---|---|
| Telephoning friends | −0·68 |
| Taking photographs | −0·59 |
| Listening to records | −0·54 |
| Cooking | −0·51 |
| Ten-pin bowling | −0·50 |
| Tape recorder | −0·46 |
| Going to parties or picnics | −0·35 |
| Putting | −0·34 |
| Sewing, knitting or crocheting | −0·33 |
| Rounders | −0·32 |
| Playing with pets | −0·31 |
| Gardening | −0·31 |

(f) Junior non-conformist activities

| Factor | Factor loadings |
|---|---|
| Having 'dates' | 0·54 |
| Smoking | 0·44 |

(g) Junior general outdoor activities

| Factor | Factor loadings |
|---|---|
| Riding a bicycle | −0·64 |
| Playing in the sand | −0·60 |
| Fishing | −0·49 |
| Swinging | −0·48 |
| Wading in water | −0·48 |
| Boating or canoeing | −0·47 |
| Roller skating | −0·45 |
| Building or watching bonfires | −0·42 |
| Climbing trees | −0·41 |
| Swimming | −0·40 |
| Blackberry picking | −0·40 |
| Chewing gum | −0·40 |
| Flying kites | −0·39 |
| Throwing stones | −0·37 |
| Hop scotch | −0·33 |
| Rolling a car tyre | −0·33 |
| Playing with mud | −0·32 |
| Turning handsprings or cartwheels | −0·31 |
| Dominoes | −0·30 |

## TABLES 26A (a), (b), (c), (d), (e), (f), (g)
### Senior play inventory factors

(a) Senior mature activities

| Factor | Factor loadings |
|---|---|
| Listening to records | −0·61 |
| Telephoning friends | −0·53 |
| Ice skating | −0·51 |
| Going to the pictures | −0·48 |
| Going to parties or picnics | −0·47 |
| Dancing | −0·47 |
| Reading or looking at magazines | −0·36 |
| Having 'dates' | −0·33 |

(b) Senior younger outdoor activities

| Factor | Factor loadings |
|---|---|
| Playing with a ball against a wall | −0·70 |
| Swinging | −0·59 |
| Just playing catch or throw | −0·55 |
| Sliding on playground slide | −0·53 |
| Skipping | −0·51 |
| Chewing gum or bubble gum | −0·40 |
| Hop scotch | −0·34 |
| Just running about | −0·33 |

| TABLE 27 (b)—*continued* | *Factor loadings* |
| --- | --- |
| *Factor* | |
| Rounders | −0·33 |
| Looking at comics | −0·30 |

**(c) Senior non-conformist activities**

| *Factor* | *Factor loadings* |
| --- | --- |
| Smoking | 0·59 |
| Having 'dates' | 0·56 |
| Shooting with air rifle | 0·46 |
| Reading books (negatively associated) | 0·32 |
| Chewing gum or bubble gum | 0·30 |

**(d) Senior purposeful activities**

| *Factor* | *Factor loadings* |
| --- | --- |
| Playing other musical instruments | 0·53 |
| Swimming | 0·38 |
| Making or assembling radios or other electrical apparatus | 0·34 |
| Gardening | 0·32 |
| Riding a bicycle | 0·32 |
| Reading books | 0·31 |
| Painting with water colours | 0·30 |

**(e) Senior athletic activities**

| *Factor* | *Factor loadings* |
| --- | --- |
| Long jump | 0·87 |
| High jump | 0·81 |
| Running races | 0·71 |
| Leap frog | 0·52 |
| Tennis | 0·33 |
| Swimming | 0·30 |

**(f) Senior feminine activities**

| *Factor* | *Factor loadings* |
| --- | --- |
| Stringing beads | −0·63 |
| Sewing, knitting or crocheting | −0·55 |
| Hopscotch | −0·51 |
| Playing five-stones or jinks | −0·51 |

| (f)—*continued* | *Factor loadings* |
| --- | --- |
| *Factor* | |
| Telling fortunes | −0·50 |
| Skipping | −0·46 |
| Other hopping games | −0·46 |
| Playing cowboys and Indians | −0·45 |
| Playing nurse | −0·40 |
| Follow your leader | −0·39 |
| Picture puzzles | −0·39 |
| Football | 0·38 |
| Combing a friend's hair | −0·38 |
| Dressing up | −0·36 |
| Cooking | −0·36 |
| Telling or guessing riddles | −0·35 |
| Telling stories | −0·33 |
| Shopping | −0·33 |
| Listening to stories | −0·32 |
| Just imagining things | −0·32 |

**(g) Senior masculine activities**

| *Factor* | *Factor loadings* |
| --- | --- |
| Digging caves or holes or dens | 0·70 |
| Wrestling | 0·69 |
| Toy trains, ships, cars or lorries | 0·69 |
| Boxing | 0·64 |
| Building a dam | 0·62 |
| Flying model aircraft | 0·66 |
| Playing soldiers | 0·57 |
| Using hammer, saw or nails | 0·50 |
| Playing with mud | 0·50 |
| Pillow fights | 0·49 |
| Wading in water | 0·49 |
| Climbing trees | 0·48 |
| Throwing stones | 0·44 |
| Playing in sand | 0·41 |
| Making or assembling radios or other electrical apparatus | 0·40 |
| Playing cowboys and Indians | 0·37 |
| Rolling a car tyre | 0·35 |
| Camping out | 0·30 |
| Playing 'chase' or 'he' | 0·30 |

## 3  A list of all items appearing in both Play Inventories

1. Football
2. Playing with a ball against a wall
3. Just playing catch and throwing
4. Rounders
5. Tennis
6. Boxing
7. Wrestling
8. Doing crossword puzzles
9. Draughts
10. Chess
11. Dominoes
12. Marbles
13. Roller skating
14. Swinging
15. Riding in a car
16. Riding a bicycle
17. Rolling a car tyre
18. Telling stories
19. Listening to stories
20. Excursions to woods, parks, country
21. Fruit picking
22.[1] Blackberry picking
23.[1] Gathering nuts
24. Picking flowers
25. Collecting stamps
26. Walking
27. Going to the pictures
28.[1] Attending the theatre
29. Sight-seeing
30. Visiting or entertaining friends or relatives
31. Chewing gum
32. Smoking
33. Having 'dates'
34. Just sitting about
35. Dancing
36. Card games
37. Going to social clubs
38. Listening to the radio
39. Playing the piano (for fun)
40. Playing other musical instruments (for fun)
41. Looking at comics
42. Reading jokes or funny sayings
43. Reading the newspapers
44. Reading or looking at magazines
45. Reading books
46. Looking at daily comic strip
47. Telling or guessing riddles
48. Writing letters
49.[1] Writing poems
50. Fishing
51.[1] Telling fortunes or fortune told
52. Boating or canoeing
53. Camping out
54. Building or watching bonfires
55. Climbing trees
56. Turning handsprings or cartwheels
57. Watching T.V.
58. Just running about
59. Running races
60.[1] Hop, skip and jump
61. Long jump
62. High jump
63. Leap frog
64. Hop scotch
65. Skipping
66. Other hopping games played on the pavement
67. Following-your-leader
68. Throwing stones
69. Playing five-stones or jinks
70. Pillow fights
71. Teasing somebody
72. Teasing birds or animals
73.[1] Bow and arrows
74. Wading in water
75. Playing in the sand
76. Building a dam
77. Swimming
78. Dressing up
79.[1] Playing circus
80.[1] Playing house
81.[1] Playing horse

[1]  Not common to both (Junior and Senior) schedules.

82.[1] Playing shop
83.[1] Playing school
84.[1] Playing Sunday school
85. Cooking
86.[1] Playing nurse
87. Playing soldiers
88. Playing cowboys and Indians
89. Train driver, engineer or guard
90.[1] Building dens
91.[1] Playing robbers and police
92.[1] Playing actor and actress
93.[1] Playing other make-believe games
94. Just imagining things
95.[1] Playing statues
96. Going to parties or picnics
97. Playing with mud
98. Plasticine or clay modelling
99. Drawing with pencil, pen, chalk or crayon
100. Painting with water colours
101. Cutting paper things with a scissors
102. Making a scrapbook
103. Taking photographs
104. Stringing beads
105. Sewing, knitting or crocheting (for fun)
106. Using a hammer, saw or nails (for fun)
107. Digging caves or holes
108.[1] Spinning tops
109.[1] Flying kites
110.[1] Walking on stilts
111. Flying model aircraft
112. Toy trains, ships, cars or lorries
113. Looking at pictures
114.[1] Toy horn or toy drum
115.[1] Doll, doll carriage, doll clothes
116. Picture puzzles
117. Making or assembling a radio or other electrical apparatus
118. Playing with pets
119. Helping somebody with his work
120.[1] Combing a friend's hair
121.[1] Sides (netball)
122.[1] Sword fighting
123. Table tennis
124. Gardening
125.[1] Hide and seek
126. Listening to records
127. Telephoning friends
128. Shopping
129. Putting
130.[1] Ten-pin bowling
131.[1] Volley ball
132.[1] Shooting with an air rifle
133. Tape recorder
134. Darts
135. Playing 'chase' or 'he'

## TABLE 27
*Numbers of children in the two areas*

|  | Stevenage | Southwark | Totals |
|---|---|---|---|
| Junior Boys | 216 | 213 | 429 |
| Junior Girls | 249 | 217 | 466 |
| Totals | 465 | 430 | 895 |
| Senior Boys | 231 | 142 | 373 |
| Senior Girls | 273 | 244 | 517 |
| Totals | 504 | 386 | 890 |
| Area Totals | 969 | 816 | 1,785 |

1 Not common to both (Junior and Senior) schedules.

# Appendix III

## Material Relating to the Ten-Borough Survey, Children and Playgrounds (Chapter 10)

### 1  The Multiple Regression Analysis: Factors influencing playground attendance

A multivariate analysis of the survey data was performed to determine the main factors influencing the attendance at children's playgrounds, and at the same time to produce a multiple regression equation for predicting attendance.

In the playground survey each child entering the playground was interviewed and at each hour, on the hour, a count was taken of the number of children in the playground. These give two figures which could be used as a measure of playground use, the total attendance at a playground, and the total hourly count from 10 a.m. to 6 p.m. for each playground, which was the total number of child-hours spent at each playground. The ratio of attendance to counts varied considerably between playgrounds from as high as $1 : 5 \cdot 56$ at Mayflower Park, Southampton, to as low as $1 : 0 \cdot 46$ at Stonebridge Recreation Ground, Brent.

Both the attendances and the total counts were used as the dependent variables in order to study any differences in the significant variables.

A multiple regression analysis was performed on each of the three types of playground and on all playgrounds together using the following variables (this gave a total of eight multiple regression analyses).

Dependent Variables:    1. Total attendance.
                              2. Total hourly count 10 a.m.–6 p.m.
Independent Variables:  1. Number of competing playgrounds within catchment area. (Competition.)
                              2. Child population within catchment area.

Independent Variables cont.: 3. Size of playground.
                                    4. Paddling pool.
                                    5. Team games area.
                                    6. Sand pit.
                                    7. Play leader.
                                    8. Adventure facilities.
                                    9. Units of formal equipment.[1]

The following proved to be the significant variables.

## TABLE 38
### *The significant variables*

| *Dependent variable* | *Total attendance* | *Total hourly count* |
|---|---|---|
| All Playgrounds (109) | Catchment Population<br>Paddling Pool<br>Formal Equipment<br>Team Games Area<br>Size of Playground | Team Games Area<br>Paddling Pool<br>Size of Playground<br>Formal Equipment<br>Competition |
| *Type* 1 (44)<br>Playgrounds in Parks and Recreation Grounds | Paddling Pool<br>Catchment Population<br>Team Games Area | Team Games Area<br>Paddling Pool<br>Formal Equipment |
| *Type* 2 (40)<br>Playgrounds with Equipment | Team Games Area<br>Formal Equipment<br>Catchment Population | Competition<br>Catchment Population<br>Size of Playground<br>Team Games Area |
| *Type* 3 (25)<br>Play Streets and Play Areas with no Equipment | Team Games Area | Team Games Area |

Table 39 gives the number of times each independent variable was a significant factor in explaining the dependent variables. The number of times each independent variable was included in an analysis is also shown.

1   The provision of formal equipment was expressed either as the number of units of formal equipment where three swings and each other item of equipment counted as one unit, or as individual items of equipment in the five main categories of swings, slides, see-saws, round-abouts and tunnels and climbing bars.

TABLE 39

| Independent variable | Attendance as the dependent variable | Count as the dependent variable |
|---|---|---|
| Team Games Area | 4 out of 4 | 4 out of 4 |
| Paddling Pool | 2 out of 2 | 2 out of 2 |
| Catchment Population | 3 out of 4 | 2 out of 4 |
| Formal Equipment | 2 out of 3 | 2 out of 3 |
| Size of Playground | 1 out of 4 | 2 out of 4 |
| Competing Playground | 0 out of 4 | 2 out of 4 |
| Play Leader | 0 out of 4 | 0 out of 2 |
| Adventure Facilities | 0 out of 2 | 0 out of 2 |
| Sandpits | 0 out of 3 | 0 out of 3 |

The following tables show the significant variables for each of the multiple regression runs and the extent to which they explain the variation in the dependent variable. For example, when considering all playgrounds for total attendance, the five significant variables explain 66 per cent of the variation with over one-third of this being explained by changes in the catchment population for each playground. The multiple regression on all variables is also given and this shows what an insignificant increase in the multiple correlation coefficient is obtained by introducing the other non-significant variables.

## TABLES 40 AND 41
## Multiple regression analysis on all playgrounds

Order of significance of the independent variables and their contribution to the overall multiple correlation coefficient ($R^2$).

40. With *Total Attendance* as the dependent variable.

| Significant Independent Variables | Contributor to $R^2$ |
|---|---|
| Catchment Population | 0·235 |
| Water—Paddling Pool | 0·157 |
| Formal Equipment | 0·150 |
| Team Games Area | 0·092 |
| Size of Playground | 0·030 |
| Total $R^2$ for a Multiple Regression on all significant variables | 0·664 |
| Multiple Regression on all variables, including the non-significant variables: Number of competing Playgrounds, Play leader, Sandpit, Adventure Facilities | 0·678 |

41. With *Total Hourly Counts* as the dependent variable.

| Significant Independent Variables | Contributor to $R^2$ |
|---|---|
| Team Games Area | 0·162 |
| Water—Paddling Pool | 0·147 |
| Size of Playground | 0·073 |
| Formal Equipment | 0·067 |
| Number of Competing Playgrounds | 0·043 |
| Total $R^2$ for a Multiple Regression on all significant variables | 0·492 |
| Multiple Regression on all variables, including the non-significant variables: Catchment Population, Play leader, Sandpit, Adventure Facilities | 0·528 |

TABLES 42 AND 43
*Multiple regression analysis on type 1 playgrounds*

Playgrounds in Parks and Recreation Grounds.
Order of significance of the independent variables and their contribution to the overall multiple correlation coefficient ($R^2$).

42. With *Total Attendance* as the dependent variable.

| Significant Independent Variables | Contributor to $R^2$ |
|---|---|
| Water—Paddling Pool | 0·266 |
| Catchment Population | 0·218 |
| Team Games Area | 0·132 |
| Total $R^2$ for a Multiple Regression on all significant variables | 0·616 |
| Multiple Regression on all variables, including the non-significant variables: Size of Playground—Formal Equipment—Sandpit—Number of competing Playgrounds | 0·656 |

43. With *Total Hourly Counts* as the dependent variable.

| Significant Independent Variables | Contributor to $R^2$ |
| --- | --- |
| Team Games Area | 0·277 |
| Water—Paddling Pool | 0·152 |
| Formal Equipment | 0·107 |
| Total $R^2$ for a Multiple Regression on all significant variables | 0·536 |
| Multiple Regression on all variables, including the non-significant variables: Catchment Population—Size of Playground—Number of competing Playgrounds, Sandpit | 0·560 |

## TABLES 44 AND 45
### *Multiple regression analysis on type 2 playgrounds*

Playgrounds with Equipment.
Order of significance of the independent variables and their contribution to the overall multiple correlation coefficient ($R^2$).

44. With *Total Attendance* as the dependent variable.

| Significant Independent Variables | Contributor to $R^2$ |
| --- | --- |
| Team Games Area | 0·202 |
| Formal Equipment | 0·113 |
| Catchment Population | 0·110 |
| Total $R^2$ for a Multiple Regression on all significant variables | 0·425 |
| Multiple Regression on all variables, including the non-significant variables: Size of Playground —Playleader—Sandpit—Adventure Facilities— Number of competing Playgrounds | 0·479 |

**45.** With *Total Hourly Counts* as the dependent variable.

| Significant Independent Variables | Contributor to $R^2$ |
|---|---|
| Number of competing Playgrounds | 0·367 |
| Catchment Population | 0·243 |
| Size of Playground | 0·111 |
| Team Games Area | 0·098 |
| Total $R^2$ for a Multiple Regression on all significant variables | 0·819 |
| Multiple Regression on all variables, including the non-significant variables: Formal Equipment —Playleader—Sandpit—Adventure Facilities | 0·837 |

## TABLES 46 AND 47
*Multiple regression analysis on type 3 playgrounds*

Play Streets and Play Areas with no equipment.
Order of significance of the independent variables and their contribution to the overall multiple correlation coefficient ($R^2$).

**46.** With *Total Attendance* as the dependent variable.

| Significant Independent Variables | Contributor to $R^2$ |
|---|---|
| Team Games Area | 0·309 |
| Total $R^2$ for a Multiple Regression on all significant variables | 0·309 |
| Multiple Regression on all variables, including the non-significant variables: Catchment Population—Size of Playground—Competition | 0·389 |

**47.** With *Total Hourly Counts* as the dependent variable.

| Significant Independent Variables | Contributor to $R^2$ |
|---|---|
| Team Games Area | 0·467 |
| Total $R^2$ for a Multiple Regression on all significant variables | 0·467 |
| Multiple Regression on all variables, including the non-significant variables: Catchment Population—Size of Playground—Number of competing Playgrounds | 0·589 |

The method of analysis was the calculation of multiple regression equations of the form

$$Y = b_0 + b_1X_1 + b_2X_2 + \ldots + b_p X_p$$
$$(B_0) \quad (B_1) \quad (B_2) \qquad (B_p)$$

where

$Y$ is the dependent variable, playground attendance.

$X_1 \ldots X_p$ are the independent variables, the factors influencing attendance.

$p$ is the number of variables being considered.

$b_1 \ldots b_p$ are the coefficients of the independent variables.

$b_0$ is a constant.

$B_0 \ldots B_p$ are the standard errors of the appropriate coefficients.

A number of equations were calculated using a different combination of variables each time.

If the coefficient $b$ of a variable X is equal to zero, then it can be stated quite definitely that this variable has no influence upon attendance. This very rarely happens and so a test is carried out on each coefficient to see whether it differs significantly from zero. The value

$$t = \frac{b}{B}$$

is calculated for each coefficient and then referred to the $t-$ distribution for $(n - p - 1)$ degrees of freedom where $n$ is the number of playgrounds. For example, if the value of $t$ for a coefficient of type 1 playgrounds when three variables are being considered was equal to 2·02, then it could be stated with 95 per cent confidence that the variable had a significant influence upon the level attendance. Throughout this analysis the 95 per cent confidence level was taken as the critical level. In the above example, therefore, a value of $t$ greater than 2·02 would indicate that the variable had a significant influence on attendance since the confidence level would be above 95 per cent. A value of $t$ lower than 2·02 where confidence level would be less than 95 per cent, would be taken to indicate that the variable did not have a significant influence on attendance.

A number of equations were calculated for the three types of playground using a different combination of factors each time. The tests of significance performed on the coefficients indicated which of the eight factors did in fact influence the level of attendance and which could be discounted as having no influence.

A deeper analysis into the influences of different types of formal equipment was performed using as the dependent variable the totalled hourly counts of children using the formal equipment. This revealed that at type 1 playgrounds swings and climbing frames and tunnels were the most significant items of formal equipment while slides were shown to be marginally so. The other two items, see-saws and round-abouts, were highly insignificant. On the other hand at type 2 play-grounds, none of the individual items appeared significant. But the constant term in this equation was significantly high suggesting that it is the presence of any type of equipment that is attracting children rather than any individual item.

A multiple regression equation was then constructed for each type of playground to use in predicting attendance at playgrounds. The following is that for playgrounds in parks and recreation grounds (type 1)

$Y$ = Total attendance in one day in fine weather on a Saturday in the summer or on a weekday in the school summer holidays.

$X_1$ = Total child population under fifteen years of age living within the catchment area. (Catchment area radius = 1,760 yds. (1 mile).)

$X_2$ = Weighted index of equipment.

The previous results indicated the weighting systems for the equipment index.

|  | Type 1 |
|---|---|
| Provision of a paddling pool | 100 |
| Provision of a sand pit | 25 |
| Provision of a team ball games area | 60 |
| For each unit of formal equipment | 3 |
| For each 1,000 sq. yds. of playground area | 7 |
|  | (max. of 35) |

The marks for a playground are totalled to give the equipment index.

$$Y = 5 \cdot 28 + X_1\, 0 \cdot 0085 + X_2\, 1 \cdot 45$$
$$\quad (9 \cdot 10) \qquad (0 \cdot 0010) \qquad (0 \cdot 07)$$
$$R^2 = 0 \cdot 931$$
$$n = 44$$
$$\overline{Y} = 168$$

$R^2$ is the coefficient of multiple correlation, $n$ is the number of play-grounds and $\overline{Y}$ is the average attendance. Estimated standard errors are shown in parentheses beneath the appropriate coefficients.

The degree of accuracy in explaining the variation in the attendance of the playgrounds that were surveyed was high for type 1 playgrounds; 93 per cent of the variation in attendance can be attributed to variations in the number of children living in the catchment area and the equipment index, whereas for the 40 type 2 playgrounds, 73 per cent of the variation in attendance can be explained in this way. But for the type 3 playgrounds only about 26 per cent of the variation in attendance can be attributed to the variation in the two variables, size of playground and the number of children living in the catchment area, leaving 74 per cent of the variation unexplained.

These differences in the correlation coefficients are not really surprising since the same method of analysis is being attempted on quite different types of playground. Children attending playgrounds in parks and recreation grounds (type 1) have to make a special journey to reach the playground, usually quite a long journey. It is a very different situation at play areas with no equipment (type 3) and especially the play streets where children have only to walk outside their own homes to play. In this case a far more detailed survey is required as to the reason children use the play area and the alternative forms of play.

The 95 per cent confidence limits for a predicted attendance which can be calculated from the above information will give a large range for the expected attendance. But this does not detract from the usefulness of the equations, since they are only meant as a rough guide to the possible attendance at a playground. When used predictively the equation will only give an estimate of attendance for a fine day in the summer, since the survey data relates to this time of year, and is probably about the maximum daily attendance that could be expected at a playground. No estimate can be made of the yearly total or of the seasonal variation in attendance from these equations.

## 2 The relationship between size of a playground and its attendance

In Table 48, only those playgrounds of types 1 and 2 that were used in the regression analysis have been considered. The type 3 playgrounds were usually play streets and other similar open areas which are not purpose-built playgrounds and where other factors determine their size.

The average attendance increases with size up to about a size of 3,000 sq. yds. where there is a levelling off. On the other hand the total count continues to increase with size.

So it would seem that the larger the playground the longer children will spend playing there, but that the total number of children attending the playground only increases up to a size of about 3,000 sq. yds., after which any increase in size ceases to increase attendance.

TABLE 48
## Size and attendance

| Size, sq. yds. | Number of playgrounds | Average attendance | Average count |
|---|---|---|---|
| Under 500 | 12 | 94 | 109 |
| 500–1,000 | 21 | 115 | 123 |
| 1,000–2,000 | 14 | 137 | 142 |
| 2,000–4,000 | 20 | 177 | 287 |
| Over 4,000 | 18 | 172 | 378 |

## 3  Definition of Units of formal equipment
Each item of equipment *except swings* is coded as one unit. Count swings to the nearest three to obtain the number of units.

e.g. Each slide          = 1 unit
     3 swings             = 1 unit
     Steam roller         = 1 unit
     7 swings and 2 slides = 4 units

9 or more units should be coded 9.

N.B.—Mobile equipment, e.g. bicycles or tricycles, rope for tug-of-war, shuttles, model boats (where there is a place to float them), etc. Where these are provided at a playground they should be noted as 'special facilities'.

## 4  Definition of 'Major Roads'
For the purposes of the survey a major road is one that satisfies one or more of the following conditions:

(a) a road carrying an off-peak bus flow of four or more buses per hour;

(b) a classified road (Ministry of Transport standards—trunk roads and class 1, 2 or 3 roads);

(c) a road known to be carrying traffic flows of more than 8,000 vehicles per 16-hour day.

## TABLE 49

*Analysis of hourly counts by the children's activities for the three types of playgrounds*

| | | Type 1 (64 Playgrounds) | | | Number of playgrounds with this equipment | Average per playground |
|---|---|---|---|---|---|---|
| Children's Activities | | Total children—all day | | | | |
| | | Male | Female | Total | | |
| Playing Pitch Area | | 856 | 186 | 1,042 | 16 | 65 |
| | Ratio | 460 : 100 | | 7% | | |
| Sand Pit | | 327 | 233 | 560 | 14 | 40 |
| | Ratio | 140 : 100 | | 4% | | |
| Water Feature | | 1,231 | 937 | 2,168 | 10 | 217 |
| | Ratio | 131 : 100 | | 15% | | |
| Formal Equipment | | 2,410 | 2,533 | 4,943 | 55 | 90 |
| | Ratio | 95 : 100 | | 35% | | |
| General Activities — Constructional Play | | 77 ⎤ | 30 ⎤ | 107 | | |
| | Ratio | | | | | |
| General Activities — Singing, etc. | | 59 | 87 | 146 | | |
| | Ratio | | | | | |
| General Activities — Imaginative Games | | 87 ⎬ 278 | 155 ⎬ 333 | 242 ⎬ 611 4% | 64 | 10 |
| | Ratio | 83 : 100 | | | | |
| General Activities — Drama, Music, etc. | | 6 | 8 | 14 | | |
| | Ratio | | | | | |
| General Activities — Painting, etc. | | 16 | 14 | 30 | | |
| | Ratio | | | | | |
| General Activities — Quiet Games | | 33 ⎦ | 39 ⎦ | 72 | | |
| | Ratio | | | | | |
| Relaxing—Talking | | 1,724 | 1,633 | 3,357 | 64 | 52 |
| | Ratio | 106 : 100 | | 24% | | |
| Free Play | | 918 | 622 | 1,540 | 64 | 24 |
| | Ratio | 148 : 100 | | 11% | | |
| Totals | | 7,744 | 6,477 | 14,221 | 64 | 222 |
| | Ratio | 120 : 100 | | 100% | | |

*of Playground*

| Type 2 (54 Playgrounds) | | | | | Type 3 (30 Playgrounds) | | | | |
|---|---|---|---|---|---|---|---|---|---|
| Total children—all day | | | Number of playgrounds with this equipment | Average per playground | Total children—all day | | | Number of playgrounds with this equipment | Average per playground |
| Male | Female | Total | | | Male | Female | Total | | |
| 578 | 264 | 842 | 14 | 60 | 452 | 179 | 631 | 11 | 57 |
| | 219 : 100 | 8% | | | | 233 : 100 | 23% | | |
| 302 | 305 | 607 | 10 | 61 | — | — | — | — | — |
| | 99 : 100 | 6% | | | | | | | |
| — | — | — | — | — | — | — | — | — | — |
| 1,401 | 1,676 | 3,077 | 52 | — | — | — | — | — | — |
| | 84 : 100 | 29% | | | | | | | |
| 21 | 12 | 33 | | | 3 | 1 | 4 | | |
| 28 | 175 | 303 | | | 28 | 31 | 59 | | |
| 41 | 91 | 232 | | | 60 | 63 | 123 | | |
| 64 | 96 | 160 | 54 | 32 | 0 | 2 | 2 | 30 | 7 |
| 52 | 235 | 387 | | | 1 | 0 | 1 | | |
| 308 | 328 | 636 | | | 7 | 9 | 16 | | |
| 814 | 937 | 1,751 | | | 99 | 106 | 205 | | |
| | 87 : 100 | 17% | | | | 93 : 100 | 7% | | |
| 1,266 | 1,253 | 2,519 | 54 | 47 | 762 | 545 | 1,307 | 30 | 44 |
| | 101 : 100 | 24% | | | | 140 : 100 | 47% | | |
| 973 | 732 | 1,705 | 54 | 32 | 458 | 186 | 644 | 30 | 21 |
| | 133 : 100 | 16% | | | | 246 : 100 | 23% | | |
| 5,334 | 5,167 | 10,501 | 54 | 194 | 1,771 | 1,016 | 2,787 | 30 | 93 |
| | 103 : 100 | 100% | | | | 174 : 100 | 100% | | |

# Appendix IV

## Material relating to the Survey of Facilities in Nineteen Boroughs (Chapters 11-13)

In summary the material analysed in this survey related to the following:[1]

19 boroughs
36 review areas selected as follows:
    3 areas in 7 boroughs
    2 areas in 3 boroughs
    1 area in 3 boroughs
    6 boroughs reviewed as a whole

| | |
|---|---|
| Largest child population per area | 24,149 |
| Smallest child population per area | 6,860 |

192 wards

| | | |
|---|---|---|
| Maximum number per review area | 12 | |
| Minimum number per review area | 2 | |
| Largest child population per ward | | 10,500 |
| Smallest child population per ward | | 760 |

467 playgrounds

| | |
|---|---|
| Largest number per review area | 48 |
| Smallest number per review area | 1 |

### TABLE 64
### Boroughs investigated

| Region | City | Population size | Number of areas investigated |
|---|---|---|---|
| Northern | Newcastle | 257,000 | 3 areas |
| | Darlington | 83,000 | Total town |
| North West | Liverpool | 728,000 | 3 areas |
| | Kirkby | 57,000 | Total town |

[1] See note on p. 210

| Region | City | Population size | Number of areas investigated |
|---|---|---|---|
| Yorkshire and Humberside | Bradford | 295,000 | 1 area |
| East Midlands | Derby | 129,190 | 2 areas, covering total town |
| | Lincoln | 77,180 | Total town |
| West Midlands | Coventry | 330,000 | 3 areas |
| | Worcester | 67,580 | Total town |
| South West | Bristol | 437,048 | 3 areas |
| | Swindon | 97,460 | 2 areas, covering total town |
| | Gloucester | 69,773 | Total town |
| Wales | Swansea | 167,322 | 2 areas, covering total town |
| South East (excluding London A.C.) | Southampton | 204,543 | 1 area |
| | Norwich | 119,123 | 1 area |
| | Stevenage | 55,000 | Total town |
| London A.C. | Brent | 296,030 | 3 areas |
| | Camden | 245,707 | 3 areas |
| | Southwark | 313,413 | 3 areas |

## TABLE 65
*Borough child population and number of play spaces*

| Borough | Child population 0–14 (in thousands) | Number of play spaces | | |
|---|---|---|---|---|
| | | Equipped | Unequipped | Total |
| Gloucester | 17·0 | 15 | 1 | 16 |
| Lincoln | 18·4 | 13 | — | 13 |
| Stevenage | 18·8 | 20 | 28 | 48 |
| Newcastle | 63·4 | 43 | 5 | 48 |
| Worcester | 16·9 | 12 | 4 | 16 |
| Swindon | 24·9 | 27 | — | 27 |
| Swansea | 38·3 | 35 | 3 | 38 |
| Norwich | 26·8 | 16 | — | 16 |
| Southampton | 50·1 | 28 | n/a | 28 |
| Bristol | 96·6 | 92 | 3 | 95 |
| Coventry | 74·7 | 38 | — | 38 |
| Camden | 39·2 | 43 | 29 | 72 |
| Kirkby | 24·1 | 24 | 2 | 26 |
| Derby | 28·6 | 16 | — | 16 |
| Darlington | 18·9 | 9 | — | 9 |
| Bradford | 70·3 | 22 | — | 22 |
| Liverpool | 195·3 | 67 | 41 | 108 |
| Brent | 55·0 | 20 | 1 | 21 |
| Southwark | 69·9 | n/a | n/a | n/a |

## TABLE 66

### Review areas grouped by borough showing population, acreage and density

| Borough | Area | Total child population | 15+ population | Total population | Size in acres | Overall density |
|---|---|---|---|---|---|---|
| Liverpool | A | 18·8 | 44·5 | 63·4 | 700 | 90·6 |
| | B | 18·3 | 49·3 | 67·7 | 3,588 | 18·9 |
| | C | 16·6 | 47·9 | 64·6 | 5,275 | 12·2 |
| Bristol | A | 6·8 | 30·6 | 37·4 | 998 | 37·5 |
| | B | 15·0 | 28·9 | 43·9 | 3,249 | 13·5 |
| | C | 16·0 | 41·1 | 57·1 | 7,278 | 7·9 |
| Coventry | A | 9·9 | 44·0 | 54·0 | 1,548 | 34·1 |
| | B | 11·5 | 43·6 | 55·2 | 2,853 | 19·3 |
| | C | 11·8 | 39·1 | 51·0 | 4,629 | 11·0 |
| Southwark | A | 19·8 | 66·3 | 86·2 | 1,131 | 76·3 |
| | B | 19·3 | 63·3 | 82·6 | 1,368 | 60·4 |
| | C | 19·0 | 73·5 | 92·6 | 3,114 | 29·8 |
| Brent | A | 14·3 | 60·1 | 74·4 | 1,384 | 53·8 |
| | B | 9·2 | 44·1 | 53·4 | 2,266 | 23·8 |
| | C | 10·4 | 44·1 | 54·5 | 2,897 | 18·9 |
| Bradford | A | 13·6 | 43·7 | 57·4 | 6,378 | 9·0 |
| Newcastle | A | 11·4 | 35·5 | 46·9 | 1,223 | 38·4 |
| | B | 10·2 | 31·8 | 42·1 | 1,490 | 28·2 |
| | C | 7·5 | 35·6 | 43·1 | 2,562 | 16·8 |
| Camden | A | 8·7 | 46·8 | 55·7 | 982 | 56·7 |
| | B | 11·9 | 51·6 | 63·6 | 1,245 | 51·1 |
| | C | 9·5 | 42·9 | 58·8 | 1,957 | 30·0 |
| Southampton | A | 13·1 | 36·7 | 49·8 | 2,415 | 20·6 |
| Swansea | A | 21·0 | 67·5 | 88·5 | 10,291 | 8·6 |
| | B | 17·3 | 61·4 | 78·7 | 11,309 | 7·0 |
| Derby | A | 15·0 | 50·0 | 65·5 | 3,981 | 16·4 |
| | B | 15·1 | 51·5 | 66·7 | 4,135 | 16·1 |
| Norwich | A | 12·9 | 42·4 | 55·4 | 4,259 | 13·0 |
| Swindon | A | 13·7 | 38·8 | 52·6 | 3,545 | 14·8 |
| | B | 11·1 | 27·9 | 39·1 | 2,814 | 13·9 |
| Darlington | T | 18·9 | 63·9 | 82·9 | 6,498 | 12·8 |
| Lincoln | T | 18·4 | 58·7 | 77·1 | 7,518 | 10·3 |
| Gloucester | T | 17·0 | 52·7 | 69·7 | 5,295 | 13·2 |
| Worcester | T | 16·9 | 50·6 | 67·5 | 6,170 | 10·9 |
| Kirkby | T | 24·1 | 27·9 | 57·3 | 4,688 | 11·3 |
| Stevenage | T | 18·6 | 36·4 | 55·0 | 3,040 | 18·1 |

Note: Discrepancies between some of the population breakdowns and the totals are due to the fact that they were only estimates.

**TABLE 67**

*Provision of sports facilities (other than swimming and gymnasia) in the review areas*

| Review Areas | | Large Pitches Football, etc. | Cricket | Tennis, Basket-ball Courts | Athletics | Bowling | Fishing | Golf | Other | Total number Sports Areas |
|---|---|---|---|---|---|---|---|---|---|---|
| Liverpool | A | | | 1 | | 1 | | | | 2 |
| Camden | A | | | 2 | | | | | | 2 |
| Southwark | B | 2 | | 2 | | | | | | 2 |
| Bristol | B | 1 | | | | | | | | 1 |
| Coventry | A | | | 1 | 1 | | | | | 2 |
| Southwark | A | 1 | | | | | | | | 1 |
| Brent | A | 1 | 1 | 1 | 1 | 1 | | | 2 | 3 |
| Newcastle | A | 1 | | 1 | | 1 | Not specified | | | 2 |
| Liverpool | B | 2 | 1 | 1 | | 2 | | | | 5 |
| Newcastle | B | 2 P/F | | 1 | | | | | | 3 |
| Coventry | B | 3 | | 1 | | 1 | | | 1 | 3 |
| Camden | B | 1 | 1 | 1 | | | | | 1 | 2 |
| Brent | B | 3 | 3 | 1 | | 1 | | | | 3 |
| Bristol | A | 1 | | 1 | | 2 | | | | 2 |
| Derby | B | 5 | 1 | 4 | | 4 | 1 | 1 | 2 | 8 |
| Swansea | B | 13 | 7 | 8 | | 8 | | | | 16 |
| Southwark | C | 3 | 2 | 4 | 1 | 2 | | 1 | 2 | 6 |
| Darlington | T | | | | | | | | | n/a |

TABLE 67—continued

| Review Areas | | Large Pitches Football, etc. | Cricket | Tennis, Basket-ball Courts | Athletics | Bowling | Fishing | Golf | Other | Total number Sports Areas |
|---|---|---|---|---|---|---|---|---|---|---|
| Bradford | A | 4 | 2 | 3 | | 3 | | | | 5 |
| Kirkby | T | 8 | | 3 | | 2 | | | 3 | 10 |
| Southampton | A | 2 P/F | | | | | | | | 2 |
| Swindon | B | 7 | 4 | 2 | | 2 | | | | 8 |
| Derby | A | 8 | 2 | 5 | | 2 | 1 | | 1 | 9 |
| Brent | C | 1 | 2 | 3 | | 2 | | | | 3 |
| Worcester | T | 8 P/F | | 2 | | 1 | | | | 10 |
| Norwich | A | 4 | 1 | 2 | | 1 | 1 | | 1 | 6 |
| Stevenage | T | 7 P/F | | 4 | 1 | 2 | | | 2 | 8 |
| Swindon | A | 4 | 2 | 2 | | 3 | | | | 5 |
| Swansea | A | 8 | 7 | 9 | 1 | 8 | | 1 | | 18 |
| Coventry | C | 4 | | | | | | 1 | | 4 |
| Lincoln | T | 5 | 1 | 1 | | | | 2 | | 8 |
| Liverpool | C | 7 | 3 | 4 | | 3 | | 1 | | 10 |
| Gloucester | T | 5 P/F | 3 | 4 | | | | | | 8 |
| Camden | C | 2 | 1 | 2 | 1 | 1 | 1 | | 3 | 4 |
| Newcastle | C | | | 1 | | 2 | | | 1 | 3 |
| Bristol | C | 5 | 2 | 2 | | 1 | | | 1 | 6 |

P/F = Playing Field.
n/a = not available.

Note: The areas in this table are in ascending order of public recreational space provision. The total areas may contain one or more of the other categories of provision.

TABLES 68 AND 69

*Equipped and unequipped playground situations in greater detail in the two categories 'Parks, etc.' and 'Other'*

TABLE 68

Playgrounds situated in:

| | General category: Parks, etc. | | | | | |
|---|---|---|---|---|---|---|
| | Equipped | | Unequipped | | | Total |
| | No. | % | No. | % | No. | % |
| Parks | 83 | 49 | 3 | 33·3 | 86 | 47 |
| Municipal Gardens | 27 | 15 | 3 | 33·3 | 30 | 17 |
| Commons, Heaths | 12 | 7 | 2 | 22·3 | 14 | 8 |
| Recreation Grounds | 49 | 29 | 1 | 11·1 | 50 | 28 |
| Total | 171 | 100 | 9 | 100 | 180 | 100 |

TABLE 69

Playgrounds situated in:

| | General category: 'Other' Equipped | |
|---|---|---|
| | No. | % |
| Off Street | 10 | 29 |
| Public open space, waste land, etc. | 9 | 26 |
| Old housing areas, redevelopment areas, etc. | 6 | 18 |
| Shopping centres, etc. | 5 | 15 |
| Private Property[1] | 4 | 12 |
| Total | 34 | 100 |

1 Of the four private property playgrounds two belonged to private sports grounds and two to private blocks of flats.

# Appendix V

## A. *Legislation*[1] *under which play and recreation facilities may be assisted from public funds*

Recreation Grounds Act, 1859
Public Improvements Act, 1860
Town Gardens Protection Act, 1863
Public Health Act, 1875
Public Health Amendment Act, 1890
Local Government Act, 1894
Open Spaces Act, 1906
Public Health Amendment Act, 1907
Public Health Act, 1925
Physical Training and Recreation Act, 1937
Street Playground Act, 1938
Social and Physical Training Grant Regulations, 1939
Education Act, 1944
National Health Service Act, 1946
Local Government Act, 1948
Nurseries and Child Minders Act, 1948
Children Act, 1948
Housing Act, 1957
Local Government Act, 1958
Recreational Charities Act, 1958
Charities Act, 1960
Public Health Act, 1961
Local Government (Financial Provisions) Act, 1963
Children and Young Persons Act, 1963
Commons Registration Act, 1966
Local Government Act, 1966
Health Services and Public Health Act, 1968

1  For details of relevant sections and powers under these Acts and Regulations see Owen (1967).

# B. Some organisations[1] in the U.K. concerned with, or in some way connected with, children's play provision, which may be approached for advice or which publish useful information

Committee for Children's Playthings,
   255, Hill Road, Cambridge.
   (A new independent body set up by Children's Play Activities Ltd.; particularly concerned with objective assessment of, and reporting on, toys and other equipment for play.)

Handicapped Adventure Playground Association,
   2, Poultons Street, London, S.W.3.
   (Will give information on adventure playgrounds for the handicapped.)

Institute of Landscape Architects,
   12, Carlton House Terrace, London, S.W.1.
   (Will advise on playground design.)

International Playground Association,
   Hon. Sec. Mr W. D. Abernethy,
   57B, Catherine Place, London, S.W.1.
   (An international organisation, particularly noted for a most informative Newsletter and interesting biennial conferences.)

Kindergartens for Commerce,
   59, Rectory Road, Beckenham, Kent.

[1] A number of local authorities now run play schemes; there are also many local voluntary associations exclusively concerned with children's play provision, and other local voluntary organisations such as Councils of Social Service who provide different forms of play services. These have been felt to be too numerous to list, but information concerning their activities may always be obtained from local authority Council offices, local Councils of Social Service, or through the national organisations listed above.

London Adventure Playground Association,
    4, Lansdowne Road, London, W.1.
(Will give advice and guidance on the setting up of adventure playgrounds.)

National Campaign for Nursery Education,
    74, Sydney Road, Muswell Hill, London, N.10.

National Playing Fields Association,
    57B, Catherine Place, London, S.W.1.
(Will give direct advice and guidance to the sponsors—either local authority or voluntary organisation—of individual schemes on playgrounds and play leadership. Has extensive range of publications and films. The Association also gives technical and legal advice on playing-field schemes and in certain circumstances offers grant aid.)

National Society for Mentally Handicapped Children,
    5, Bulstrode Street, London, W.1.

Nursery School Association,
    89, Stamford Street, London, S.E.1.

OMEP
Organisation Mondiale pour l'Education Pré-scolaire,
    (World Organisation for Early Childhood Education)
    The Housing Centre, 13, Suffolk Street, London, W.1.

Save the Children Fund,
    29, Queen Anne's Gate, London, S.W.1.
(Will consider requests for assistance in setting up play groups and will give advice. Will also advise on Hospital play groups.)

Youth Service Information Centre,
    NCTYL, Humberstone Drive, Leicester.
(Although primarily concerned with services for youth, information on children's play facilities is also available.)

Pre-School Playgroups Association,
    87A, Borough High Street, London, S.E.1.

# C. Road accident figures for children[1]

| | All children 1967 | Fatal 885 | Serious 15·186 | Slight 46·945 | Total 63·016 |
|---|---|---|---|---|---|

Circumstances of fatal road accidents to children under 15 in Great Britain, January–December 1967

| Circumstances | Under 1 | 1 | 2 | 3 | 4 | 5 | 6 | 7 | 8 | 9 | 10 | 11 | 12 | 13 | 14 | Total |
|---|---|---|---|---|---|---|---|---|---|---|---|---|---|---|---|---|
| Cyclists turning right | | | | | | 1 | | 1 | 2 | | 7 | 5 | 3 | 3 | 3 | 25 |
| Cyclists/tricycles failing to stop at major roads | | | | | | 1 | 3 | 1 | 2 | 1 | 2 | 5 | 3 | 3 | 4 | 25 |
| Cyclists/tricycles losing control | | | | 1 | 1 | | | 1 | 1 | | 6 | 3 | 6 | 5 | 5 | 29 |
| Cyclists colliding with vehicles turning/overtaking | | | 2 | 1 | 2 | 1 | 1 | 1 | 2 | 1 | 2 | 9 | 4 | 9 | 6 | 41 |
| Cyclists with faulty equipment | | 1 | | | | | | | | | 1 | | 1 | | 1 | 4 |
| Playing near delivery vehicles | | 9 | 7 | | 1 | 1 | 1 | 1 | 1 | | 1 | 1 | | | | 23 |
| Hanging on to moving vehicles (with/without bicycle) | | 1 | | | 2 | 1 | 1 | 1 | 1 | 1 | 1 | 1 | 1 | 1 | | 12 |
| Losing control of toys | | | 1 | | | 1 | 1 | | | | | | 1 | | | 4 |
| On footpath/verge/pavement | | 6 | | 1 | 6 | 1 | 1 | 4 | 2 | 1 | 3 | 2 | 1 | 3 | 2 | 33 |
| On zebra crossing with centre refuge | | | | | | | 1 | 1 | | 1 | | | | | | 3 |
| On zebra crossing without centre refuge | | | | | 1 | 1 | 1 | 2 | | | 1 | | 2 | | | 8 |
| Dashing into road/across road | 1 | 3 | 14 | 35 | 29 | 34 | 35 | 27 | 29 | 17 | 6 | 9 | 2 | 11 | 6 | 258 |
| Running across road to join mother/friends, etc. | | | | | | | | | 2 | 1 | 1 | 1 | 1 | 1 | 1 | 8 |
| Crossing road masked by moving vehicles | | 1 | | | | | | | | | 1 | | 1 | | | 3 |
| Crossing road masked by stationary vehicles | | 1 | 11 | 18 | 27 | 16 | 18 | 11 | 6 | 9 | 5 | 7 | 3 | 5 | 5 | 142 |
| Alighting from bus (school/p.s.v.) | | | | | | 2 | 1 | | 1 | | 1 | 1 | 1 | 3 | 2 | 12 |
| Playing in street/near busy road | | 3 | 4 | 2 | 1 | 5 | 1 | 2 | 1 | | 1 | 2 | | | | 22 |
| Children escaping control of adults/older children | | 3 | 2 | 4 | 2 | 1 | | | 1 | | | | | | | 13 |
| Crossing road to/from ice-cream van | | 4 | 3 | | | | | | 2 | | | 1 | | 1 | | 11 |
| Crossing road without due care (not running) | | 2 | 6 | 4 | 2 | 8 | 8 | 4 | 2 | 7 | 3 | 4 | 6 | 5 | 6 | 67 |
| Crossing road masked by concealed entrance/hedge, etc. | | | | | | | | 1 | | | | | | | | 1 |
| Playing near stationary vehicle other than delivery | | 3 | 2 | 2 | | | | | | | | | | | | 7 |
| Others | 2 | 4 | 2 | 2 | | 2 | 1 | 1 | 1 | | 1 | | 1 | 3 | 1 | 21 |
| Passengers | 10 | 15 | 16 | 9 | 3 | 4 | 4 | 6 | 7 | 6 | 8 | 3 | 5 | 4 | 13 | 113 |
| **Total** | 13 | 56 | 70 | 92 | 79 | 78 | 76 | 61 | 61 | 47 | 49 | 52 | 40 | 56 | 55 | 885 |

1 Royal Society for the Prevention of Accidents (1968).

# D. Some space standards

## (1) Provision for open space

The following breakdown shows a comparison between the existing and proposed situation of open space provision per 1,000 population derived from a sample of Ministry of Housing and Local Government urban categories.[1]

| Urban category | Existing situation | Proposed situation |
|---|---|---|
| (a) County boroughs | 8·1 | 10·5 |
| (b) Metropolitan town map areas | 11·9 | 13·8 |
| (c) Large town map areas (over 10,000 pop.) | 15·1 | 15·2 |
| (d) Small town map areas (under 10,000 pop.) | 26·0 | 25·1 |
| (e) New towns | 9·8 | 11·1 |

(This is used by the author to underline his thesis that there is no evidence for the criticisms of New Town planning of 'low density housing, the overpowering space, an eternity of wideness . . . the lack of compact layout and the scattered two-storey dwellings separated by great spaces'.[2] It does not, however, take account of space distribution).

Open space standards differ both from one New Town to another and from the original recommendations by the New Towns Committee.

## (2) Open space in relation to housing density

Ministerial recommendation for minimum standard of incidental open space:

One acre per 1,000 population[3] irrespective of any other provision for public open space and playing fields.

(This is based on daylight requirements and is achievable through layout and height with dwelling densities up to 300 per acre.)

1 Best (1964), p. 57.
2 *Ibid.*, p. 49.
3 Ministry of Housing and Local Government (1952), p. 33.

288

## (3) *Provision for recreational open space*

(a) Ministerial recommendation:[1]
   7 acres per 1,000 population
      (6 acres of playing space plus 1 acre for parks)
(b) National Playing Fields Association Recommendation:
   6 acres of playing space (inclusive of children's play space) per 1,000 population.
   (This standard was formulated in 1925 and reconsidered in 1951 and was based upon an analysis of the age groups of the then population.)

This analysis indicated that approximately half the population were between the ages of ten and forty years. Of this 500 per 1,000 it was assumed that probably 150 did not want to, or were prevented from, playing games, while a further 150 would be catered for during the term at schools and colleges—which leaves a land requirement for 200 per 1,000. It was estimated that six acres of playing fields (accommodating 2 football pitches, 2 netball pitches, 1 cricket table, 1 bowling green, 2 tennis courts and a half-acre children's playground) would be the minimum allocation per (200) 1,000 population.

The reduction in the proportion of young to old revealed by the 1951 census was considered not to affect the above requirements owing to prolongation of active life and improved games standards.[2] (A marked increase in the population of 10–20 year olds as shown in the 1961 census returns, still does not bring the figure up to the original one on which the standard was based.)

(c) Examples of Local Authority proposed standards:

Greater London—7 acres per 1,000 population,[3] of which four acres should be within the County and three acres outside.

Liverpool—approximately three acres per 1,000 population[4] within the County Boundary, plus approximately one acre outside.

1  (a) Ministry of Housing and Local Government (1943).
   (b) Ministry of Housing and Local Government (1956).
   (c) The Ministry of Housing and Local Government and the Department of Education and Science (in circulars 49 and 11) recommended local authorities to review recreational space provision in their respective areas.
2  National Playing Fields Association (1963), pp. 96, 97.
3  (a) County of London Plan 1943 (see Carter and Goldfinger, 1945).
   (b) Greater London Plan 1944.
4  Liverpool Open Space Report 1964.

(*d*) New Towns:
Harlow as an example[1]

| *Situation in* 1969 | *Per* 1,000 *population* |
|---|---|
| Public playing fields and sports grounds, all ages | 3 acres |
| Town multi-sport centre | ½ acre |
| Private playing fields and sports ground | 1 acre (1963 recommended) |
| Parks and parkways | 1 acre |
| | 5·5 acres[2] |

(*e*) U.S.A. (recommended):
National Recreation Association[3] claim accepted standard to be 10 acres per 1,000 population.
46 of the largest cities have 7 acres per 1,000
11 of the 46 have 10 acres or more per 1,000.

## (4) *Open space attached to schools* (mandatory):

The Standards for School Premises Regulations 1954 specify minimum space requirements. These include reference to:

(*a*) a paved area;

(*b*) playing field accommodation.

The requirements depend on the number of classes and of pupils, and the following are examples:

(*a*) 'In the case of a school or department of eight or more classes provided wholly for infants, the paved area shall comprise two areas each of 110 feet by 60 feet.'

(*b*) Boys 3 form entry secondary school (450 pupils)—appropriate playing field area shall be 9 acres.

## (5) *Children's play facilities:*

(*a*) Relating to distribution and size of 'neighbourhood' playgrounds:

(i) National Playing Fields Association recommendation:[4]
Provision of playgrounds at intervals of not more than half a mile in built up residential areas.
Further N.P.F.A. recommendation:[5]
Half an acre per 1,000 population calculated as part of a 6-acre site (see above, (3) (*a*)).

1 Unpublished source.
2 This total must be viewed in the light of generous provision of other forms of open space, e.g. woodlands, school playing fields.
3 Owen (1965) p. 12.
4 Gooch (1963).
5 *Ibid.*

Size of playground should be not less than 1,000 sq. yds.

(ii) New Towns have adopted the N.P.F.A. standard of half an acre per 1,000 population.

(iii) Local Authority examples:

Liverpool—half an acre per 1,000 population[1] (proposed) calculated as follows:

135 sq. ft. per child playing, subject to two acres maximum and half an acre minimum size.

(iv) International examples:

U.S.A. National Recreation Association:

A recommended standard of one acre of playground per 800 population.

'There should be a playground within a $\frac{1}{4}$ to $\frac{1}{2}$ mile of every home.'[2]

The same double standard appears to occur here as in the N.P.F.A. recommendations (see above, (5) (a), (i)), the playground size to be dependent on the population:

| Population | Size needed |
|---|---|
| 2,000 | 3·25 acres |
| 3,000 | 4·00 acres |
| 4,000 | 5·00 acres |
| 5,000 | 6·00 acres |

*Sweden* (recommended):

'Every closely populated area with at least 500 children under sixteen should have a play park within a walking distance of 400 metres and when the number of children in an area is considered permanently to exceed 1,200 more play parks should be provided.

'In every area with more than 1,000 children there should be at least one play park open the whole year with indoor accommodation for play. If the number exceeds 3,000 at least two play parks should be open all the year round.'[3]

*Yugoslavia* (mandatory):

An overall minimum of 15 square metres per inhabitant.[4]

(b) Relating to location in housing areas:

(i) Ministry of Housing and Local Government[5] (recommended):

1  Liverpool Open Space Report 1964.
2  Butler, G. D. (1958), p. 2.
3  Wretlind-Larsson (1965).
4  Milincovic (1961).
5  Ministry of Housing and Local Government (1961), p. 42.

'Space should be set aside for children's play calculated on the basis of at least 20 to 25 sq. ft. per person on the estate,[1] not counting people in one- and two-person dwellings. At least 5/- per sq. ft. more than the cost that would otherwise be incurred on grassing should be spent on surfacing and equipment of the play areas. On a typical 12-acre scheme at about 140 habitable rooms per acre, the amount of space required is likely to be between 4,300 and 5,400 sq. yds. in all, that is in the region of an acre.'[2]

(ii) Some local authority examples:

*Liverpool* (proposed):
50 sq. ft. per child playing;
subject to maximum of 400 sq. yds.;
spaces to be within 200 yards of dwelling.[3]

*Birmingham* (proposed):
(a) 'A toddlers' play area with every block of flats of four storeys or more.'
(b) 'Play facilities for older children within the 5–12-year-old age group depending on the density, location of the nearest park or open space and the amount of ground available within the housing unit.'[4]

*Southwark* (proposed):
Larger estates should have one toddlers' play space of at least 400 sq. ft. for every hundred homes, discounting one- and two-person dwellings . . . junior playgrounds of at least 900 sq. ft. for every 200 houses for three persons and above . . . development housing upwards of a thousand people which are more than half a mile from a full-sized adventure playground should have a supervised 'mini adventure playground' of half an acre . . . a large size kick-around area (100 ft. × 60 ft.) should be provided for every 500 dwellings and a medium-size area (80 ft. × 40 ft.) for every 250 dwellings.

These standards should be considered as flexible . . . the most important consideration is that on any housing estate in

1 This standard has since been changed to that of '15–20 sq. ft. per bed space, with a minimum of 10 sq. ft. in exceptionally favourable circumstances, such as where an estate has existing playgrounds readily accessible in the immediate vicinity'. See Ministry of Housing and Local Government Circular 36/67 (1967), p. 14.
2 Ministry of Housing and Local Government (1961), p. 42.
3 Liverpool Open Space Report 1964.          4 Mitchell (1963), p. 12.

a dense urban area there should be 25 sq. ft. of play space per household of three persons or more.[1]

*Harlow New Town* (recommended):
For toddlers under five within housing areas where density is sixteen dwellings per acre or more: 1 play space per 200 dwellings; minimum size 200 sq. yds. It is expected, however, that housing layouts should include additional safe playing areas suitable for small children.[2]

(iii) International examples:

(*a*) *Denmark* (mandatory):
Under the Copenhagen Building Act and Building Regulations, 1939, 'All tenement houses open space is to be secured for joint use of the inmates, as also a sufficiently large and free area to provide a recreation area and playground for the children.'[3]

(*b*) *Yugoslavia* (mandatory):
In Belgrade and Zagreb:
5 to 7 sq. m. per child.[4]

(*c*) *Germany*—'The Golden Plan'[5] (a guide only):
Playgrounds for infants aged 3–6:
0·50 sq. m. of usable playing area per inhabitant in completely built-up areas.
0·25 sq. m. of usable playing area in less intensely developed areas.
Area: approximately 150 sq. m.
Distance: at the most 100 m.

Playgrounds for children aged 7–12:
0·50 sq. m. of play space as for younger children.
Area: 100 sq. m.
Distance: 500 m. maximum.

Playgrounds for 13–17-year-olds:
1·00 sq. m. per head of population.
Area: 7·000 sq. m.
Distance: 10 minutes maximum.

1 Southwark Interim Report (1966).
2 Unpublished source.
3 European Seminar on Playground Activities Report (1958), p. 21, and see Chapter 3.
4 Milincovic (1961).
5 Rupprecht (1966).

# References

AARON, D. 'Childsplay.' Harpers Row, N.Y., 1965.

ABERNETHY, W. D. 'Playleadership.' National Playing Fields Association, 1968.

ALLEN OF HURTWOOD, Lady. 'Design for Play.' The Housing Centre Trust, 1962.

ALLEN OF HURTWOOD, Lady. 'New Playgrounds.' The Housing Centre Trust, 1964.

ALLEN OF HURTWOOD, Lady. 'Planning for Play.' Thames and Hudson, 1968.

ARVILL, Robert. 'Man and Environment.' Penguin Books, 1967.

BENJAMIN, J. 'In Search of Adventure.' National Council of Social Service, 1966.

BENTLEY, B. Gilbert. 'The evolution of national insurance in Great Britain.' Michael Joseph, 1966.

BERG, Leila, in *The Observer*, April 24, 1965.

BESSEY, Gordon. 'The Community School.' *R.I.B.A. Journal*, Vol. 75, No. 8, 1968.

BEST, Robin H. 'Land for New Towns.' Town and Country Planning Association, 1964.

BOYD, William. 'The Educational Theory of Jean Jacques Rousseau.' Longmans, Green & Co., 1911.

BRITISH TRAVEL ASSOCIATION, UNIVERSITY OF KEELE, Pilot National Recreation Survey, Report No. 1, July 1967.

BROADY, Maurice. 'Social Theory and the Planners.' *New Society*, February 16, 1967.

BUTLER, George D. 'Playgrounds: Their Administration and Operation.' The Ronald Press Co., N.Y., 1960.

BUTLER, George D. 'Recreation Areas.' The Ronald Press Co., New York, 1958.

BYNNER, J. M. 'The Young Smoker.' Government Social Survey, SS 383, 1969.

CAILLOIS, Roger. 'Man the Sacred.' The Free Press of Glencoe, U.S., 1959.

CAILLOIS, Roger. 'Man Play and Games.' The Free Press of Glencoe, U.S., 1961.

CAMPBELL, Janet M. 'Report on the Welfare of Children and Mothers.' Carnegie U.K. Trust, Vol. 2, 1917.

CARTER, E. J., and GOLDFINGER, Ernö. 'The County of London Plan.' Penguin Books, 1945.

CENSUS OF ENGLAND AND WALES, 1961.

CENTRAL ADVISORY COUNCIL FOR EDUCATION (ENGLAND). 'Out of School.' 1948.

CENTRAL ADVISORY COUNCIL FOR EDUCATION (ENGLAND). 'Children and Their Primary Schools,' Vols. I and II, 1967. H.M.S.O. Known as the 'Plowden Report.'

CHAPMAN, Colin, in *The Sun*, November 12, 1964.

CHESHIRE RECREATION PRELIMINARY REPORT (K. O. Males, County Planning Officer). 'Recreation in Cheshire: A Survey of Existing Facilities in Sport and Physical Recreation', 1967.

CHILDREN AND YOUNG PERSONS ACT, 1963.

COHEN, Stanley. 'The Nature of Vandalism,' *New Society*, February 12, 1968.

COLES, Robert. 'The Strength of the Child,' *New Society* No. 295, May 1968.

COMMITTEE ON LOCAL AUTHORITY AND ALLIED PERSONAL SOCIAL SERVICES, Report of, 1968. H.M.S.O. Known as the 'Seebohm Report.'

COUNTY OF LANCASHIRE. Survey of Existing Facilities for Sport and Recreation, Preliminary Report, January 1967.

CRICK, Bernard, and GREEN, Geoffrey. 'People and Planning', *New Society*, September 5, 1968.

DAVIES, Hunter. 'The Other Half.' Heinemann, 1966.

DIDUSENKO, A. 'Soviet Children.' Progress Publishers, 1964.

DOUGLAS, J. W. B. 'Home and School.' McGibbon and Kee, 1964.

EDUCATION ACT, 1944.

EUROPEAN SEMINAR on Playground Activities, Objectives and Leadership Report, United Nations, Geneva, 1958.

FANNING, D. M. 'Families in Flats', *British Medical Journal* No. 5576, 1967.

FLETCHER, Ronald. 'The Family and Marriage.' Penguin Books, 1962.

FREUD, Sigmund. 'Beyond the Pleasure Principle', 1920. The Standard Edition of the Complete Psychological Works, Vol. XVIII, The Hogarth Press, 1955.

FROEBEL, F. 'Education of Man.' New York, 1826.

GESELL, A., and ILG, F. 'The Child, from Five to Ten.' Hamish Hamilton, 1946.

GIDDENS, A. 'Notes on the Concepts of Play and Leisure', *Sociological Review* I, Vol. 12, 1964.

GOOCH, R. B. 'Selection and Layout of Land for Playing Fields and Playgrounds.' National Playing Fields Association, 1963.

GROOS, K. 'The Play of Animals.' D. Appleton & Co., N.Y., 1898.

GROOS, K. 'The Play of Man.' D. Appleton & Co., N.Y., 1901.

*The Guardian*, March 17, 1966.

HALL, G. Stanley. 'Adolescence, Its Psychology.' London, 1904.

HANMER, Jalna. 'Girls at Leisure.' London Union of Youth Clubs and London Young Women's Christian Association, 1964.

HARLOW, Harry F. *et al.* 'Social Deprivation in Monkeys', *Scientific American*, 1962.

HASLUCK, E. L. 'Local Government in England.' Cambridge University Press, 1948.

HELANKO, R. 'Theoretical Aspects of Play and Socialisation.' Turku University Press, Finland, 1958.

HENDRIKSON, A. E., and WHITE, P. O. 'Promax. A quick method for rotation to oblique simple structure.' *British Journal of Statistical Psychology*, Vol. 17, pages 65-70.

HIMMELWEIT, Hilda T., OPPENHEIM, A. N., and VINCE, Pamela. 'Television and the Child.' Oxford University Press, 1958.

HOLE, Vere. 'Children's play on housing estates.' National Building Studies. Research Paper 39, H.M.S.O., 1965.

HOME OFFICE. 'Children in Care in England and Wales, Cmnd 3893.' 1968.

HOME OFFICE. 'Statistics relating to approved schools, remand homes and attendance centres in England and Wales for 1967.' 1968.

HUIZINGA, Johan. 'Homo Ludens, A study of the play element in culture.' Routledge and Kegan Paul, 1949.

HUNT, Audrey. 'A Survey of Women's Employment.' 1968. A survey carried out on behalf of the Ministry of Labour by Government Social Survey in 1965. SS 379, 1968.

INTERBUILD ARENA. N. J. Habraken's 'support system' and the work of the S.A.R., the Dutch Foundation for Architects' Research, pp. 12-19, October 1967.

INTERNATIONAL PLAYGROUNDS ASSOCIATION NEWSLETTER. Vol. 11, No. 4.

JACOBS, Jane. 'The Death and Life of Great American Cities.' Penguin Books, 1964 (first published U.S. 1961).

JENNINGS, Hilda. 'Societies in the Making.' Routledge and Kegan Paul, 1962.

LASLETT, Peter. 'The World we have lost.' University Paperbacks, 1965.

LAZARUS, M. 'Uber die Reise des Spiels.' Berlin, 1883.

LEDERMANN, A., and TRACHSEL, A. 'Playgrounds and Recreation Spaces.' Architectural Press, 1959.

LIVERPOOL OPEN SPACE REPORT, 1964. City of Liverpool Development and Planning Committee.

LOCAL GOVERNMENT INFORMATION OFFICE. 'The Cost of Vandalism to Local Authorities.' 1964

LOWENFELD, Margaret. 'Play in Childhood.' Victor Gollancz, 1935.

LYNCH, K. 'Site Planning.' The M.I.T. Press, Cambridge, Mass., 1962.

MACE, D. and V. 'The Soviet Family.' Hutchinson, 1963.

MCKAY, Henry D. 'The Neighbourhood and Child Conduct' in 'Cities and Societies' edited by Hatt and Ross, The Free Press of Glencoe, 1961.

MACKENZIE, N. Leslie. 'Scottish Mothers and Children.' Carnegie U.K. Trust, Vols. 2 and 3, 1917.

MCKENNEL, A. C., and BYNNER, J. M. 'Self-images and smoking behaviour among schoolboys', *Brit. Journal of Ed. Psychology*, Vol. 36, 1969.

MAIZELS, Joan. 'Two to Five in High Flats.' The Housing Centre Trust, 1961.

MANCHESTER AND SALFORD POLICE. 'The Closing of Streets to Motor Vehicles.' 1965.

MARCH, Lionel. 'Towards a Garden of Cities', *The Listener*. March 21, 1968.

MARTY, F., in *International Playgrounds Association Newsletter* No. 8, 1966.

MAYS, John Barron. 'Adventure in Play.' Liverpool Council of Social Service, 1957.

MILINCOVIC, S., in *International Playgrounds Association* Conference Report, 1961.

MINISTRY OF HOUSING AND LOCAL GOVERNMENT CIRCULAR No. 5. 1943.

MINISTRY OF HOUSING AND LOCAL GOVERNMENT. 'Density of Residential Areas.' 1952.

MINISTRY OF HOUSING AND LOCAL GOVERNMENT TECHNICAL MEMORANDUM. 1956.

MINISTRY OF HOUSING AND LOCAL GOVERNMENT. 'Homes for Today and Tomorrow.' 1961. Known as 'The Parker Morris Report'.

MINISTRY OF HOUSING AND LOCAL GOVERNMENT, Sociological Research Section. 'Families Living at High Density.' 1964.

MINISTRY OF HOUSING AND LOCAL GOVERNMENT. Written Evidence to the Royal Commission on Local Government in England. H.M.S.O., 1967.

MINISTRY OF HOUSING AND LOCAL GOVERNMENT CIRCULAR 36/37. 'Housing Standards, Costs and Subsidies.' 1967.

MINISTRY OF LAND AND NATURAL RESOURCES. 'Leisure in the Countryside.' Cmnd 2928, H.M.S.O., 1966.

MITCHELL, Mary, in *International Playgrounds Association Newsletter*, No. 5, 1963.

MITCHELL, Mary, in *International Playgrounds Association Newsletter*, Vol. II, No. 2, 1965.

MORRIS, B., in *International Playgrounds Association Newsletter*, Vol. II, No. 5, 1965.

MUSSEN, P. H., CONGER, J. J., and KAGAN, J. J. 'Child Development and Personality.' 2nd ed. Harper Row, London, 1964.

MYCROFT, David R. 'Juvenile Vandalism.' A Diploma of Psychology thesis, University of London, 1964.

NATIONAL PLAYING FIELDS ASSOCIATION. 'Making the Most of School Playing Fields.' 1960.

NATIONAL PLAYING FIELDS ASSOCIATION LEAFLET. 'Sandpits, Construction and Maintenance.'

NATIONAL PLAYING FIELDS ASSOCIATION. 'Recreational Planning.' Report of Local Authorities Conference, 1964.

NATIONAL UNION OF TEACHERS. 'The State of our Schools.' 1962.

NEUMANN, J. Van, and MORGANSTERN, Oskar. 'Theory of Games and Economic Behaviour.' Science Edition. John Wiley, N.Y., 1964.

NEWSON, John and Elizabeth. 'Four Years Old in an Urban Community.' George Allen and Unwin, 1967.

NOBLE, Eva. 'Play and the Sick Child.' Faber and Faber, 1967.

*The Observer.* February 19, 1967.

OPIE, Iona and Peter. 'The Lore and Language of Schoolchildren.' Oxford University Press, 1959. Oxford Paperbacks 1967.

OPPENHEIM, A. N. 'Questionnaire Design and Attitude Measurement.' Heinemann, 1966.

OSWIN, Maureen. 'The Empty Hours', *Our Children*, Council for Children's Welfare. Autumn 1968.

OWEN, Rowland. 'Recreation in the U.S.A.', *International Playgrounds Association Newsletter*, Vol. II, No. 4, 1965.

OWEN, Rowland. 'Statutes and Constitutions.' National Playing Fields Association, 1967.

PATRICK, Thomas G. 'The Psychology of Relaxation.' Houghton Mifflin Co., 1916.

PAVIOLO, A., in *International Playrgounds Association Newsletter*, Vol. II, No. 4, 1964.

PIAGET, Jean. 'Play, Dreams and Imitation in Childhood.' Heinemann, 1951.

POLAND. No. 2., February 1967. Polish Interpress Agency, Warsaw.

REANEY, M. Jane. 'The Place of Play in Education.' Methuen & Co., 1927.

REGIONAL SPORTS COUNCILS' PRELIMINARY REPORTS. Eastern; South Western; Wales; Yorkshire and Humberside, 1967.

RITTER, Paul. 'Planning for Man and Motor.' Pergamon Press, 1964.

ROYAL SOCIETY FOR THE PREVENTION OF ACCIDENTS. 'Road Accident Statistics for 1967, 1968.

RUPPRECHT, H., in International Playgrounds Association Newsletter, Vol. II, No. 6, 1966.

RYAN, T. M. 'Day Nursery Provision Under the Health Service, England and Wales 1948–1963.' National Society of Children's Nurseries, 1964.

SANDELS, Stina. 'Survey of Activities 1958–1964 of the Research Institute on Developmental Psychology at Stockholm University— Stockholm School of Education', Sociala Meddelanden Kungl Social-styrelsen, Stockholm, 1965.

SCHILLER, F. 'Essays Aesthetical and Philosophical.' George Bell & Sons, London, 1875.

SCHOOLS COUNCIL. The Working Paper No. 17. 'Community Service and the curriculum.' H.M.S.O., 1968.

SCHWAGENSCHEIDT, Walter. 'Die Nordweststadt: Idee und Gesteldtung.' Krämer, Stuttgart, 1964

SHEPPARD, D. 'Play Spaces for Children on Estates.' A survey under-taken for D.S.I.R. by Government Social Survey in 1959; SS 295, 1964.

SIGSGAARD, Jens. 'The Playground in Modern Danish Housing.' Reprint from Danish Foreign Office Journal, No. 54, 1965.

SLOTKIN, J. S. 'Social Anthropology.' New York, 1950.

SMITH, W. D. Lester. 'Education in Great Britain.' Oxford University Press, 1964.

SOUTH LONDON PRESS, January 1876. Quoted in 'Survey of London', Vol. XXV, ed. Sir Howard Roberts, L.C.C. 1955.

SOUTHWARK INTERIM REPORT (F. O. Hayes, Borough Architect and Planner). 'Recreation in Southwark: An Introductory Report of Continuing Studies', August 1966. Revised September 1967.

SPENCER, H. 'Principles of Psychology.' Williams and Norgate, 1872.

SPENCER, R. J., TUXFORD. J., and DENNIS, N. 'Stress and Release in an Urban Estate.' Tavistock Publications, 1964.

STEVENAGE DEVELOPMENT CORPORATION (E. C. Claxton, Chief Engineer). 'Stevenage Traffic Accident Survey 1957–1966.' 1967.

STEVENSON, Anne, MARTIN, Elaine and O'NEILL, Judith. 'High Living. A Study of Family Life in Flats.' Melbourne University Press (Cambridge University Press), 1967.

STEWART, Mary. 'Leisure Activities of School Children.' Workers Educational Association, 1960.

SWAIN, Henry. 'Brief for Community Schools.' *R.I.B.A. Journal*, Vol. 75, No. 8, 1968.

SYKES, Gresham M. 'Crime and Society.' Random House, 1956.

TERMAN, L. M. 'Psychological Sex Differences', in Manual of Child Psychology, ed. Carmichael, L. New York. John Wiley and Sons, 1946.

TERMAN, L. M. *et al.* 'Mental and Physical Traits of a Thousand Gifted Children', in 'Genetic Studies of Genius'. Vol. I. Stanford University Press, 1925.

*Times Educational Supplement.* November 29, 1968.

U.K. NATIONAL COMMITTEE of the World Organisation for Early Childhood (O.M.E.P.). 'Play in Hospital.' Housing Centre Trust, 1967.

WARD, Joyce. 'Children out of School.' A survey carried out on behalf of the Central Advisory Council for Education by Government. Social Survey, 1948.

WHITE, L. E. 'Community and Chaos.' National Council of Social Service, 1950.

WHITING, B. B. 'Six Cultures: Studies of Child Rearing.' John Wiley, N.Y., 1963.

WHITING, J. W. M. 'Becoming a Kwoma.' Institute of Human Relations, Yale University Press, 1941.

WITTY, P. A. 'A Study of Deviates in Versatility and Sociability in Play Interest' (a thesis). Teachers College, Columbia University, New York, 1931.

WRETLIND-LARSSON, Stina. 'Parkleken', *International Playgrounds Association Newsletter*, Vol. II, No. 4. August 1965.

YOUNG, M., and WILLMOTT, P. 'Family and Kinship in East London.' Routledge and Kegan Paul, 1957. Penguin Books, 1962.

YUDKIN, Simon. 'o-5—A report on the care of Pre-School Children.' George Allen and Unwin for National Society of Children's Nurseries, 1968.

YUDKIN, Simon, and HOLME, Anthea. 'Working Mothers and their Children.' Michael Joseph, 1963. Sphere Books, 1969.

# Additional Bibliography

## Relating to Play Theory

APPLETON, L. E. 'A comparative study of the play activities of adult savages and civilized children.' The University of Chicago Press, 1960.

AXLINE, V. M. 'Play therapy.' Boston Houghton, 1947.

BECKER, H. S. 'Through Values to Interpretation.' Duke University Press, 1950.

BENTOVIM, A. 'The psychological importance of play.' *Proceedings* of the 74th Royal Society of Health Conference 1967.

BERLYNE, D. E. 'Conflict, arousal and curiosity.' McGraw-Hill Book Company Inc. 1960.

BERNSTEIN, B., BOWLBY, J., DOWNES, M., HINDLEY, C., LEACH, P., and TRASLER, G. 'The Formative Years.' BBC, 1968.

BRUNER, J. S. 'The Process of Education.' Harvard University Press, Cambridge, 1960.

CASSIRER, E. 'An Essay on Man.' Yale University Press, 1944.

CLAPAREDE, E. 'Experimental Pedagogy.' Trans. M. Louch and H. Holman. Longmans & Green & Co. New York, 1911.

DENNIS, Wayne. 'The Hopi Child.' D. Appleton Century Company, 1940.

ERIKSON, E. H. 'Childhood and Society.' 2nd ed. W. W. Norton & Co., New York, 1963.

ERIKSON, E. H. 'Youth: Change and Challenge.' Basic Books, New York—London, 1963.

FLAUELL, J. H. 'The developmental Psychology of Piaget.' Princeton, Van Nostrand University Series in Psychology, 1963.

GOODENOUGH, F. L. 'Developmental Psychology.' The Century Psychology Series, D. Appleton Century Company N.Y.—London, 1934.

HARTLEY, R. E. *et al.* 'Understanding Children's Play.' Routledge & Kegan Paul, Columbia University Press, 1952.

INHELDER, B., and PIAGET, J. 'The Growth of Logical Thinking from Childhood to Adolescence.' Basic Books, 1958.

INHELDER, B., and PIAGET, J. 'Early Growth of Logic in the Child.' Routledge & Kegan Paul, 1964.

LINDZEY, G. (ed.) 'Handbook of Social Psychology.' 2 vols. Cambridge, Mass., Addison-Wesley, 1954–56.

LLOYD, Arnold. 'Creative Learning.' Inaugural lecture as Professor of Education, University of Natal, 1953.

MACFARLANE, J. W. 'A Developmental Study of Behaviour Problems.' University of California Press, Berkeley and Los Angeles, 1954.

MEAD, Margaret and WOLFENSTEIN, M. 'Childhood in Contemporary Cultures.' University of Chicago Press, 1955.

MILLAR, Susanna. 'The Psychology of Play.' Penguin Books, 1968.

MITCHELL, Elmer D., and MASON, Bernard S. 'The Theory of Play.' A. S. Barnes & Co., New York, 1948.

NEWCOMB, T. M. 'Social Psychology.' Tavistock Publications, 1952.

OPLER, M. E. 'An Apache Way of Life.' University of Chicago Press, 1941.

PARSONS, T., and BALES, R. F. 'Family, Socialisation and Interaction Process.' The Free Press, 1955.

PELLER, L. 'Libidinal Phases, Ego Development and Play.' Psychoanalytical Study of the Child. University Press, 1954.

PIAGET, J. 'The Child's Conception of the World.' Routledge & Kegan Paul, 1929.

PIAGET, J. 'Social Evolution and the New Education.' New Education Fellowship, London, 1932.

PIAGET, J. 'The Moral Judgment of the Child.' Routledge & Kegan Paul, 1932.

PIAGET, J. 'A Child's Construction of Reality.' Routledge & Kegan Paul, 1955.

REANEY, M. Jane. 'The psychology of the organised game.' *The British Journal of Psychology*, Monograph Supplements IV, Cambridge University Press, 1916.

ROBERTS, M. P. 'A Study of Children's Play in the Home Environment.' State University of Iowa. *Studies in Child Welfare*, Vol. 8, 1934.

ROMANES, George J. 'Animal Intelligence.' 9th ed. Routledge & Kegan Paul, 1960.

WATSON, R. I. 'Psychology of the Child.' John Wiley & Sons, N.Y. 1959.

WALL, W. D. 'Child of our Times.' National Children's Home, London, 1959.

## Relating to the Urban Environment

AMERICAN PUBLIC HEALTH ASSOC. Committee on the Hygiene of Housing. 'Planning the Neighbourhood; Standards for Healthful Housing.' Chicago Public Admin. Service, 1948.

BRACEY, H. C. 'Neighbours.' Routledge & Kegan Paul, 1964.

CENTRAL OFFICE OF INFORMATION. 'Town and Country Planning in Britain.' H.M.S.O. second impression, 1968.

CHERMAYEFF, Serge and ALEXANDER, Christopher. 'Community and

Privacy.' Towards a New Architecture of Humanism. Penguin Books, 1966. (First published U.S.A., 1963).

CULLINGWORTH, J. B. 'Town and Country Planning in England and Wales'—An Introduction. George Allen & Unwin, 1964.

DAVIE, M. R. 'Problems of City Life.' John Wiley & Sons, New York, 1932.

DURANT, R. 'Watling: Survey of Social Life on a New Housing Estate.' P. S. King & Co., 1939.

ECKBO, Garrett. 'Urban Landscape Design.' McGraw-Hill Book Company, New York, 1964.

GIBBERD, F. 'Town Design.' Archit. Press. First Ed. 1953, Fourth Ed. 1962.

GREBLER, Leo. 'Urban Renewal in European Countries.' Oxford University Press, 1964.

HALL, Peter. 'London 2000.' Faber & Faber, 1963.

INSTITUTE OF LANDSCAPE ARCHITECTS. 'The Urban Scene, Design for Pleasure and Hard Use.' Institute of Landscape Architects, 1960. (now out of print).

JENNINGS, N. 'Societies in the Making.' Routledge & Kegan Paul, 1962.

KUPER, L. 'Living in Towns.' The Cresset Press, 1953.

MADGE, J., SMEE, M., and BLOOMFIELD, R. 'People in Towns'. A course of twenty radio programmes on urban sociology. BBC, 1968.

MINISTRY OF HOUSING AND LOCAL GOVERNMENT. 'The Deeplish Study.' HMSO, 1966.

MINISTRY OF TRANSPORT REPORT. 'Traffic in Towns—A Study of the longterm problems of traffic in urban areas.' HMSO, 1963. Known as 'The Buchanan Report'.

NEW TOWNS ACT, 1946. Reports of the Development Corporations for the period ended March 31, 1964. HMSO 1964.

ORLANS, H. 'Stevenage.' Routledge & Kegan Paul, 1952.

PURDOM, C. B. 'The Building of Satellite Towns.' Dent, 1949.

ROYAL INSTITUTE OF BRITISH ARCHITECTS. 'The Urban Scene.' Report of Symposium RIBA, 1960.

SELF, P. 'Regional Planning in Britain.' *Urban Studies*, Vol. 1, No. 1. May, 1964.

SALFORD, CITY OF, 'Facilities on Housing Estates.' Report of Town Clerk, *et al.* July, 1963.

SENIOR, Derek. 'The Regional City.' Longmans. 1966.

SEGAL, W. 'Home and Environment.' Leonard Hill, 1953.

SHANKLAND, COX AND ASSOCIATES. 'Social Survey: Childwall Valley Estate, Liverpool.' 1967.

SOCIAL SCIENCE RESEARCH COUNCIL AND CENTRE FOR URBAN STUDIES. 'The Future of the City Region.' Conference Report, 1968.

*Town and Country Planning.* Special Issue. 'New Towns Come of Age.' Jan., Feb., 1968.

VEREKER, C., and MAYS, J. B. 'Urban Redevelopment and Social Change.' Liverpool University Press, 1961.

WHITE, L. E. 'New Towns.' National Council of Social Service, 1951.

## *Relating to Recreation and Play*

CASS, Joan E. 'The Under Fives in the Welfare State.' Published by the Nursery School Association of Great Britain and Northern Ireland. (now out of print)

DAIKEN, L. H. 'Children's Games throughout the Year.' B. T. Batsford, London, 1949.

GARDNER, D. E. M. 'Children's Play Centres.' Its psychological value and place in the training of teachers. Methuen & Co., 1937.

OMAN, Julia, and JOHNSON. 'Street Children.' Hodder & Stoughton, 1964.

OUTDOOR RECREATION RESOURCES REVIEW COMMISSION. 'Outdoor Recreation for America.' A Report (U.S. Govt. publication), Washington, D.C., 1962.

RUIMTE VOOR DE JEUGD. 'Youth and Residential Environment.' European Conference on Space for Youth 1966.

SAVE THE CHILDREN FUND, THE. 'The Play Needs of the Town Child.' Report prepared by a sub-committee of the Junior Clubs Committee of the Save the Children Fund. Save the Children Fund, 1962.

TRADES UNION CONGRESS. 'School Holiday Amenities: A Survey.' 1968.

WILLIAMS, Wayne R. 'Recreation Places.' Reinhold Publishing Corp. N.Y., 1958.

## *Relating to Play Schemes and Under-Five Play Groups*

ALLEN OF HURTWOOD, Lady. 'Adventure Playgrounds.' National Playing Fields Association, reprinted 1961.

ALLEN OF HURTWOOD, Lady. 'Play Parks.' Housing Centre Trust.

BATSFORD RURAL DISTRICT COUNCIL. 'Eighteen Thousand Happy Hours'—A Report of an Experiment in Play Leadership. 1964.

BERTELSEN. 'The Daily Round on a Junk Playground.' Danish Outlook Vol. VI, No. 6, 1953.

BBC Publications. 'How to form a Playgroup.' 1968.

CRAWLEY COMMUNITY ASSOCIATION ADVENTURE PLAYGROUND COMMITTEE. 'Crawley Adventure Playground.' 1955.

GLENFIELD ADVENTURE PLAYGROUND GROUP—A Report. 1964.

HEMEL HEMPSTEAD COUNCIL OF SOCIAL SERVICE. (1) 'Two Studies from the New Towns on Children's Play.' Jan. 1966. (2) 'Report of a Conference held at Hemel Hempstead May 29, 1965.'

MATTERSON, E. M. 'Play with a Purpose for Under-Sevens.' Penguin Books, 1965.

MAY, Dorothy E. 'Suggestions for Play Activities for Young Children.' Save the Children Fund, 1967.

NATIONAL PLAYING FIELDS ASSOCIATION. 'Play Leadership on Recreation Grounds.' Beckenham, Dagenham, Lewisham, Stevenage, Wandsworth. 1955 (revised 1961).

NATIONAL PLAYING FIELDS ASSOCIATION. 'Adventure Playgrounds.' A Progress Report. June 1960, Reprinted October 1961.

SVENSEN. 'Junk Playgrounds.' Danish Outlook, Vol. IV, No. 1. 1951.

TURNER, H. S. 'Something Extraordinary'. Michael Joseph, 1961.

WHITE, L. E. 'Adventure at Harlow.' Reprint from 'Playing Fields', April–June 1964.

WINN, Marie, and PROCTOR, Mary Ann. 'The Playgroup Book.' Souvenir Press, 1968 (first published USA).

## Relating to Methodology

DENNIS, W. 'Current Trends in Psychology.' University of Pittsburg Press, 1947.

FESTINGA, L., and KATZ, D., eds. 'Research Methods in the Behavioural Sciences.' New York, Holt, 1954.

FESTINGA, L. et al. 'Social Pressures on Informal Groups.' Tavistock Publication, London, 1964.

FISHER, R. A. 'The Design of Experiments.' Oliver and Boyd, 4th edn., 1947.

FISHER, R. A. 'Statistical Methods for Research Workers.' Edinburgh, 1925.

LAZARSFELD-JAHODA, Marie. 'Research Methods in Social Relations.' Free Press of Glencoe, 1959.

LAZARSFELD, P. F., and STOUFFER, S. A. 'social research to test ideas.' Free Press of Glencoe, 1962.

MOSER, C. A., and SCOTT, W. Y. 'British Towns. A Statistical Study of Social and Economic Differences.' Centre for Urban Studies, Oliver & Boyd, 1961.

## *Miscellaneous*

CENTRAL ADVISORY COUNCIL FOR EDUCATION (ENGLAND) REPORT. 'Half our Future.' 1963. Known as 'The Newsom Report'.

MINISTRY OF EDUCATION. 'Physical Education in Primary Schools.' 1952/3.

MINISTRY OF HOUSING AND LOCAL GOVERNMENT CIRCULAR No. 42/66. 'Public Expenditure.'

UNITED NATIONS. 'Declaration on the Rights of the Child.' November 1959.

# Index